ANGLISTIK UND ENGLISCHUNTERRICHT

Herausgegeben von
Gabriele Linke
Holger Rossow
Merle Tönnies

Band 86

SONJA FRENZEL
BIRGIT NEUMANN (Eds.)

Ecocriticism – Environments in Anglophone Literatures

Universitätsverlag
WINTER
Heidelberg

Bibliografische Information der Deutschen Nationalbibliothek
Die Deutsche Nationalbibliothek verzeichnet diese Publikation in der Deutschen Nationalbibliografie; detaillierte bibliografische Daten sind im Internet über *http://dnb.d-nb.de* abrufbar.

Herausgeber:
Prof. Dr. Gabriele Linke
PD Dr. Holger Rossow
Prof. Dr. Merle Tönnies

ISBN 978-3-8253-6843-2
ISSN 0344-8266

Imprimé en Allemagne · Printed in Germany
Druck: Memminger MedienCentrum, 87700 Memmingen

Gedruckt auf umweltfreundlichem, chlorfrei gebleichtem und alterungsbeständigem Papier

Den Verlag erreichen Sie im Internet unter:
www.winter-verlag.de

Acknowledgements

The volume ermged from an international conference held at Heinrich Heine University Duesseldorf, Germany, in April 2016, which was generously funded by the German Research Foundation and the Freunde und Förderer of Heinrich Heine University. We gratefully acknowledge their support. We would also like to thank all authors for their stimulating contributions as well as for their patience while the volume was in production. Our special thanks go to Judith Rahn, Mareike Ilsemann, Yvonne Kappel and Marvin Harder for their careful editorial work.

Table of Contents

Sonja Frenzel and Birgit Neumann

Introduction: Environments in Anglophone Literatures

1. Environment Matters

The current discussions surrounding the Anthropocene as a new geological and bio-genetic age in which the earth's ecosystems are decisively shaped by human influences have rapidly expanded academic research on the relationships between human beings and their environments.[1] Climate change, environmental crises, resource shortages, species extinction and infrastructure design have drawn attention to the extent to which humans have themselves become a geological and climatological force[2], inevitably shaping, making and destroying various forms of life on our planet. Proceeding from the premise that narratives crucially shape our understanding of nature and environment, ecocriticism has turned to literary and cultural representations of environmental issues. Broadly speaking, ecocriticism seeks to examine how literature represents (natural) environments, how it articulates environmental knowledge and how it might possibly foster the development of a shared environmental consciousness or indeed a "planetary imagination"[3].

The notion of the Anthropocene has been subject of numerous controversies regarding its periodisation as well as its premises and consequences.[4] No matter how precisely one might define the Anthropocene, it is clear that this new epoch offsets and "even scrambles some crucial categories by which people have made sense of the world and their lives"[5]. Referring to "a world-historical phenomenon that has arrived"[6], the Anthropocene challenges us into re-considering our personal, seemingly local actions and routines on a planetary scale. What, for instance, are the planetary ramifications of someone's routine use of aluminium coffee capsules, a daily practice that may appear inconsequential on a local scale, but that takes on considerable political and ethical urgency on the planetary scale? Timothy Clark is certainly right in noting that the "planetary scale of the Anthropocene compels us to think and act as if already citizens of a world polity"[7]. While we are required, in other words, to think beyond the local, we are also called upon to think beyond the contemporary: The Anthropocene is both retrospective in identifying human beings' historical impact upon the earth's geological development and, at the same time, prospective, or rather: anticipatory, as it "indicat[es] humanity's probable impacts on geophysical and biological systems for millennia to come"[8].

To think and act on a planetary scale and thus to relate daily practices to other, frequently far-away places and distant times involves immense cognitive, imaginative and affective efforts. Literature, we maintain, is conducive to promoting these efforts.[9] One defining characteristic of literature is its capacity to establish imaginative links between different, physically unconnected spaces and to juxtapose diverse dimensions of time. In so doing, literature brings into being new, imaginative environments and offers readers opportunities to observe possibilities and consequences of interacting in and with specific environments.[10] Literature, therefore, provides a particularly effective anf affective arena in which planetary "scale effects"[11] of locally grounded actions can be explored and in which the abstract, often intangible complexities of the 'Anthropocene' can be translated into concrete experiences. As it stages the complex interactions between human and natural histories,[12] literature may allow humans to reflect on their agency as geological agents, while also indicating the very limits of human agency and reason.

If the Anthropocene draws attention to the role of humans in shaping environments, then "[r]econceptualising the 'Anthropos' in the Anthropocene"[13] has indeed political urgency. As human interactions with nature and environment continue to propel the global environmental crisis, a number of scholars have drawn attention to the fact that these interactions are pervasively shaped by prevalent discourses, epistemologies and ontologies. Bruno Latour in particular has highlighted the fact that western epistemologies and the so-called 'Modern Constitution' they have engendered fundamentally rely on binary oppositions, such as those between humans vs. nonhumans, mind vs. body, culture vs. nature. These epistemic models prefigure possibilities of understanding and interacting with nature and environment.[14] Ultimately building on and expanding the Cartesian mind-matter dualism, the binary oppositions underlying western epistemologies work together to posit nature as the radical other of culture and subjectivity, namely as passive, inert matter devoid "of all experience, intrinsic value, internal purpose, and internal relations"[15]. This also means that modern epistemologies have played a vital role in separating the human from the nonhuman realm and in defining humans' relation to nature primarily in terms of consumption, "mastery and possession"[16].

And indeed, the influence of modern epistemologies on a number of socio-political projects and configurations can hardly be overestimated. The extent to which the oppositions between culture and nature, the human and nonhuman underwrite imperial ideologies is well-documented. The decoupling of nature from history, as e.g., Mary Louise Pratt has cogently argued, helped obscure colonialism's histories of conquest, exploitation and violence and ultimately naturalised Europeans' global presence by construing a seemingly natural, undifferentiated and abstract space.[17] 'Abstract space' works to dissimulate imperialism's violence and to impose reciprocity, unity and communality instead.[18] Arguably, the construction of such an abstract space within a larger imperialist rhetoric also provided the basis for relegating colonised peoples to the realm of nature and configuring them as resources to be civilised, exploited and mastered. Closely connected to imperial modes of othering and dispossession naturalised by western epistemologies are sexist and racist forms of stigmatisation. A number of scholars have illustrated the extent to which the binary oppositions underlying western epistemic models have provided and continue to provide the implicit basis for various – past and contemporary – forms of racism and sexism, which, to a certain extent, are part and parcel of European humanism and its Eurocentric ideal of 'Man'.[19]

Seeking to establish more responsible, politically and ethically sound epistemologies and ontologies, ecocritical theories – in tandem with other ecological and materialist approaches – have stressed the need to overcome the binary oppositions that have long structured western epistemologies and to focus instead on their reciprocal and dynamically changing interactions. Rather than conceiving of nature and culture as opposites, current scholarship addresses their mutual entanglements and stresses the vibrant, self-organising and emergent force of (living) matter.[20] Broadly speaking, this line of reasoning can be traced back to

Alfred North Whitehead's process philosophy, which understands being as a mode of becoming and transformation and which counters the prevalent view according to which matter is a mere essence. In his seminal studies *An Enquiry Concerning the Principles of Natural Knowledge* (1919), *The Concept of Nature* (1920) and *Process and Reality* (1929),[21] Whitehead develops a generative ontology that is based on the reconceptualisation of matter as an open and transformative force. Stressing the potentialities of matter, Whitehead not only challenges the substance materialism that has been dominating western philosophy since Aristotle and that ultimately gave rise to the Cartesian mind-matter dualism. Rather, he also opens ontology and its underlying concept of matter for the generative and unpredictable dynamics of events and, accordingly, understands "Time, Space, and Material" as "adjuncts of events"[22].

Whitehead's process philosophy has considerably influenced ecocritical concepts of matter and nature[23] and has been taken up and taken on by a number of ecocritical scholars. From their respective vantage points, these scholars stress the dynamics of matter and suggest replacing the rigid boundaries between nature and culture, which inevitably distance humans from nature and environment, by a relational, "non-dualistic understanding"[24] of nature-culture and human-nonhuman interactions. From this perspective, matter and nature are understood as nonhuman actors in their own right, which are endowed with a specific, "protean agency"[25]. It is such an agency that accounts for the "plurality, unpredictability, and compromised condition of the natural world"[26]. This also means that conceptualisations of difference between human and nonhuman actors need to be re-thought beyond hierarchical dualisms. According to ecocritical approaches, human and nonhuman actors do not constitute distinct and rigidly separate entities; rather, they occupy ever-shifting positions along a continuum: They share a "coextensive materiality"[27] and emerge only "through relationality"[28]. Such notions of a coextensive materiality, of "vibrant matter"[29] and "single matter energy"[30], of entanglements and interactions between human and nonhuman actors, have far-reaching consequences for western discourses, ideas and practices: They invite us to rethink and restructure existing epistemologies and ontologies and to develop a – politically and ethically relevant – awareness of the extent to which humans and nonhumans, culture and nature, semiotics and matter, subjects and objects are "inextricably enmeshed in a dense network of relations"[31].

The special issue *Ecocriticism: Environments in Anglophone Literatures* explores the cultural, social, ethical and theoretical challenges that concepts of nature and environment pose from a perspective in literary studies. We seek to take stock of the state of the art in ecocriticism and to analyse literary explorations of nature, environment, ecologies and environmental knowledge with particular interest in Anglophone literatures. More specifically, we intend to shed light on the historicised and localised interrelationships between nature, culture and literature, and to examine how literary texts possibly prefigure new, relational and processual ontologies that may come to operate on a planetary scale. Moving beyond the divide between cultural constructions and natural processes[32], we thus follow Latour's assumption that the importance of ecology lies not so much in a 'green' reaffirmation of nature's value, but in the ways in which environmental concerns (and their articulation in a variety of discourses) challenge traditional binaries between nature vs. culture, body vs. mind, etc., and incite us to imagine new, open and interrelational modes of thinking and being.[33] Literature, we argue, provides a powerful site in which relations between human and nonhuman forces can be probed and in which the emergence of environments, i.e., of dynamic relations and associations between diverse agents, times and places, can be dramatised. Environmentally-oriented Anglophone literatures frequently foreground the changing and open connections between natural history, human history and agency in the wake of colonialism, migration and globalisation, and model new, non-anthropocentric configurations of human and nonhuman forces. Entering into a critical dialogue with literary depictions of nature and environment therefore promises to lay bare formerly hidden, latent histories and to reveal new ontologies that are based on horizontal rather than hierarchical relations.

Literary engagements with nature and environment, their histories and power to affect exceed the so-called content of a text.[34] Rather than focusing solely on the referential, mimetic or didactic dimensions of literary texts, which – maybe inevitably – perpetuate the dichotomy between the given (nature, environment, etc.) and the constructed (literature, culture, etc.), the essays focus on the transformative agency of literary poetics and aesthetics themselves. This also means that they seek to do justice to the formative role of matter and materiality in signifying processes. The term material-semiotic practice indexes this constitutive interplay between the material and semiotic dimensions of a text.[35] Hence, while acknowledging the importance of language and semiotics in our understanding of nature and environment, the contributions to this volume also stress the need to conceive matter as a force in its own right.

2. From Nature Writing to Aesthetic Agencies: Towards an Ethics of Re-Enchantment

Looking back on ecocriticism's history of almost half a century, it remains utterly impressive to survey the ongoing developments and the wide-ranging scope of this field. While the 1970s witnessed the rise of such critical paradigms as gender studies and race studies, each thriving on the contested relations between matter and discourse as well as between political activism and academic theory, it was only with the foundation of the *Association for the Study of Literature and the Environment* (ASLE) in 1992 that ecocriticism became an institutionalised strand in and across the humanities disciplines. Accommodating a heterogeneous "alliance of academic critics, artists, environmental educators, and green activists"[36], ecocriticism has since remained an utterly multi-faceted domain, held together by two interrelated objectives: From their grounding in literary studies, ecocritical approaches have aimed, firstly, at revaluating the relations between "wordscape" and "worldscape"[37] so as to shed new light upon human beings' intimate entanglements with their environments.[38] Secondly – both simultaneously and consequently – ecocritical approaches have sought to devise ways out of the environmental crisis. In these endeavours to translate between world and text as well as between ethical commitments and academic theories, ecocriticism has expanded literary contextualisations from society and culture to nature-culture configurations and environments.[39]

Proceeding from these premises, ecocriticism has been developing in three concurrent waves. First wave ecocriticism has re-examined literary representations of nature in canonical and, later, in non-canonical texts.[40] For instance, Karl Kroeber and Laurence Buell critically revaluate Romantic nature writing and the pastoral tradition,[41] whereas Lawrence Coupe's *Green Studies Reader* comprehensively traces the "Green Tradition"[42] from Romanticism and its legacies to contemporary critiques of modernity. Second wave ecocriticism meets these critiques of modernity by integrating notions of gender, race and/or class differences into its theories, models and methods.[43] At the same time, ecocritical theories have increasingly sought to overcome the boundary lines of the academic "compartmentalisation of knowledge"[44] into human, social and natural sciences. By entering into critical conversations and, thereby, into "a more literal and potentially more antagonistic confrontation between scientific and literary descriptions of nature"[45], ecocritics from various disciplines have aimed at devising interdisciplinary ecological frameworks for tackling ecocriticism's academic and political objectives.[46]

And yet, while acknowledging the reciprocal relationships that connect literary texts and semiotic procedures on the one hand with nature and environment on the other, both ecocriticism's first and second wave approaches have perpetuated – albeit often unintentionally so – the dichotomous opposition between nature and culture. This may at least partly be due to the fact that ecocriticism's transformative impact stems from its initial rejection of the oft-cited legacies of the linguistic turn[47], which have been widely perceived as an outright "abandon or dismissal of matter and materiality"[48]. The capacity to signify has thereby been restricted to the realm of human culture, while nature and environment have been regarded as powerless and voiceless and, by extension, as devoid of meaning. Ecocriticism has endeavoured to "reconnect the work of (environmental) writing and criticism with environmental experience – meaning in particular the *natural* world"[49]. Yet, in so doing, most first and second wave approaches have upturned the hierarchies of the nature-culture divide in favour of nature, rather than translating them into non-dualist models.

Current third-wave approaches in ecocriticism rely on new materialist conceptualisations of shared materiality in order to circumvent the dualisms between matter and meaning or nature and culture. Accordingly, and as argued above, materiality is recognised as "an emergent property created through dynamic interactions between physical characteristics and signifying strategies"[50]. 'Physical characteristics' cannot define fixed substance or inert nature any more, as 'matter' becomes a fluid category that co-emerges with its discursive meanings in "a continuing process of dynamic materialisation and differentiation over time and space"[51]. This emergent materiality engenders crucial re-conceptualisations of agency:

Emanating from a pool of acoustic, visual, corporeal, and imaginative energies[52], material agencies become mutually entangled into temporary configurations with 'signifying strategies'. Material-semiotic practices undermine the dualistic oppositions of nature and culture, materiality and semiotics, ontologies and epistemologies, and translate them into historically contingent configurations along a nature-culture-continuum[53] within material-discursive networks[54] or relational onto-epistemologies[55]. More crucially, still, they critically traverse Cartesian dualisms of self and other, man and woman, and thereby undermine the persistent hierarchies of difference, be it racialised or gendered. Donna Haraway makes a particularly valuable point when, in adapting Bruno Latour's actor-network-theory into a feminist ecological framework, she foregrounds the transformative agency of thinking the multiple assemblages of natureculture as a form of kinship embracing all life on this planet.[56]

Capitalising on these perpetual processes of transformation and translation, new materialist ecocritical theories may meet ecocritical ethics in a transformative "framework related to issues of being, knowing, and doing"[57]. In sum, these ecocritical theories and ethics seek to transform modernity's hierarchical dualisms into horizontal relations[58], and it is in these endeavours that they come to bear the potential to alter human beings' places and practices within them.

Evidently, this ecocritical approach proceeds from a rethinking of environment. Rather than referring to a given, static entity that merely surrounds human beings, environments need to be recognised in their multi-dimensional plurality and in their autopoietic dynamics. Above all, environments are emergent materialities themselves, into which organisms are intricately entangled.[59] Following Jakob von Uexküll's early observations, environments are seen as relative to the agents they enfold and develop along with the relationships these agents form with one another.[60] As environments continuously transform themselves, "ravelling here and unravelling there"[61], ecocritical theories, models and methods seek to analyse these processes and partake in their dynamic onto-epistemologies. With theory thus intimately related to practice, ecocritics, too, are ever more compelled to retain a self-reflexive awareness of their own entanglement within the environments they study. They are agentic forces among multiple other emerging human and nonhuman agencies, which jointly weave these environments. Ultimately, in this dynamic and open co-mingling of semiotics and materiality, environment "comes to be seen clearly as a multiplicity of complex interchanges between innumerable agentic forces"[62]. It is within such a scenario of interdependence and intertwining that literature and literary texts acquire aesthetic agency and reveal their unique potential of bringing environments into being.

Connecting these relational configurations of environment to literary and cultural studies, material ecocriticism[63] suggests "that we can read the world as matter endowed with stories [...] designated as 'storied matter', or 'material expressions' constituting an agency with signs and meanings"[64]. Not only does material ecocriticism[65] thus expand the boundary lines of agency to cultural artefacts, matter and literary texts; rather it also yields new conceptualisations of aesthetic agency and of the role of literature within a network of diverse human and nonhuman agencies.[66]

Recent third-wave ecocriticism embraces new materialist approaches in tracing these material stories "as they happen through the formation of content and expression, that is, through the entanglement of materiality and meaning in the widest sense of the word"[67]. This also means being open to the processes in which literary texts, too, emerge in their respective processes of materialisation, both as material words on the page (as writing or *écriture*) and as semiotic practices. As aesthetic agencies signify in diverse, often conflicting and disjunctive ways, they are "never entirely exhausted by their semiotics"[68]. As such, literary texts become entangled in their own environments, through their multi-faceted interactions and associations with other – human and nonhuman – agencies and their respective co-emergent materialisations. It is the ensuing shared "onto-tale"[69] of enmeshed ontologies and epistemologies that creates and perpetually re-creates (literary) environments.

The relational configurations of human and nonhuman agencies within (literary) environments testify to ecocriticism's interest in developing more sustainable ways of inhabiting this world. Attributing agency to humans and nonhumans alike calls for expanding the claims of moral philosophy. When ethics is directed at nonhuman agents who do not – and cannot – share human(ist) values and ideas, hitherto prevalent approaches to dealing with difference and alterity need to be translated into horizontal relationships so as to accommodate radical – nonhuman – otherness.[70] These challenges have been explored with particular focus on animals,[71] whereas (material) ecocriticism has further extended them to notions of nature and environment. Theorising agency in terms of materialisations emerging from and through "Thing-Power"[72] and its "internal experience, agentive creativity, and vitality"[73] raises pertinent ethical questions of how to respond to diverse signifying capacities and effects produced by human and nonhuman agents. Literary environments are challenged into accommodating the otherness of aesthetic agencies and their material-semiotic articulations, as they rely on a diverse repertoire of expressions and significations. Along these lines, some ecocritical approaches have called for an "ethics of relinquishment"[74], in which humans surrender their anthropocentric position in favour of ecocentric perspectives and approaches. Critically interrogating the possibility of such ecocentricism, which is invariably articulated from a human vantage point, new materialist perspectives propose, instead, an ethics of (re-)enchantment.[75] As Kate Rigby summarises: "Perhaps, then, it might be more helpful to seek in the work of ecopoiesis, not so much a voicing of the more-than-human natural world, but, more humbly, simply a response […] a merely human response at that, to the call of nature's self-disclosure, its *autopoiesis.*"[76] It is this response, we contend, that resonates with particular force in Anglophone literatures and that may re-invigorate literary theory and practice as well as translate them into ethically sound and sustainable relationships between humans and nonhumans

3. Postcolonial Ecocriticism and Literary Environments

A number of historians, most prominently Alfred Crosby, have drawn attention to the close relationship between western imperialism and ecology, a relationship that is expressed by the term 'ecological imperialism'[77]. With an eye to the devastating effects of western imperialism on various ecosystems, it is hardly surprising that ecological issues figure particularly prominently in postcolonial literatures. And yet, though postcolonial studies and ecocriticism share a number of critical concerns and concepts, to date there have been relatively few attempts to systematically link these fields of research.[78] We suggest that relating ecocritical and postcolonial approaches can productively enhance both fields of research, as each of them aims to transform hierarchical oppositions into horizontal relationships of entanglement and seeks to challenge the traditional distinction between the human and it's others.

Most importantly, postcolonial ecocriticism promises to reveal how the manifold entanglements of literature, nature and culture continue to be traversed by global power structures and how articulations of nature and environments are used in negotiating political and epistemological hierarchies in our increasingly entangled, though asymmetrically structured world. Time and again Anglophone postcolonial literatures, by authors such as Olive Senior, Grace Nichols, Derek Walcott, Margret Atwood, Eden Robinson, Lorna Goodison and Amitav Ghosh, portray how various – human, material, and biotic – processes of translocation bear on seemingly 'natural' landscapes. They dramatise the extensively and irreversibly destructive effects of western colonialism, neo-liberal capitalism and global tourism on local ecosystems, while – by means of their poetics – allowing readers to experience the making and re-making of environments.[79] Revolving around environmental damage, such as soil degradation, floods, droughts, global warming and species extinction, texts such as Ghosh's *The Hungry Tide* (2004) or Senior's poetry cycle *Gardening in the Tropics* (1994) radically challenge the conventional split between singular, localized dwelling places and the disparate places of economic support and consumption.[80] As they portray the planetary "scale effects"[81] of western colonialism, capitalism and life-style, they respond to genuine environmental concerns and invite readers into an interpretive process that explores the meanings of environmental justice in a transculturally connected, though uneven world.[82] Moreover, by revealing the frequently devastating effects of human aims and routines on nature, literary texts – just think of Walcott's *Tiepolo's Hound* (2001) or Nichols's *i is a long memoried woman* (1983) – problematize the very notion of natural environments and their conventional disjunction from histories, cultures and agency.[83] Suggesting that nature is not a given essence but a dynamic and generative phenomenon, these texts model alternative, non-Eurocentric conceptualisations of nature and culture. Such imaginative articulations allow readers to probe new associations with their environments – associations that build on multiple linkages, connections and interactions rather than hierarchies and boundaries.

In creatively engaging with the historicity and agential powers of nature, postcolonial literatures also respond to the fundamental challenge of grounding individual existences in the social fabric of dominant onto-epistemologies, concepts and aesthetic forms. As is well known, colonial travellers, settlers and missionaries often tried to capture the alterity of foreign lands in familiar terms and therefore gave established names to the unknown flora and fauna. To change this situation and to reclaim local and frequently marginalised knowledge, a number of postcolonial texts inscribe colonially established codes with localized creative traditions and situated knowledge. In so doing, these texts also work towards creating new, pluralised onto-epistemologies in which the (epistemic) violence of the imperial projects is imaginatively redressed. As such, postcolonial literatures provide a particularly rich source for analysing how literature may respond to the fragility of environments in the age of the Anthropocene and how they work through established western epistemes. Foregrounding its transformative agency, literature compels readers to consider the processes through which we bring environments into existence and how we respond to them.[84] Ecological poetics and ethics in Anglophone literatures are therefore not only about imagining new, more responsible relations between culture and nature, human and nonhuman forces, meaning and matter, "but about responsibility and accountability for the lively relationalities of becoming of which we are a part"[85].

If, as Timothy Clark argues, the Anthropocene indeed represents "the demand upon a species consciously to consider its impact, as a whole and as a natural/physical force"[86], then literature – by means of its material-semiotic operations – can certainly enhance such a consideration. Some of the key questions to be asked in this volume are thus the following: Which material-semiotic operations and practical procedures are used to create new literary environments and how do these environments interact with and reflect on other environments? What is specific of literary environments and how can these environments induce us to rethink the relations between nature and culture? And if, as Manuel De Landa puts it, "rocks and winds, germs and words, are all differential manifestations of [a] dynamic material reality"[87], then how do literary environments express themselves?

4. Explorations

The special issue at hand is based upon an international symposium held at Heinrich Heine University Düsseldorf, Germany, in April 2016, which was generously funded by the German Research Foundation and the Freunde und Förderer of Heinrich Heine University. Bringing together international scholars working in the fields of ecocriticism and postcolonialism, the event pursued the overall objective to trace affinities and divergences of these prolific fields of research, which – though sharing a number of topical concerns and interests – have only rarely converged. Thought-provoking papers and lively discussions critically examined the current state of the art in ecocriticism and postcolonial studies, and shed new light on the role of literature in modelling shared environments. In particular, they offered insights into the manifold and often conflicting relations between environments, ecocriticism, and ethics in Anglophone literatures that further provided valuable impulses for rethinking the role of literature in the making of environments – impulses that the essays gathered in this collection take up and take on.

The essays thus provide a number of new perspectives on the aesthetic agency of literature as well as on the intersections between ecocriticism and postcolonial studies. First and foremost, the essays engage with the potential of Anglophone literatures to involve readers in open processes of making, experiencing and reflecting on environment and nature. We hope that these explorations will not only stimulate new debates about the intersections between literature and environment but will also prompt our readers to think about new projects which take the topics introduced here to their next critical level.

Three individual papers with conceptual foci open this collection. Roman Bartosch's and Sonja Frenzel's contributions each engage with relationality and movement as two pivotal concepts in contemporary ecocriticism. Their essays theorise attempts at overcoming modernity's rigid oppositions of matter and meaning, nature and culture, ontologies and epistemologies, and translate these observations into didactic and po(i)etic practices. Roman Bartosch's "Æsthetic Æffect. Relationality as a Core Concept in Environmental Studies and Education" sets out to challenge the notion of representation and its inherent dualism of text and world. Following phenomenological approaches in positing relationality as a constitutive element of onto-epistemologies, Bartosch suggests that aesthetics "foster[s] or engender[s] affective relationality". It is this 'æffect' that offers itself as a pertinent didactic tool, not only in teaching environmental awareness, but also in proposing connections with the effects of an aesthetic agency.

Sonja Frenzel correlates this affective relationality with dynamic processes of becoming and stresses its potential to pervasively challenges concepts of literature as product or stable structure. Accordingly, she explores the creative potential of matter's onto-epistemological co-emergences by tracing their material and aesthetic agencies. Not only does this agency unfold in matter's capacities to affect and to be affected in turn, but this affective agency sets in motion the dynamics of relationality and becoming alike. Critically interrogating the alleged linearity of the widely used ecocritical notion of 'storied matter', this contribution devises an ecopoetics of rhizomatic errantry and posthuman affect, that stresses the ever-shifting as-sociations of material agencies and of literature's aesthetic agency in particular.

Subsequently, Wendy Wheeler's chapter "A Feeling for Form: Biosemiotics and the Primacy of Aesthetic Knowing" opens up an innovative and interdisciplinary perspective on material becoming and material affect through exploring aesthetic form. Identifying aesthetic agency as matter's potential to signify, Wheeler traces signifying processes beyond human prerogatives and into the realm of nonhuman semiotics. How this biosemiotics has evolved within the larger context of pertinent academic developments in critical theory of the past 50 years offers invaluable ecocritical insights into the dynamic interplay between semiotics and materiality may be regarded as characteristic of literary environments.

These dynamic conceptualisations of human and nonhuman materialities and their distinctive signifying agencies are further spelled out in the following contributions on Anglophone literatures from the Caribbean. Indeed, exploring the aesthetic agency of (Caribbean) environments considerably expands notions of onto-epistemological becoming, of relationality, and of the agency of literature.

Timo Müller's and Jan Rupp's contributions show how engaging with literary environments may revaluate pertinent cultural tropes. Müller's "The Road in the Garden" critically engages with the dynamics of spatial experience through the motif of the road in two Anglophone Caribbean novels. Their articulations of movements in and through Caribbean island spaces present pertinent insights into the dynamics of ecological becoming and allow for a non-canonical appreciation of the American pastoral tradition.

Turning to Caribbean poetry, Jan Rupp's contribution introduces the concept of geopoetics as a useful tool for studying Anglophone Caribbean literatures in their intimate relations with island geographies and histories of continuous displacement. The author's thorough engagement with geophysics and materiality correlates current approaches in both geopoetics and aesthetics. Zooming in on *Zong!*, Rupp opens up new ethical perspectives on prominent topoi and tropes in contemporary Anglophone literary and cultural studies.

In their shared endeavor to historicise (Caribbean) nature and environment, Müller's and Rupp's contributions draw attention to questions of ethics that have permeated the field of ecocriticism for considerable time. Extending human ethics to nonhuman life forms raises crucial questions about the boundary lines between human beings and animal beings, and will, ultimately, lead to new conceptualisations of species, life forms, and signification.

John Thieme's contribution takes up these relations as it examines the figure of the theriantrope as one potentially productive strategy for countering human appropriations of nonhuman life forms. In "Theriantropes Past and Future: Transformative Figures in Colonial and Postcolonial Writing", he provides a concise historical survey of this age-old trope and relates its transformative potentials of Anglophone writing. It is particularly the underlying ethical-political dimension of his essay that opens up future perspectives on human-animal relations and their significations.

The particular ethical urgency of material-semiotic relationality between human and nonhuman agents is taken up, too, in the following two contributions. Jonathan Skinner's ecopoetical piece "Call the Pulsing Home" engages with sonic materials of life as they are articulated in bird song and whale song and as they find entrance in pieces of ecopoetry, the author conceptualises human-nonhuman communications through the notions of fascination and resonance. Eventually, he argues, these observations may call upon us to re-consider the role of poetry as eco-poiesis and, thereby, offer new perspectives on the heterogeneous ways in which new forms of attachments and associations may be articulated.

Pieter Vermeulen and Ioannis Tsitsovits' explorations of "Big Data, Deep Time, and the Writing of Life" takes these insights one step beyond animal agencies. By touching upon the realm of the technological, they illustrate how human processes of signification may come to operate as a mode of geological inscription. This decidedly anthropocentric perspective "blurs the distinction between human action and writing, as all action now becomes a form of writing". As the essay shows, this take on material-semiotic practices radically alters literary environments, both for human and nonhuman life forms, opening them up for various forms of in-between-ness.

While the majority of contributions foregrounds material agencies in the aesthetic evocation of environments in Anglophone literatures, it cannot be denied that these environments frequently remain traversed by modernity's axes of differentiation. Rainer Emig turns to exploring the political aspects of human relations to nature and environment. Capitalising on gender aspects in contemporary Welsh poetry, he not only illustrates how notions of gender and ethics bear on our understanding and interaction with environments; what is more, he shows how widespread associations of nature and femininity may be undermined in ecopoetic articulations of masculinity.

Finally, Alexa Weik von Mossner's contribution titled "When Everything is Up for Grabs" pursues a cognitive approach to environmental narratives. Weik illustrates how cognitive and affective narratology may provide new insights into the aesthetic evocation of ecological catastrophe and may, in fact, achieve a didactic goal. Our reading of satirical and self-ironically unreliable narratives like *Grand Canyon, Inc* may succeed in creating a new awareness of the contemporary state of our environment – both in terms of ethics and politics – and may thus be seen to culminate in an ever more urgent call for action.

In sum, this special issue brings together a wide range of interrelated perspectives on environments, ecocriticism, and ethics in Anglophone literatures. Its contributions enter into critical dialogue with one another and thereby stress the lively and ongoing debates in the bourgeoning academic fields of ecocriticism and postcolonialism. While each contributor necessarily addresses these conceptual relations as well as their dynamic inter- and intra-relations from a particular, theoretically and methodologically informed angle, his or her writing is intimately entangled with the texts of the other contributors. It is in answering to ecocriticism's major objectives of exploring material-semiotic practices in their agentic entanglements that each contribution offers a number of didactic impulses for rethinking the role of literature in the Anthropocene. Accordingly, this collection models and perpetually re-models a literary environment of its own, into which, it is hoped, readers will interweave their own lines of critical inquiry.

Notes

[1] Haraway (2015).
[2] Braidotti (2013:5).
[3] Spivak (2003:96). Note that Spivak uses the term 'planetary imagination' in a different context, namely for the development of a new comparative literature.
[4] For this debate see, for instance, Parham, and Westling (2017).
[5] Clark (2015:9).
[6] Trexler (2015:4).
[7] Clark (2015:9).
[8] Trexler (2015:1).
[9] For an overview of the role of literature in ecocriticism see, e.g., the impressive volumes by Zapf (2016), Sammells (1998); Parham and Westling (2017).
[10] James (2015:33) stresses in her book on econarratology and postcolonial narratives that "literary narratives offer up virtual representations of physical environments for their readers to inhabit and experience."
[11] Clark (2015:72-73).
[12] Cf. Chakrabarty (2009).
[13] Palsson (2013:8).
[14] Cf. Latour (1993).
[15] Griffin (2007:8).
[16] Rigby (2012:152).
[17] Cf. Pratt (1992).
[18] Cf. Lefebvre (1991 [1974]:49).
[19] Cf. Davies (1997); Merchant (2003); Plumwood (2002); Braidotti (2013). Bennett, for example, stresses that the notion of the nonhuman world as passive and inanimate, "feeds human hubris and our earth-destroying fantasies of conquest and consumption" (Bennett (2010:ix); by contrast, recognising the vitality of nonhuman entities might enable us to see "a fuller range of the nonhuman powers circulating around and within human bodies" (*Ibid.*:ix).
[20] Cf. Bennett (2010); Alaimo (2010); Iovino (2012); Oppermann (2012); Braidotti (2013).
[21] Whitehead (1919); Idem (1920); Idem (1929).
[22] Cf. Neumann (2017a).
[23] See, for instance, Iovino (2012)
[24] Braidotti (2013:3).
[25] Bennett (2010:13).

[26] Clark (2014:80).
[27] Iovino (2012:64).
[28] Kirby (2011:76).
[29] Bennett (2010:title).
[30] De Landa (2000:21).
[31] Bennett (2010:13).
[32] Cf. Kirby (2011); Barad (2007); De Landa (2000).
[33] Latour (2004). "How to Talk About the Body? The Normative Dimension of Science Studies." *Body & Society* 10.2-3, 205-229.
[34] Cf. Belsey (2002).
[35] Cf. Haraway (1992).
[36] Buell (2005:6).
[37] *Ibid.* (2005:39).
[38] Cf. also Glotfelty and Fromm (1996); Garrard (2014).
[39] Cf. Rigby (2014).
[40] Cf. Glotfelty and Fromm (1996); Rigby (2014).
[41] Cf. Kroeber (1994); Buell (1995).
[42] Coupe (2000:vii).
[43] Cf. Rigby (2014:162); cf. also Bate (1991); Buell (2005); Garrard (2014); Nixon (2005).
[44] Rigby (2014:152).
[45] Heise (1997:6).
[46] Cf. Love (2003); Heise (1997); Idem (2015); Zapf (2008).
[47] Cf. Oppermann (2006); Idem (2012).
[48] Iovino (2012:52); cf. also Buell (2005:10); Glotfelty and Fromm (1996).
[49] Buell (2005:6) (emphasis in the text); cf. also Glotfelty and Fromm (1996).
[50] Hayles (2005:3).
[51] Iovino (2012:56).
[52] Cf. Borsò. 13 February 2015. Web. 18 October 2015 <https://grk1678.hypotheses.org/373>.
[53] Cf. Braidotti (2013).
[54] Cf. Barad (2007).
[55] Cf. Serpil Oppermann (2014:26).
[56] Cf. Haraway (2016).
[57] Iovino (2012:55).
[58] For further explication, please refer to Dolphijn and van der Tuin (2012); Coole and Frost (2010).
[59] Cf. Stengers (2005); Simondon (2008 [1958]); Hörl (2013).
[60] Cf. Ingold (2011).
[61] *Ibid.* (2011:71).
[62] Oppermann (2012:43).
[63] Cf. Iovino (2012); Iovino and Oppermann (2014).

[64] Oppermann (2014:21).
[65] Material ecocriticism (Iovino (2012); Iovino and Oppermann (2014)) connects relational configurations of environment to literary and cultural studies. Yet, the anthropomorphising notions of 'story' and 'narrative' subsume the diverse signifying capacities of human and nonhuman agencies into human concepts, which ultimately maintain human beings' superior – interpretive – position.
[66] Cf. Latour (2005); *Idem* (2013).
[67] Dolphijn and van der Tuin (2012:91).
[68] Bennett (2010:5). Ecosemiotic approaches (Maran and Kull (2014)) have explored relationships between human beings and their environment with particular focus on sign systems; they have, however, not only retained the dichotomies between nature and culture which material ecocriticism seeks to overcome, but also pursue a strong anthropocentric focus.
[69] Bennett (2010:117-118).
[70] Cf. Claviez (2006); Idem (2012).
[71] Cf. Derrida (2002); Abram (2010); Peterson (2013).
[72] Bennett (2010:4).
[73] Oppermann (2014:21).
[74] Buell (2005).
[75] The notion of re-enchantment has been embraced by a wide variety of theoretical approaches ranging from ecophenomenology (Abram (2010); Peterson (2001); Idem (2013).) to new materialism (Bennett (2010), Alaimo (2010)). While the former have revolved mainly around forming ethical relationships between human beings and animals, the latter have taken into account the re-enchantment of nature and environment, too.
[76] Rigby (2004:438).
[77] Crosby (1993).
[78] Exceptions are, e.g. DeLoughrey, Gosson and Handley (2005); Huggan and Tiffin (2010); Bartosch (2013); DeLoughrey, Didur and Carrigan (2015).
[79] Neumann (2017b).
[80] Cf. Clark (2015:116), who draws on the Australian philosopher Val Plumwood.
[81] *Ibid.*, 72-73.
[82] On the concept of environmental justice see Adamson (2001).
[83] Cf. DeLoughrey and Handley (2011:4).
[84] Indeed, the aesthetic agencies of literary texts become entangled not only with other worldly human and nonhuman agencies, but also with the agencies of theory and critical practice themselves.
[85] Barad (2007:393).
[86] Clark (2014:86).
[87] De Landa (2000:21).

Works Cited

Abram, David (2010). *Becoming Animal. An Earthly Cosmology*. New York: Vintage Books.

Adamson, Joni (2001). *American Indian Literature, Environmental Justice, and Ecocriticism: The Middle Place*. Tuscon: The University of Arizona Press.

Alaimo, Stacy (2010). *Bodily Natures. Science, Environment, and the Material Self*. Bloomington: Indiana University Press.

Barad, Karen (2007). *Meeting the Universe Halfway: Quantum Physics and the Entanglement of Matter and Meaning*. Durham: Duke University Press.

Bartosch, Roman (2013). *EnvironMentality. Ecocriticism and the Event of Postcolonial Fiction*. Amsterdam and New York: Rodopi.

Bate, Jonathan (1991). *Romantic Ecology. Wordsworth and the Environmental Tradition*. New York: Routledge.

Belsey, Catherine (2002). *Critical Practice*. London and New York: Routledge.

Bennett, Jane (2010). *Vibrant Matter. A Political Ecology of Things*. Durham and London: Duke University Press.

Borsò, Vittoria. "Interview: Prof. Vittoria Borsò zu den Schlüsselbegriffen des GRK1678" *GRK 1675*. Heinrich-Heine-Universität Düsseldorf, 13 February 2015. Web. 18 October 2015 <https://grk1678.hypotheses.org/373>.

Braidotti, Rosi (2013). *The Posthuman*. Cambridge: Polity.

Buell, Lawrence (1995). *The Environmental Imagination. Thoreau, Nature Writing, and the Formation of American Culture*. Cambridge, MA and London: The Belknap Press of Harvard University Press.

--- (2005). *The Future of Environmental Criticism*. Malden: Blackwell Publishing.

Chakrabarty, Dipesh (2009). "The Climate of History: Four Theses." *Critical Inquiry* 35, 199-201.

Clark, Timothy (2014). "Nature, Post Nature." *The Cambridge Companion to Literature and the Environment*. Ed. Louise Westling, 75-89.

--- (2015). *Ecocriticism on the Edge. The Anthropocene as a Threshold Concept*. London and New York: Bloomsbury.

Claviez, Thomas (2006). "Ecology as Moral Stand(S). Environmental Ethics, Western Moral Philosophy and the Problem of the Other." *Nature in Literary and Cultural Studies. Transatlantic Conversations on Ecocriticism*. Eds. Catrin Gersdorf and Sylvia Mayer. Amsterdam and New York: Rodopi, 435-454.

--- (2012). "Jamming What Exactly? Some Notes on the 'Anthropological Machine' and Ethics in Derrida, Agamben, Calarco, and Latour." *Literature, Ecology, Ethics. Recent Trends in Ecocriticism*. Eds. Timo Müller and Michael Sauter. Heidelberg: Winter, 69-80.

Coole, Diana, and Samantha Frost (eds.) (2010). *New Materialisms. Ontology, Agency, and Politics*. Durham and London: Duke University Press.

Coupe, Laurence (ed.) (2000): *The Green Studies Reader. From Romanticism to Ecocriticism*. London and New York: Routledge.

Crosby, Alfred (1993). *Ecological Imperialism: The Biological Expansion of Europe, 900-1900*. Cambridge: Cambridge University Press

Davies, Tony (1997). *Humanism*. London: Routledge.

De Landa, Manuel (2000). *A Thousand Years of Nonlinear History*. Cambridge, MA and London: MIT Press.

DeLoughrey, Elizabeth M., Jill Didur and Anthony Carrigan (eds.) (2015). *Global Ecologies and the Environmental Humanities: Postcolonial Approaches*. New York and London: Routledge.

---, Renée K. Gosson and George B. Handley (eds.) (2005). *Caribbean Literature and the Environment: Between Nature and Culture*. Charlottesville and London: University of Virginia Press.

---, and George Handley (2011). "Introduction: Toward an Aesthetics of the Earth." *Postcolonial Ecologies. Literatures of the Environment*. Eds. E. D. and G. H. Oxford: Oxford University Press. 3-39.

Derrida, Jacques (2002). "The Animal Therefore I Am (More to Follow)." *Critical Inquiry* 28.2, 369-418.

Dolphijn, Rick, and Iris van der Tuin (2012). *New Materialism: Interviews and Cartographies*. Ann Arbor: Michigan University Press.

Garrard, Greg (ed.) (2014). *The Oxford Handbook of Ecocriticism*. Oxford: Oxford University Press.

Glotfelty, Cheryll, and Harold Fromm (eds.) (1996). *The Ecocriticism Reader. Landmarks in Literary Ecology*. Athens: University of Georgia Press.

Griffin, David Ray (2007). *Whitehead's Radically Different Postmodern Philosophy: An Argument for Its Contemporary Relevance*. Albany: State University of New York Press.

Haraway, Donna (1992). "The Promises of Monsters: A Regenerative Politics for Inappropriate/d Others." *Cultural Studies*. Eds. Lawrence Grosberg, Cary Nelson and Paula Treichler. New York and London: Routledge, 295-337.

--- (2015). "Anthopocene, Capitalocene, Plantationocene, Chthulucene. Making Kin." *Environmental Humanities* 6, 159-165.

--- (2016). *Staying With the Trouble*. Durham, NC and London: Duke University Press.

Hayles, N. Katherine (1999). *How We Became Posthuman. Virtual Bodies in Cybernetics, Literature, and Informatics*. Chicago and London: University of Chicago Press.

--- (2005). *My Mother was a Computer: Digital Subjects and Literary Texts*. Chicago: University of Chicago Press.

Heise, Ursula K. (1997). "Science and Ecocriticism." *The American Book Review* 18.5, 4, 6.

--- (2015). "Environmental Literature and the Ambiguities of Science." *Anglia* 133.1, 22-36.

Hörl, Erich (2013). "A Thousand Ecologies: The Process of Cyberneticization and General Ecology." *The Whole Earth: California and the Disappearance of the Outside*. Eds. Diedrich Diederichsen and Anselm Franke. Berlin: Sternberg Press, 121-130.

Huggan, Graham, and Helen Tiffin (2010). *Postcolonial Ecocriticism: Literature, Animals, Environment*. Abingdon: Routledge.

Ingold, Tim (2011). *Being Alive: Essays on Movement, Knowledge and Description*. London: Routledge.

Iovino, Serenella (2012). "Material Ecocriticism. Matter, Text, and Posthuman Ethics." *Literature, Ecology, Ethics. Recent Trends in Ecocriticism*. Eds. Timo Müller and Michael Sauter. Heidelberg: Winter, 51-68.

Iovino, Serenella, and Serpil Oppermann (eds.) (2014). *Material Ecocriticism*. Bloomington and Indianapolis: Indiana University Press.

James, Erin (2015). *The Storyworld Accord. Econarratology and Postcolonial Narratives*. Lincoln and London: University of Nebraska Press.

Kerridge, Richard, and Neil Sammells (eds.) (1998). *Writing the Environment. Ecocriticism and Literature*. London and New York: Zed Books Ltd.

Kirby, Vicki (2011): *Quantum Anthropologies. Life at Large*. Durham, NC: Duke University Press.

Kroeber, Karl (1994). *Ecological Literary Criticism. Romantic Imagining and the Biology of Mind*. New York: Columbia University Press.

Latour, Bruno (1993). *We Have Never Been Modern*. Cambridge, MA: Harvard University Press.

--- (2004). "How to Talk About the Body? The Normative Dimension of Science Studies." *Body & Society* 10.2-3, 205-229.

--- (2005). *Reassembling the Social: An Introduction to Actor-Network-Theory*. Oxford: Oxford University Press.

--- (2013). *An Inquiry into Modes of Existence*. Cambridge, MA: Harvard University Press.

Lefebvre, Henri (1991 [1974]). *The Production of Space.* Trans. Donald Nicholson-Smith. Malden, MA: Blackwell.

Love, Glen (2003). *Practical Ecocriticism. Literature, Biology, and the Environment*. Charlottesville: University of Virginia Press.

Maran, Timo, and Kalevi Kull (2014). "Ecosemiotics. Main Principles and Current Developments." *Geografiska Annaler* Series B, 41-50.

Merchant, Carolyn (2003). *Reinventing Eden: The Fate of Nature in Western Culture*. New York: Routledge.

Neumann, Birgit (2017a). "Von der eigentümlichen Macht der Materie in der englischen Literatur des 18. Jahrhunderts – 'Sounding Bodies' und 'Passive Brains'." *Die Materie des (bildenden) Geistes. Der ,material turn' im Kontext von Bildungs- und Literaturgeschichte um 1800*. Eds. Roman Bartosch and Sigrid Grimm. Heidelberg: Winter. [in press]

--- (2017b). "Referring Leaves to their Originals': Multiplying Environments in Derek Walcott's *Tiepolo's Hound.* " *Configurations*. [under review]

Nixon, Rob (2005). "Environmentalism and Postcolonialism." *Postcolonial Studies and Beyond*. Eds. Ania Loomba et al. Durham and London: Duke University Press.

Oppermann, Serpil (2006). "Theorizing Ecocriticism. Toward a Postmodern Ecocritical Practice." *Interdisciplinary Studies in Literature and Environment* 13.2, 103-128.

--- (2012). "Rethinking Ecocriticism in an Ecological Postmodern Framework. Mangled Matter, Meaning, Agency." *Literature, Ecology, Ethics. Recent Trends in Ecocriticism*. Eds. Timo Müller and Michael Sauter. Heidelberg: Winter, 35-50.

--- (2014). "From Ecological Postmodernism to Material Ecocriticism: Creative Materiality and Narrative Agency." *Material Ecocriticism*. Eds. Serenella Iovino and Serpil Oppermann. Bloomington: Indiana University Press.

Palsson, Gisli, et al. (2013). "Reconceptualizing the 'Anthropos' in the Anthropocene: Integrating the Social Sciences and Humanities in Global Environments Change Research." *Environmental Science & Policy* 28, 3-13.

Parham, John, and Louise Westling (eds.) (2017). *A Global History of Literature and the Environment.* Cambridge: Cambridge University Press.

Peterson, Anna (2001). *Being Human. Ethics, Environment, and Our Place in the World*. Berkeley and Los Angeles: University of California Press.

--- (2013). *Being Animal. Beasts and Boundaries in Nature Ethics*. New York and Chichester: Columbia University Press.

Plumwood, Val (2002): *Environmental Culture. The Ecological Crisis of Reason*. London and New York: Routledge.

Pratt, Mary Louise (1992). *Imperial Eyes: Travel Writing and Transculturation*. London: Routledge.

Rigby, Kate (2004). "Earth, World, Text: On the (Im)possibility of Ecopoiesis." *New Literary History* 35.3, 427-442.

--- (2012). "Ecocriticism." *Introducing Criticism at the Twenty-First Century*. Ed. Julian Wolfreys. Edinburgh: Edinburgh University Press, 151-178.

--- (2014). "Romanticism and Ecocriticism." *The Oxford Handbook of Ecocriticism*. Ed. Greg Garrard. Oxford: Oxford University Press, 60-79.

Simondon, Gilbert (2008 [1958]). *Du Mode d'Existence des Objets Techniques*. Paris: Aubier.

Spivak, Gayatri Chakravorty (2003). *Death of a Discipline*. New York: Columbia University Press.

Stengers, Isabelle (2005). "Introductory Notes on an Ecology of Practices." *Cultural Studies Review* 11.1, 183-196.

Trexler, Adam (2015). *Anthropocene Fictions: The Novel in a Time of Climate Change*. Charlottesville, VA: University of Virginia Press

Whitehead, Alfred North (1919). *The Principles of Natural Knowledge*. Cambridge: Cambridge University Press.

--- (1920). *The Concept of Nature: the Tarner Lectures Delivered in Trinity College, November 1919*. Cambridge: Cambridge University Press.

--- (1929). *Process and Reality, an Essay in Cosmology*. New York: Macmillan.

Zapf, Hubert (2008). "Literary Ecology and the Ethics of Texts." *New Literary History* 39.4, 847-868.

Zapf, Hubert (ed.) (2016). *Handbook of Ecocritcism and Cultural Ecology*. Berlin and Boston: de Gruyter.

Roman Bartosch (Köln)

Æsthetic Æffect. Relationality as a Core Concept in Environmental Studies and Education

1. Entangling Aesthetics

The current times, it is becoming increasingly clear, are precarious in multiple ways. As the twenty-first century commences, we find ourselves in the midst of a whirl that radically reshapes long-standing certainties and truths, ranging from the political and socio-economical to the ecological as well as the epistemological and ontological. Writing about this time of transition and emergence, Donna Haraway asks,

> What happens when human exceptionalism and bounded individualism [...] become unthinkable in the best sciences, whether natural or social? Seriously unthinkable: not available to think with. [...] What happens when the best biologies of the twenty-first century cannot do their job with bounded individuals plus contexts, when organisms plus environments, or genes plus whatever they need, no longer sustain the overflowing richness of biological knowledges, if they ever did?[1]

Haraway in this passage points to a number of complex entanglements, also recently analysed in much detail by Karen Barad (2007) and Bruno Latour (2004). They constitute what she and Latour describe as 'naturecultures', a term that testifies to the fact that the facile equations 'individuals plus contexts', 'nature plus cultures', 'environments plus humans' seem no longer to add up, or that they have begun adding up to an incalculable sum. It is with regard to the dawning understanding of complex enmeshment and the quest for a term to contain it that Haraway cries out: "Surely such a transformative time on earth must not be named the Anthropocene!"[2] I agree that a terminology that culminates multiverse and emergent networks into the story of 'Species Man' is an "almost laughable rerun of the great phallic humanizing and modernizing Adventure, where man, made in the image of a vanished god, takes on superpowers in his secular-tragic ascent."[3] However, as Haraway implies, such a rejection of linear explanatory frameworks – 'Man', 'Capitalism' and so forth – warrants an alternative that may help us to understand these perilous times.

Many branches of the environmental humanities have therefore more or less unanimously agreed on another slogan: 'everything is connected to everything else'.[4] Yet, what exactly does it help to assume that *every*thing connects with *every*thing else – for politics, ethics, pedagogy, and, not least, cultural analyses? The *how* of the interconnection is, it seems to me, much more interesting than the very fact that complete interconnection means that the world is (and, probably, always was!) enormously complex. As it were, stating the obvious – 'the world is complex' – turns out to become just another facile explanation, even if it may incite a certain humility before all that which cannot be known and mastered. "Nobody", Haraway succinctly remarks, "lives everywhere; everybody lives somewhere. Nothing is connected to everything; everything is connected to something."[5] Environments, aesthetics, ethics and education need to be rethought, and it seems about time to do this rethinking by paying closer attention to the specificities of their multiform relations and, as I will be doing in this chapter, to relationality as a core concept of the environmental humanities.

So, instead of the one-size-fits-all explanation of complexity, we need to sharpen our senses and readjust our frames of perception for an acute awareness of the relations that constitute naturalcultural environments, understood here as necessarily subjective phenomenal sites that implicate both perceiver and perceived in more-than-dualist relations. This has already been attempted in quite a number of philosophical and intellectual schools and theories, some of which I will be pointing to here briefly. My main argument, however, will be that literature is of great value in this endeavour because its aesthetic figurations ground in a sense and experience of relations and thus engenders ways of perceiving and feeling relationality. This, in turn, has important implications for the ways in which literary texts are read and taught, which is why I will conclude my argument by remarking on questions of education and the implementation of literary studies in schools and universities. The kinds of thinking that are fostered by reading literary texts are the kinds of thinking we might need right now; reading, in other words, is not a luxurious or idle pastime but a catalyst of creativity and an exercise in relational thinking and feeling. This is why we should reconsider its place in or absence from curricula and policy documents.

Relationality as a figure of thought and epistemological as well as ontological figuration surely has a long history in psychoanalysis and its poststructuralist refashioning by thinkers such as Gilles Deleuze and Félix Guattari or in the cultural theory of Édouard Glissant; it has played an important role in the sociology of Norbert Elias and his concept of *homines aperti*; it influences current thought in the new materialisms of Karen Barad and Jane Bennett and has of course also left a mark in contemporary ecocritical research, for instance in material ecocriticism.[6] Despite the individual differences of these approaches, they all share a desire to spell out non- or more-than-dualist accounts of being and becoming and challenge notions of a stable and transcendent human identity in strict separation from natural and cultural ecology. Some scholars have therefore suggested speaking of a 'relational turn'.[7] In any case, it seems worthwhile to consider in how far all of these approaches to relationality share an interest in the role of experience and individual involvement – notions, that is, that are central to aesthetic communication and that will allow me to include the discourses of art and the role of reading literary fiction in this context. Engaging, through affect and interpretations, with literature draws on this very sense of relationality that thinkers as diverse as the motley crew mentioned above have tried to fathom in most insightful ways. No hermeneutic understanding, no feeling-with in literature without relationality – between texts and readers, words and worlds, or within the polyphony of characters and intertextual family ties.

After a brief overview of the history of this idea in literary studies and, more particularly, ecocriticism, I will elaborate on the notion of aesthetic relationality by describing two of its specific ways – 'morphing' and 'scaling' in my terminology. In the third and fourth section of the essay, I describe scaling and morphing as pivotal aspects of the effect of aesthetic discourse, and frame the experience of relationality in fiction in terms of the notion of affect,[8] or, in my terminology, as 'æsthetic æffect'.[9] In doing so, I am trying to highlight that in the experience of the literary, relations precede relata too: reading effects affect, and affect effects the meaning and significance of literature. This has important implications for the teaching of literature as well as its role in education which is why I will conclude the essay by discussing educational philosophy and practice in light of literary relationality and æsthetic æffect.

2. Relationality and Environmental Literary Criticism

Relationality has from its very beginnings played a major role for the epistemological and ethical trajectories of ecocriticism. At the heart of much ecocritical theory and interpretive praxes has always been the question of ecological interrelatedness and the ethical entanglements of humans with their environments or nonhuman co-inhabitants. These forms of relational thinking thus constitute the main focus of this chapter that sets out to describe them in more general terms as foundational operations of aesthetic reading with crucial pedagogical and ethical implications. Therefore, rather than presenting a close reading or in-depth analysis of a single text, my aim is to briefly review how narratives spell out different forms of relationality and relational experientiality in order to describe what I call 'æsthetic æffect' as the most important contribution of literature to current debates in the environmental humanities. I am hereby inspired by existing work in (environmental) aesthetics, especially Gernot Böhme's recent work on atmospheres and Kate Rigby's place-based take on the idea of a distribution of aesthetic force that includes the human, which she dubs "ecstatic dwelling".[10] Diffusion and relationality are at the heart of both, and my aim here is to better describe the possible trajectory of such aesthetic ecstasies[11] in terms of 'æsthetic æffect'.

'Scaling' and 'morphing' are central aspects of æsthetic æffect and constitute two ways of describing aesthetic relationality between texts and readers that I conceive of as affective ones.[12] Affect, in this sense, is understood as "the corporeal instantation of recognition […] which accumulate[s] over time, fostering a sense of self-worth"[13], assigning a particular value to æsthetic æffect for onto-epistemological as well as pedagogical praxes. The pedagogical dimension of affective experience has indeed long been recognised; I will here try to add to the many findings on the social dimension of (affective) learning the role of literary fiction in the process of engendering an entangled notion of selfhood. Before that, however, a few words of caution on what I do *not* mean to do.

Together with other approaches to thinking embodiment and phenomenal dwelling, ecocriticism has pointed to the importance of considering and thinking through the importance of space. As Lawrence Buell writes, "There never was an is without a where."[14] In its early phases, with its emphasis on nature writing and what has been described as a post-poststructuralist attitude to the reality of a world within which cultural and fictional narratives are situated, ecocriticism has thus gained much of its analytical relevance from the insight that "[p]lace is the specific resource of environmental imagination."[15] This return to the stuff of earthly existences has not remained undisputed: postcolonial ecocriticism in particular has criticised the Western-based conceptions of place at work in environmental(ist) thinking, and it has emphasised the culture-specific notion of wilderness underlying an alleged 'direct' relation between wordscape and worldscape.[16] This is part of the reason why the more theoretically inclined writing of 'second-' and 'third-wave' ecocritics generally again foregrounds the discursive dimensions of our cultural imaginaries in order to point out that, even for an environmentalist, there is nothing 'outside the text'. Hence, while the assumption that the/an "environment matters", as Sonja Frenzel and Birgit Neumann's introduction puts it, is an uncontested axiom of ecocritical thought, the contours of this 'aesthetic agency' are less unequivocally stated. I therefore think it is crucial that ecocriticism returns to the specific questions of the 'literary' in the context of reading spaces and our place within them as well as human entanglements with the nonhuman. What does literature have to offer for ethical, onto-epistemological worlding processes?

In asking for the *differentia specifica* of literary fiction in the context of ecocritical analyses of environments, I am endorsing a functional approach[17] to imaginative writing grounded in aesthetic theory and phenomenological approaches to reading fiction. This allows to conceptualise what may be genuine to (some) literary texts by highlighting the role and nature of affect rather than certain literary representational modes. Such a predominant interest in representation, I argue with Derek Brewer, is an example of the "mimetic fallacy", as it assumes that "actions, people and things can and should be closely imitated in words."[18] It shows in what Tim Morton describes as 'ecomimesis'[19] just as well as in many debates over 'ecocentric writing' in which 'the' ecosystem is taken as an allegedly unambiguous measurement and indicator of 'nature', disregarding its anthropogenic and anthropocentric dimensions. An ecosystem is defined, after all, by humans and grounded in specific scientific and metaphysical assumptions concerning the nature and regulation of systems, and so forth.[20] This is how Morton's call for an 'ecology without nature' can be read as well: It is not only our metaphysical and romantic conception of nature, which Morton discusses in terms of what he calls the 'beautiful soul syndrome', but our scientific hold on environments as ecosystems, conceived of with a supposedly objective view from nowhere, that frames – and possibly distorts – our perception of the world. As an analytical yard stick for what Buell calls 'environmentality'[21] in texts, it may thus be misleading at best, and politically damaging and dangerous at worst.

Buell offers 'environmentality' in response to the critique of his concept of an environmental text and especially to Dana Phillips's scathing remarks on Buell's (and others) naïve reliance on the realist mode of narrative supposedly equipped best to bring home a feeling for, and an adequate image of, landscapes and environments.[22] Buell had, in his earlier *The Environmental Imagination* (1995), tried to set up a list of criteria that could be taken to define what he then called an 'environmental text', a text, that is, that could be described as 'earth-bound' and as not only aesthetically but ethically desirable for ecocritics. What Buell defined as "the study of the relationship between literature and environment *conducted in a spirit of commitment to environmental praxis*"[23] – ecocriticism or, as he called it, environmental literary criticism – thus not only makes claims about preferable representational and generic modes but also about ethical effects that stem directly from said modes. Phillips takes issue with this idea and what he believes is Buell's 'untheoretical' endorsement of concepts and terminology and concludes that "[t]o suggest that the nature depicted in a literary text [...] can be something substantial, is at odds with the fact that ideology, fantasy, and allegory are basic to literature."[24] And he concludes his diatribe against representationalist naiveté by suggesting: "[I]f this [...] is intended as ecocriticism, then ecocriticism needs to be given a strong dose of formalism."[25] I will return later to the question in how far Formalism might provide a way out of the representational/ethical dilemma of ecocriticism; for now, it might suffice to say that Buell indeed reacted to these allegations, arguing that ecocriticism should incorporate narrative modes into its reflection and read different texts against each other so as to learn to understand the complex social and natural ecologies at play in literature. "Once I thought it helpful to try to specify a subspecies of 'environmental texts'", he muses – but "[n]ow it seems to me more productive to think inclusively of *environmentality* as a property of any text"[26]. What, then, is environmentality? And if it is a property of any text – where can it be located?

In the theoretical writings of such diverse thinkers as Michel Foucault, Joachim Radkau, Timothy W. Luke, and Giorgio Agamben, the political dimension of ecological discourse has been repeatedly stressed. Luke, for instance, has, in analogy with Foucault's concept of governmentality, shown "how discourses of nature, ecology, or the environment [...] might be reinterpreted as efforts to generate systems of 'geopower'" or biopolitics, and he has described this tendency by using the term 'environmentality' as well.[27] This for sure is an environmentality different from the one Buell and other ecocritics (myself included!) had or have in mind, but the notable parallel should not go unnoticed. In both cases, an elusive 'nature' is defined and made to speak, apparently for itself and thus objectively and unequivocally, as an 'ecosystem' – be it in ecosystem management or in aesthetic and critical discourses. In both cases, ecology is anything but a value-free, neutral view from nowhere but a man-made "disciplinary environment [...] where power/knowledge operate as ensembles of geo-power and eco-knowledge"[28].

In my own engagement with what I have called 'EnvironMentality' I have, cautiously acceding to the inevitability of epistemological anthropocentrism, tried to bypass these intricacies by focussing on individual interpretive engagements with literature, understood as both material and semiotic environments, and by pointing to the word's original implication of an act of 'environing': the construction of a spatial organisation of perception that makes sense only from the restriction of the one who perceives or, in hermeneutic terms, as the 'horizon of understanding'.[29] In other words, the point is to theoretically bring together relationality and an individual perceptional and experiential position, over and against the hegemonic fantasy of a view from nowhere. The parallels between such a phenomenological ecocriticism and hermeneutics are not coincidental but point to the role and significance of reading and interpretive praxes in the context of relating with the world. This is why I have tried to contrast my own concept of engaging with literary environments with the perspective of ecological knowledge by endorsing a radically different notion of knowledge production: one that concentrates first and foremost on the encounter of the reader with word and world in ways that engender, and make felt, relationality. Knowing relations is feeling them, and an approach that concentrates on this 'thinking-feeling' (Massumi) and æsthetic æffect points to ways of negotiating environmental ethics radically different from those grounded in what is usually understood to be the 'eco-' in both ecocriticism and ecology.

Fiction, from this perspective, appears as an interdiscourse or, as proponents of cultural ecology would aver, functions on at least three discursive tiers[30] that can best be defined and understood in their relational nature. Readers *relate* to storyworlds, which in turn consist of *relating* characters and perspectives, which in turn are realised through *relations* with readerly interpretation and emotional investment: æsthetic æffect draws on countless relationalities that in sum constitute the agency of literary fiction. And these relations are a matter of aesthetic experiences rather than philological inquiry. Thus, in contrast to the predominantly intellectual ruminations on readerly inference and interpretation brought about by gaps and blanks that are in the focus of traditional reception aesthetics, and by returning to some of the basic tenets of classical aesthetics, the specific agency engendered by literary responses to textual environments consists in æsthetic æffect realising a potential relationality. And this brings us back to the role of Formalism, hinted at, maybe only rhetorically, by Dana Phillips, as mentioned above. Indeed, in Russian Formalist Viktor Shklovsky's famous formulation of the objective of narrative as understood by formalist inquiry, there is at its core what could be called an ecocriticial programme in the sense discussed by the likes of Buell, Zapf, and others: In his essay "Art as Device", Shklovsky claims that the purpose of art is "to make a stone feel stony", that is, "to allow us to perceive the object in a special way, in short, to lead us to a 'vision' of this object rather than mere 'recognition'"[31]. The choice of a stone as such an object is already remarkably 'environmental', and it becomes clear from this formulation that, according to formalist thinking, such an environmental effect cannot be bound to realist modes of representation, which would allow for a mere recognition or *effet de réel*, but for defamiliarising ways of narrative rendering that lead to a 'vision' of the world – an ethical effect indeed, if we conceive of environmental ethics in literary contexts as the reconfiguration of older, and perhaps damaging, forms of seeing the world.

As is well known, Shklovsky's term for this process is *ostraniene*. As Benjamin Sher, translator of the 2009 edition of Shklovsky's *Theory of Prose*, reminds us, this word is a neologism:

> There is no such word in Russian dictionaries. [...] It is a pretty fair assumption [...] that Shklovsky speaks of *ostraniene* as a process or act that endows an object or image with 'strangeness' by 'removing' it from the network of conventional, formulaic, stereotypical perceptions and linguistic expressions.[32]

But he continues by refuting current translations of the term as 'estrangement' or 'defamiliarization' as either too "negative and limited" or "dead wrong". In contrast, his suggestion, 'enstrangement', is "positive" as its use of the prefix *en*-, as in 'enthrall', suggests a bringing-about while "it is also strongly associated with the counterpointing 'estrange'"[33]. To my knowledge, only one publication from the field of the environmental humanities to date has explicitly discussed this particular meaning of '*en*strangement' despite its outstanding importance for the discussion of narrative and ethics.[34] But the potential of enstrangement should not go unnoticed: (Environmental) Literary perception is not about reconfirming prevalent views of familiar; it is a dialectic movement between epistemologies and knowledges that can be reconfigured in the act of reading.

The specific power of literary narrative and aesthetic communication has of course been recognised before, and it should be recognised even more in the environmental humanities and the discussion of literature and ethics. Indeed, from its beginnings in Alexander Gottlieb Baumgarten's mid-18th-century *Aesthetica*, modern aesthetic theory has grappled with the paradox that aesthesis, described by Baumgarten as *analogon rationis*, produces knowing analogous to but ultimately different from knowledge derived from rational inquiry.[35] A literary take on environments – or environmental takes on literature – ought therefore to be alert to the aesthetic specifics and agencies of literariness and come to terms with the ways in which knowledge is produced beyond the confines of intellectual reasoning as well as the role and significance of the individual receptive dimension of embodied affect.

Against the notion of an all-encompassing view from nowhere, a phenomenological environment is conceived from a first-person perspective: it is "something for a creature, a field of meanings or significance"[36]. 'EnvironMentality', from this perspective, is a relation between a living creature and its life- (or story-)world. Yet, neither creature nor world exist *a priori*; they are engendered through the relation and exist temporarily in and as space. They are not subject and object but form a complex, phenomenal mesh. And while non-dualist thinking and relationality are tropes of many different current onto-epistemologies, from actor-network theory and agential realism to new materialism and material ecocriticism, it is this phenomenological outlook that first posited relationality as a constitutive element. It must be noted that from a phenomenological perspective, such an inherent relationality is by no means restricted to literary writing; in fact, the very idea of relational thinking is that relationality is an ontic condition. However, literature can be seen as a privileged site where such onto-epistemologies can best be explored and experienced. This is what distinguishes literary fiction from the material agency of any other object, if not in kind, then by degree: by its high degree of sympoetic self-awareness, by its high degree of compositional complexity and, maybe most importantly, through a specific mode of encountering texts we as interpretive community have decided to see as 'aesthetic' ones, experiential relationality is closely tied to the process of aesthetic reading.

3. Morphing

The first category or class of experience that literary fiction is able to generate could almost go unnoticed due to its ubiquity and commonness: thinking-with other, even nonhuman, characters, and assuming another's point of view and feeling. What researchers especially in the cognitive branch of literary studies have called 'mind-reading' and related to our 'theory of mind' is obviously not restricted to fictional literature; yet literary writing seems to hold a special place when it comes to the sophistication of this form of relational experience.[37] Timothy Morton goes as far as to claim that relational feeling-with – traditionally decried as anthropomorphism or pathetic fallacy – is an anthropological constant of humans that has clear equivalents in other objects and beings as well:

> I *anthropomorphize*. It's not that I anthropomorphize in some situations but not in others. It's that, because of the fact of phenomenological *sincerity*, I can't help anthropomorphize everything I handle. [...] It is impossible for me to peel myself away from the totality of my phenomenological being. Just as I fail to avoid anthropomorphizing everything, so all entities whatsoever constantly translate other objects into their own terms. [...] The wind windpomorphizes the temperature differentials between the mountains and the flat land. The mountains are shellpomorphic piles of chalk.[38]

'Phenomenological sincerity' is a strong concept that resonates with what has been said above about the presumably neutral position 'from nowhere' against which I have tried to position the notion of relationality. In more concrete terms: when I see the confusing excitement of human beings over a "gold metal" I do not understand because I am realising Buck's perspective in Jack London's *The Call of the Wild* (1903); or when I suffer the hardships of toil and neglect as the eponymous *Black Beauty* by Anna Sewell (1877), I am doing this because of a relationality between myself-as-reader and the focalising instance of the texts, not because I can fully immerse myself in another's consciousness and know what it's like to be a dog or a horse (or, in Thomas Nagel's famous example, a bat). But this is not a limitation; it points to the fact that experience, too, is relational. What Morton calls translation thus relies on a relational nexus of sameness and difference that in current human-animal studies is discussed as 'the creaturely'.[39] And while there is some disagreement over the question whether the creaturely as a figure of thought can do away with human/animal binaries and dualist thinking concerning the nonhuman world, or whether, as a matter of fact, it re-instigates this very violent hierarchy,[40] my point here is that such creaturely relationality can be felt in literary texts of almost every type, making fiction a store-house and test-case of sympoiesis. As trope and narrative strategy, it can only ever function because of an inherent relationality realised in readerly engagements.

I have, in another context, pointed out that this kind of relationality, despite its ontic dimension, does not offer any kind of 'secure knowledge' about the other as biologist or ecological sciences fantasise about. Rather, it establishes relationality as an experience, which might lead us to a kind of "care-filled reading".[41] One of the lessons of care-filled reading, I have argued, is that

> In contradistinction to the ideal of factuality in other areas of knowledge production, the forms of knowing of aesthetic discourses are realized in relations, not in discrete data. What we can learn from reading fiction, in other words, is not facts or truth-claims about humans, animals and everything in-between but rather how an experience of creaturely poetics creates a sense of uncertainty and connectivity that eventually takes effect in a stance of wonder and, perhaps, care, or supports what Matthew Calarco has described as an "agnostic animal ethics".[42]

Such are the wonders of morphing in literature: a knowing that is not knowledge, but a knowing still, and one that cannot be replaced easily. Let's call it æsthetic æffect.

4. Scaling

My second exploration of æsthetic æffect, one that takes us from the horizontal plane of co-inhabitant critters to the vertical dimensions of time and space, is best described as 'scaling'. Scale, Timothy Clark maintains, is one of the crucial categories and conflictive quandaries of current environmental and ecocritical thought. One of his examples is the popular slogan 'Think globally, act locally': it "involves work on at least two scales at the same time. It says, in effect: try to understand ecological systems on the largest possible scale and then take action locally in accordance with that understanding"[43]. It is indeed one of the central objectives of environmental education to foster a thinking-together of such different scales, often identified as the individual, the national (or communal) and the global dimension. If only this were so easy: contemporary environmental thinking, Clark avers, is marred by 'derangements of scale' and confusing 'scale effects' in unprecedented proportions:

> Scale effects […] are confusing because they take the easy, daily equations of moral and political accounting and drop into them both a zero and an infinity: the greater the number of people engaged in modern forms of consumption then the less the relative impact of their insignificance.[44]

And, with regard to literary analyses, he goes on:

> The larger the scale, the more thing-like becomes the significance of the person registered on it [...]. Plots, characters, setting and trivia that seemed normal and harmless on the personal or national scale reappear as destructive doubles of themselves on the third scale [that is, the planetary, transnational one].[45]

Scale is thus more than just a challenge of thinking complexity because, as Derek Woods claims, it includes assemblages "of relation among ontologically different entities".[46] Paradoxically, thus, what some prefer to call the Anthropocene "names the disempowerment of human beings in relation to terraforming assemblages that draw much of their agency from nonhumans": scale effects.[47]

Yet while ontologically incompatible scales are indeed a major challenge in environmental thought and especially politics, literary fiction has always worked with an imaginative contraction, refiguration, and expanding of various scales. Urban fiction in particular almost always negotiates different scales of individual experience and the larger structures of the city;[48] one of the key features of authorial narrative situations is the jumping back and forth in time, and from Victorian novels to today's science fiction, we have spatial and temporal scales that deliberately transcend usual dimensions of thought and experience. Consider David Mitchell's *Cloud Atlas* (2004): It consists of a multiplicity of embedded stories that, while they are situated across different times and spaces, are linked through plot and motifs, thus creating a sense of conflictual harmony across the time, place, and the experientiality of humans and machines as well as the media formats of diary, letters, and novelistic narration. The harmony established by the novel's form does not resolve conflicts but at the same time creates coherence and the performative paradox that this coherence relies on spatiotemporal and medial disjunction – this is an ambivalence æsthetic æffect can explain.

In this context, Astrid Bracke notes that all of the different storylines of the novel lend themselves to ecocritical readings and together present a rather conclusive tableau of environmental concerns:

> The eighteenth-century journal of Adam Ewing – the first narrative – invites an analysis of environmental colonialism, whereas in the narrative

> describing corporacy, the fifth story, widespread environmental destruction is placed side-by-side with the complete breakdown of boundaries between humans and nonhumans.[49]

And she shows in which ways, as "a novel, [...] the structure is significant"[50]. I agree and hold that it is its structure that allows for an insight into scaling techniques as well as the inevitable derangements of scale brought about by the different dimensions on which the narrative is played out. Through its form, then, the novel achieves its environmental effect: "its complex recursive structure does not lead attention *away* from its environmental dimension, but *foregrounds* and *emphasizes* it."[51]

The point for me is that by this means of narrative scaling, a meaning is generated that is indeed greater than the sum of its parts: narrative harmonisation – the feeling of textual and storied unity despite the stories' derangement of scales – is in fact a felt and an embodied experience of relationality across the very scales the story draws on. In her discussion of the role of form in contemporary narratives, Bracke's next example is Ian McEwan's *Solar*. Recounting the critical history of, mostly, frustration and disappointment, Bracke concludes that this history is closely tied to expectations and conventions associated with novelistic form.[52] And her reading of the novel's structure and composition allow her to refute the oft-repeated claim that the unsympathetic anti-hero of the novel weakens any readerly insight into the complexity of environmental crisis and the competences needed for its 'solutions' (if such a thing exists): She concludes that

> *Solar* illustrates a pluriformity of views on nature: through a combination of characters – Beard, Melissa, and the idealistic Aldous – the novel shows the many dimensions of contemporary debates on environmental crisis and climate change, which cannot be caught in the simplistic opposition between deniers and activists.[53]

In that environmental meaning is generated across actants and even timescales, the novel moves the notion of meaning from intellectual reasoning found in both philological or biographical readings and techno-fix thinking in environmentalism and towards an affective knowing of (narrative) harmonisation. By way of presenting a 'synthesis of the heterogeneous' (Ricœur), novelistic discourse generates æsthetic æffect.

Æsthetic æffect is, however, not just a diffuse complexity where everything relates to everything else. It relies on fine mesh of relationalities that are in no way restricted to the diegetic world but expand into the readerly world where the innertextual relations are realised.

5. Æducation?

From what has been said before, we can conclude that narration and textual composition as well as readerly affective response are the crucial elements of a poetics of relationality. It should also be clear that affective reception does not come naturally but is a question of skill, habit, and diligence. Becoming response-able to literature in the way outlined hereis thus always already a question of education too, as it recognises aesthetic response to be the pivotal moment that takes us from poetics to an ethics derived from literature. Being able to respond to literature "as literature", as Derek Attridge would say,[54] is what in educational research is dubbed a competence that is highly complex and difficult to attain.[55] Let me, therefore, conclude this chapter by pointing to the role of education – or, indeed, the inextricability of narrative interpretation, affective reception, and educational praxes – in the context of environmental ethics and fiction.

If, as recent research from the fields of posthumanism, (material) feminism, and biosemiotics suggests, our sense of identity and ethical ramifications of empathy are distributed and entangled, and if, as argued above, such entanglements show in the aesthetic discourse strategies of scaling and morphing, then the experience of aesthetic communication is also a crucial educational and political issue. Since reading aesthetically shows strong parallels with, could even be said to be analogous to, experiencing a distributed sense of self, reading aesthetically also marks a pivotal point of entry for an ethics and politics based on entanglement and relationality. In other words, reading fiction and cultivating its æsthetic æffect constitute basic features of ecological politics and ethics because of the role of relationality in all of these fields.

In a sense, existing educational approaches, for instance in the context of Education for Sustainability, draw on this very insight, even though they might not spell out explicitly how and why literary fiction deserves a special place in an environmental curriculum. The UNESCO-based curriculum for 'Global Development' (2016), for example, states that pupils should be empowered to grapple with the world's complexity in social, ecological, and economical ways, and to analyse global change as well as develop plans for action, change perspectives and employ empathy for other people(s), their values, and the nonhuman world.[56] Nowhere do we find any remarks on the potential of fiction, however. The same holds true for the concept of *Gestaltungskompetenz*[57] – the notion that pupils should acquire a competence for individual and societal 'transformation', roughly translatable as 'competence of transformation'. In my view, the notion of a 'transformative competence' also seriously 'undertheorises' the potential and value of fiction. None of these approaches can truly work with the insight of early ecocriticism that "environmental crisis involves a crisis of the imagination"[58]. This is more than a flashy slogan advocating the relevance of cultural studies in an age of technoscience in crisis. Taking seriously the cultural dimension of the natural[59] means that Education for Sustainability needs to become more aware not only of the significance of literary writing but the workings and functions of aesthetics more generally.

This desideratum has also been identified in Grimm and Wanning's publication on cultural ecology and the teaching of literature: in their introduction, the editors claim that "the teaching of literature contributes to education for sustainability a specific form of knowledge that cannot be acquired in any other way"[60]. Drawing on Gerhard de Haan's concept of *Gestaltungskompetenz*, too, Grimm and Wanning show that for pupils to become able to actively transform societies, they need emotional knowledge, the ability to change and coordinate different perspectives as well as an understanding of the (cultural-)ecological potential of the imagination. One such potential, I have maintained, lies in the experience of relationality. Let me therefore briefly introduce and discuss two approaches that I think will help to spotlight challenges and potentialities of dealing with literary fiction in education and environmental contexts before I return to the question of relationality in (literary) education.

To date, the most exhaustive and stimulating attempt to theorise relationality from the perspective of pedagogy and theories of learning has come from Tobias Künkler. In *Lernen in Beziehung* ('Learning in Relations'), Künkler sets out to analyse and critique current learning theories for their lack of precision concerning the terms and ends of the various concepts of learning employed, as he avers, without sufficient awareness of the theoretical contexts from which some of these concepts – behaviourist, cognitivist, constructivist, and neuroscientific – have been taken. From this critique, he develops a substantial theory of learning based on the notion of relationality. Learning, he avers,

> needs to be thought of as a complex and mutually dependent togetherness [*Ineinander*] of self-determination and heteronomy. [...] Learning can thus be described as a process of subjectivation that brings about both emergence and submission.[61]

Drawing on theories of the body and embodiment as well as on numerous writings on subjectivity, Künkler concludes that both the process of learning and the outcome of (distributed) subjectivity must be understood as a 'relational space'[62] that learners and teachers create and enter together. The same space is opened up and explored by fiction, and in the encounter with fictional works.

While Künkler is interested in theories of learning and the terminology and set of concepts necessary to think through the many blindspots and conflicts of current pedagogical theory, Nicola Mitterer explicitly addresses the question of media and narrative when she outlines her approach to a 'theory of responsive reading'. In *Das Fremde in der Literatur* ('The Other in Literature'), she demands that the central objective of literary education should be the ability to perceive aesthetically, which means to engage with the ambiguity of poetic and literary discourse and to develop a response-ability to this abyss of meaning:

> The world that the texts opens up [...] knows no certainties. It is an abyss that everyday language tries to conceal. And yet, everything we think, do, could be beginning, lies only in this abyss, if only we move away from the limitations we call reality. The utopian potential of literature [...] has no substitute and cannot be unfolded in any other discourse.[63]

In dialogue with the writing of Bernhard Waldenfels, responsitivity – or 'response-ability', as other (eco)pedagogic texts have it – is developed as a stance through which readers learn to engage with a text on an affective, embodied, that is to say: aesthetic, level. Instead of interpretive domestication, the text and its singularity constitute the irreducible enigma of the literary, which in turn means that reading holds enormous epistemological and imaginary potentials that "take precedence over rationalist analyses".[64] Such a stance towards the epistemological potential of literary reading shares significant insights with the Formalist notion of 'enstrangement' discussed above. At the same time, and just as Künkler's endorsement of the notion of *Widerfahrnis* (i.e., an experience that someone is powerlessly subjected to), the idea of a 'responsive habitus' falls slightly short of the active nature of literary reception in the sense of æsthetic æffect. If we understand such a habitus as grounded in "a deliberate subordination of the self that temporarily lets go of its (imagined) sovereignty and surrenders to the otherness of the text" in order to foster a form of "answering questioning" that thrives on "a 'passive' stance that is made active only through the demands of the text, its question-abilities",[65] Mitterer's description of the humility before the literary artwork and the working of an 'erotics of art' (Sontag) are convincing but lack, as she concedes, a practical educational dimension that stresses the active position of the reader constructing (her) meaning.

I believe that focussing on æsthetic æffect instead, that is, an idea of literary relationality that precedes the relata of text and reader, and thus also of active and passive roles, is more helpful for our understanding of fiction for the environmental humanities classroom, and that it offers more direct methodological as well as theoretical avenues for thinking through enstrangement, imaginative thinking, and the educational value of relational reading. Such a form of reading and reaction – that I have dubbed affective reception aesthetics elsewhere[66] – would include the kind of responsiveness Mitterer demands as well as creative and individualised engagements with the texts that are read so as to foreground the relational quality of text-reader interactions. It would also call for care-filled reading praxes through which literary fiction may be understood – and, moreover, experienced! – as "a tool for guided and sensitive speculation, a complex zooanthropological machine" and explorative site of affective sympoiesis.[67]

Notes

[1] Haraway (2016:30).

[2] *Ibid.*, 31.
[3] *Ibid.*, 47.
[4] Popularised by Barry Commoner as the 'first law of ecology', the slogan has quickly become an oft-cited statement in ecocritical research as well as pedagogy. See Glotfelty (1996:xix) and Volkmann (2016:205).
[5] Haraway (2016:1). See also van Dooren (2014:60).
[6] See, for instance, Iovino and Oppermann (eds.) (2014).
[7] Künkler (2011:409).
[8] See the various contributions in Gregg and Seigworth (eds.) (2010).
[9] It was only after finalising this chapter that my attention was brought to Jondi Kean's article "Æffect: Initiating Heuristic Life", published in 2013 in *Carnal Knowledge. Towards a 'New Materialism' through the Arts*. Eds. Estelle Barrett and Barbara Bolt. London and New York: Tauris. 41-61. Although our arguments differ in important ways, readers are kindly referred to this text for another take on "the æffective."
[10] Böhme (2013) and Rigby (2004). "Ecstatic Dwelling. Perspectives in Place in European Literature." *Angelaki. Journal of the Theoretical Humanities* 9.2. 117-142.
[11] *Ibid.*, 33.
[12] Affect is here understood not as the prediscursive event that psychological research and its cultural studies applications posit as a means of distinction over and against individual, diachronic reflection. Rather, as my choice of literary reading and interpretation is intended to show, affect should be understood as a centrally *relational* engagement with a hermeneutic situation that does indeed encompass reflection, experience, and a sense of subjectivity but that can never be rationalist. The neologism 'æsthetic æffect' is meant to distinguish this sense of the affective from more orthodox usage concerning the emotional or emotive.
[13] Watkins (2010:273).
[14] Buell (2001:55).
[15] *Ibid.*, 56.
[16] See, for example, Mukherjee (2010) and Crane (2012).
[17] 'Function' in this sense must not be mistaken for semiotic determinism or the notion of a single meaning of any literary text. It is rather deployed as a means to express another form of relationality that concerns literary utterance and effect; an idea that has been discussed, for instance, in Winfried Fluck's functional literary history, Wolfgang Iser's literary anthropology and, indeed, Hubert Zapf's cultural ecology. In this sense, and with an interest in the difficulty of describing literariness in the first place as a measure of literary quality, Christoph Bode as early as 1989 advocated a "functional view" of literariness and literary quality that he described as being primarily "relational." See Bode (1989).
[18] Brewer (1988:1).
[19] Morton, (2007:31-32).

[20] For a detailed critique of the concept of ecocentrism in this respect, see Bartosch (2017). "Against Exuberant Ecocentrism: Kafka, Coetzee, and Transformative Mimesis." *From Ego to Eco. Imagining Ecocentrism in Literature, Film and Philosophy.* Ed. Tina-Karen Pusse. New York and Amsterdam: Brill/Rodopi (*forthcoming*).
[21] Buell (2008:25).
[22] Buell (1995:7) and Phillips (2003).
[23] Buell (1995: 430, emphasis original).
[24] Phillips (2003:161).
[25] *Ibid.*, 168.
[26] Buell (2008:25, emphasis added).
[27] Luke (1995). See also Agrawal (2005).
[28] *Ibid.*, 58.
[29] Bartosch (2013:143-160; 258-291).
[30] See Zapf (2006) and Bartosch (2018) "The Energy of Stories: Postcolonialism, the Petroleum Unconscious, and the Crude Side of Cultural Ecology." *Resilience* (*forthcoming*).
[31] Shklovsky (2009:10).
[32] Sher (2009: xix).
[33] *Ibid.*, xix.
[34] Robles (2016:48).
[35] For a discussion of the notion of affect in light of aesthetic inquiry since Baumgarten, see Highmore (2010).
[36] Cooper and Palmer qtd. in Clark (2014:277).
[37] See Zunshine (2012) and for a study that pays particular attention to the notion of affect Colm Hogan (2011).
[38] Morton (2012:207).
[39] See Santner (2006); Pick (2011); Vermeulen (2015); Ohrem and Bartosch (eds.) (2017).
[40] See Herman (2016).
[41] Fudge (2016) and Bartosch (2016).
[42] Bartosch (2016: 97).
[43] Clark (2011:136).
[44] Clark (2012:150).
[45] *Ibid.*, 161.
[46] Woods (2014:139).
[47] *Ibid.*, 134.
[48] See Bartosch (2015).
[49] Bracke (2014:429).
[50] *Ibid.*, 429.
[51] *Ibid.*, 431.

[52] For a comparable, form-oriented reading of the novel, see also Bartosch (2015:86).
[53] Bracke (2014:433).
[54] Attridge (2004:95).
[55] On the question of competences in the context of literary and aesthetic reading, see Abraham (2008).
[56] See *Orientierungsrahmen für den Lernbereich Globale Entwicklung* (2016). Compiled by Jörg-Robert Schreiber and Hannes Siege. Bonn: Engagement Global, 2016, 95; see also *Ibid.,* 159-173 for a detailed description of these competences in the context of teaching English
[57] Bormann and de Haan (eds.) (2007).
[58] Buell (1995: 2).
[59] See, for instance, Hulme (2009).
[60] Grimm and Wanning (2016). (my translation).
[61] Künkler (2011).
[62] See Künkler (2011: 350, my translation).
[63] Mitterer (2016) (my translation).
[64] Mitterer (2016:273, my translation), see Attridge (2004).
[65] Mitterer (2016: 272, my translation).
[66] Bartosch (2017). "Graveyard Poetry und die Wirkmacht des Körpers. Grundzüge einer affektiven Rezeptionsästhetik." *Die Materie des Geistes. Der* Material Turn *aus Sicht der Bildungs- und Literaturgeschichte.* Eds. Sieglinde Grimm and Roman Bartosch. Heidelberg: Winter (*forthcoming*).
[67] Bartosch (2016: 99).

Works Cited

Abraham, Ulf (2008). "Lesekompetemz, Literarische Kompetenz, Poetische Kompetenz. Fachdidaktische Aufgaben in einer Medienkultur." *Kompetenzen im Deutschunterricht.* Eds. Heidi Rösch. Frankfurt: Peter Lang, 13-26.

Agrawal Arun (2005). *Environmentality. Technologies of Government and the Making of Subjects.* Durham: Duke University Press.

Attridge, Derek (2004). *The Singularity of Literature.* New York and London: Routledge.

Barad, Karen (2007). *Meeting the Universe Halfway. Quantum Physics and the Entanglement of Matter.* Durham: Duke University Press.

Bartosch, Roman (2013). *EnvironMentality. Ecocriticism and the Event of Postcolonial Fiction.* Amsterdam & New York: Rodopi.

--- (2015). "Scaling the City: Urban Environments and Transcultural Consciousness in Zadie Smith's *NW* and Ian McEwan's *Saturday*." *Journal for the Study of British Cultures* 22.1, 73-88.

--- (2016). "Ciferae in the City." *American Beasts. Perspectives on Animals, Animality and U.S. Culture, 1776-1920*. Ed. Dominik Ohrem. Berlin: Neofelis, 75-100.

--- (2017a). "Against Exuberant Ecocentrism: Kafka, Coetzee, and Transformative Mimesis." *From Ego to Eco. Imagining Ecocentrism in Literature, Film and Philosophy*. Ed. Tina-Karen Pusse. New York and Amsterdam: Brill/Rodopi (*forthcoming*).

--- (2017b). "Graveyard Poetry und die Wirkmacht des Körpers. Grundzüge einer affektiven Rezeptionsästhetik." *Die Materie des Geistes. Der* Material Turn *aus Sicht der Bildungs- und Literaturgeschichte*. Eds. Sieglinde Grimm and Roman Bartosch. Heidelberg: Winter (forthcoming).

--- (2018). "The Energy of Stories: Postcolonialism, the Petroleum Unconscious, and the Crude Side of Cultural Ecology." *Resilience; Special issue*. Eds. Axel Goodbody and Bradon Smith (forthcoming).

Bode, Christoph (1989). "Literary Value and Evaluation: The Case for Relational Concepts." *Anglistentag 1988 Göttingen – Proceedings*. Eds. Heinz-Joachim Müllenbrock and Renate Noll-Wiemann. Tübingen: Max Niemeyer, 309-324

Böhme, Gernot (2013). *Atmosphäre. Essays zur neuen Ästhetik*. Berlin: Suhrkamp.

Bormann, Inka, and Gerhard de Haan (eds.) (2007). *Kompetenzen der Bildung für nachhaltige Entwicklung. Operationalisierungen, Messung, Rahmenbedingungen, Befunde*. Wiesbaden: Verlag für Sozialwissenschaften.

Bracke, Astrid (2014). "The Contemporary English Novel and its Challenges to Ecocriticism." *The Oxford Handbook of Ecocriticism*. Ed. Greg Garrard. Oxford: Oxford University Press, 423-439.

Brewer, Derek (1988). "Escape from the Mimetic Fallacy." *Studies in Medieval English Romances. Some New Approaches*. Ed. Derek Brewer. Cambridge: D. S. Brewer, 1-10.

Buell, Lawrence (1995). *The Environmental Imagination: Thoreau, Nature Writing, and the Formation of American Culture*. Cambridge, MA: Harvard University Press.

--- (2001). *Writing for an Endangered World. Literature, Culture, and Environment in the U.S. and Beyond*. Cambridge, MA: Belknap Press of Harvard University Press.

--- (2008). *The Future of Environmental Criticism. Environmental Crisis and Literary Imagination*. Malden: Blackwell.

Clark, Timothy (2011). *The Cambridge Introduction to Literature and the Environment*. Cambridge: Cambridge University Press.

--- (2012). "Derangements of Scale." *Telemorphosis: Theory in the Era of Climate Change*. Ed. Tom Cohen. Ann Harbor: Open Humanities Press, 148-165.

--- (2014). "Phenomenology." *The Oxford Handbook of Ecocriticism.* Ed. Greg Garrard. Oxford: Oxford University Press, 276-290.

Colm Hogan, Patrick (2011). *Affective Narratology. The Emotional Structure of Stories.* Nevada: University of Nebraska Press.

Crane, Kylie (2012). *Myths of Wilderness in Contemporary Narratives. Environmental Postcolonialism in Australia and Canada.* Basingstoke: Palgrave Macmillan.

van Dooren, Thom (2014). *Flight Ways. Life at the Edges of Extinction.* New York: Columbia University Press.

Fudge, Erica (2016). "Farmyard Choreographies in Early Modern England." *Renaissance Posthumanism.* Eds. Joseph Campana and Scott Maisano. New York: Fordham University Press, 145-166.

Glotfelty, Cheryll (1996). "Introduction: Literary Studies in an Age of Environmental Crisis." *The Ecocriticism Reader. Landmarks in Literary Ecology.* Eds. Cheryll Glotfelty and Harold Fromm. Athens: University of Georgia Press, xv-xxxvii.

Gregg, Melissa, and Gregory J. Seigworth (eds.) (2010). *The Affect Theory Reader.* Durham and London: Duke University Press.

Grimm, Sieglinde, and Berbeli Wanning (2016). *Kulturökologie und Literaturdidaktik.* Göttingen: Vandenhoeck und Ruprecht unipress.

Haraway, Donna J. (2016). *Staying with the Trouble. Making Kin in the Chthulhucene.* Durham and London: Duke University Press.

Herman, David (2016). "Introduction: Literature Beyond the Human." *Creatural Fictions. Human-Animal Relationships in Twentieth- and Twenty-First-Century Literature.* Ed. David Herman. Basingstoke: Palgrave Macmillan, 1-15.

Highmore, Ben (2010). "Bitter After Taste: Affect, Food, and Social Aesthetics." *The Affect Theory Reader.* Eds. Melissa Gregg and Gregory J. Seigworth. Durham: Duke University Press, 118-137.

Hulme, Mike (2009). *Why We Disagree about Climate Change. Understanding Controversy, Inaction and Opportunity.* Cambridge: Cambridge University Press.

Iovino, Serenella, and Serpil Oppermann (eds.) (2014). *Material Ecocriticism.* Bloomington and Indianapolis: Indiana University Press.

Keane, Jondi (2013). "Æffect: Initiating Heuristic Life." *Carnal Knowledge. Towards a 'New Materialism' through the Arts*. Eds. Estelle Barrett and Barbara Bolt. London and New York: Tauris, 41-61.

Künkler, Tobias (2011). *Lernen in Beziehung. Zum Verhältnis von Subjektivität und Relationalität in Lernprozessen.* Bielefeld: Transcript.

Latour, Bruno (2004). *Politics of Nature: How to Bring the Sciences into Democracy.* Cambridge, MA: Harvard University Press.

Luke, Timothy W. (1995). "On Environmentality: Geo-Power and Eco-Knowledge in the Discourses of Contemporary Environmentalism." *Cultural Critique* 31.2, 57-81.

Massumi, Brian (2008). "The Thinking-Feeling of What Happens." *Inflections* 1.1, 1-40.

Mitterer, Nicola (2016). *Das Fremde in der Literatur. Zur Grundlegung einer responsive Literaturdidaktik.* Bielefeld: Transcript.

Morton, Timothy (2007). *Ecology without Nature. Rethinking Environmental Aesthetics.* Cambridge (MA): Harvard University Press.

--- (2012). "An Object-Oriented Defense of Poetry." *New Literary History* 43.2, 205-223.

Mukherjee, U. Pablo (2010). *Postcolonial Environments. Nature, Culture and the Contemporary Indian Novel in English.* Basingstoke: Palgrave Macmillan.

Ohrem, Dominik, and Roman Bartosch (eds.) (2017). *Beyond the Human-Animal Divide. Creaturely Lives in Literature, Culture, and History.* Basingstoke: Palgrave Macmillan (*forthcoming*).

Ortiz Robles, Mario (2016). *Literature and Animal Studies.* London and New York: Routledge.

Phillips, Dana (2003). *The Truth of Ecology. Nature, Culture, and Literature in America.* Oxford: Oxford University Press.

Pick, Anat (2011). *Creaturely Poetics. Animality and Vulnerability in Literature and Film.* New York: Columbia University Press.

Rigby, Kate (2004). "Ecstatic Dwelling. Perspectives in Place in European Literature." *Angelaki. Journal of the Theoretical Humanities* 9.2, 117-142.

Santner, Eric (2006). *On Creaturely Life. Rilke, Benjamin, Sebald.* Chicago: University of Chicago Press.

Schreiber, Jörg-Robert, and Hannes Siege (2016). *Orientierungsrahmen für den Lernbereich Globale Entwicklung.* Issued by the German Federal Ministry for Economic Cooperation and Development. Bonn: Engagement Global.

Sher, Benjamin (2009). "Translator's Introduction." *Theory of Prose.* Viktor Shklovsky. Champaign and London: Dalkey Archives Press, xv-xxi.

Shklovsky, Viktor (2009). *Theory of Prose.* Champaign and London: Dalkey Archives Press.

Vermeulen, Pieter (2015). *Contemporary Literature and the End of the Novel. Creature, Affect, Form.* Basingstoke: Palgrave Macmillan.

Volkmann, Laurenz (2016). "Transcultural Learning and Ecodidactics: New Trends in Teaching English as a Foreign Language." *America After Nature. Democracy, Culture, Environment.* Eds. Catrin Gersdorf and Juliane Braun. Heidelberg: Winter, 199-217.

Watkins, Megan (2010). "Desiring Recognition, Accumulating Affect." *The Affect Theory Reader.* Eds. Melissa Gregg and Gregory J. Seighworth. Durham and London: Duke University Press, 269-285.

Woods, Derek (2014). "Scale Critique for the Anthropocene." *The Minnesota Review* 83, 133-140.

Zapf, Hubert (2006). "Literature and Ecology: Introductory Remarks on a New Paradigm of Literary Studies." *Anglia* 124.1, 1-10.

Zunshine, Lisa (2012). *Getting Inside Your Head. What Cognitive Science Can Tell Us about Popular Culture.* Baltimore: The John Hopkins University Press.

Sonja Frenzel (Düsseldorf)

An EcoPoetics of Storied Matter: Agency, Affect, and Errantry in the Anthropocene

1. Stories Matter

Contemporary debates surrounding environments, ecocriticism, and ethics thrive on ever more profoundly sustained evidence that human agencies have become decisive geological and biogenetic forces in the earth's ecosystems. This anthropocenic age supersedes, or at least powerfully re-focuses, the geological epoch of the Holocene by drawing attention to

> the growth and impacts of the human species worldwide, including all its written history, development of agriculture and major civilisations, and overall significant transition toward urban living in the present.[1]

In thus stressing the crucial influences of human life forms upon their nonhuman environments, the Anthropocene challenges us, as human beings[2], into pivotal awareness not only of our agentic powers, but also of the moral responsibilities[3] these agentic powers engender. After all, it is our human ways of being in the world that have been complicit in prompting and further propelling an ever more urgent state of ecological emergency, which has affected and will continue to affect human and nonhuman life on this planet. The present evocation of the Anthropocene thus capitalises – not unproblematically – on the scope and the manifold dimensions of human agency; and yet, more importantly, it thereby also calls for radically altered relations between the human and the nonhuman.

It may seem curious to note that contemporary ecocritical attempts at conceiving such altered relations between human and nonhuman agencies abound with ideas of story-telling. For one, Bruno Latour has argued that agency in the Anthropocene comes to be expressed in a shared "geostory"[4], which he conceives of as a narrative fabric that is concocted through the collective participation of human and nonhuman life forms in the earth's ever-evolving story. His line of argument presumes that story-telling is not an exclusively human prerogative, indeed, it is "not just a property of human language, but one of the many consequences of being thrown in a world that is, by itself, fully articulated and active"[5]. This 'fully articulated world' abounds with diverse, often conflicting and disjunctive modes of articulation, which not only exceed human practices of story-telling, but which, in fact, resist any attempts at their easy incorporation into a singular notion of story-telling. Rather, story-telling in the Anthropocene thrives on the multiple and multiply diffracted capacities to signify that come to be articulated by human and nonhuman agencies.

This essay critically examines the premises and possibilities of such story-telling in the light of material-ecocritical approaches. To this end, it sets out to trace ideas of shared story-telling along theorisations of nonhuman capacities to signify in recent ecosemiotic and ecophenomenological approaches, and proceeds to incorporate these observations into the concept of storied matter. Arguably, material story-telling reaches beyond the premises of Western-European modernity. These transformative impulses will be explored mostly along the two conceptual axes of errantry and affect, before they will, again, be brought to bear upon configurations of the Anthropocene.

2. Shared Story-Telling

The notion of a collectively shared, human and nonhuman, story-telling revaluates prevalent conceptualisations of signs and significations, of language and articulation. Rather than a property that divides the human from the nonhuman, signification and articulation come to constitute shared, albeit not common, capacities that relate the human and the nonhuman.[6] These capacities are *shared* to the extent that any human or nonhuman agency may foster them; they are, however, not *common* to the extent that available signs and languages as well as the significations and articulations they bring forth remain diffracted[7] and thoroughly diverse. The present section follows two pertinent lines of inquiry into this conundrum, namely ecosemiotics and ecophenomenology, before engaging critically with material-ecocritical conceptualisations of storied matter.

To begin with, ecosemiotic approaches[8] have traced Charles S. Peirce's trialectic semiotics in nonhuman articulations and have thereby identified "a multitude of other semiotic systems, some partly accessibly, some rather different from ours".[9] Generally speaking, ecosemiotics focuses on the accessibility or rather decipherability of nonhuman sign systems. In thus emphasising the perception of these signs, it bears a strong anthropocentric perspective on meaning-making processes and facilitates their incorporation into human story-telling.[10] Ecophenomenology shifts awareness to the perception of both human and nonhuman processes of signification. This approach argues that human and nonhuman capacities to signify derive from their shared – corporeal – materiality, which constitutes "a realm wherein the body itself speaks – by the tonality and rhythm of its sounds, by its gestures, even by the expressive potency of its poise"[11]. Such articulations are initially observed in relations between human and nonhuman animals[12], as they become enmeshed into an "earthly cosmology"[13], or a "kind of *distributed sentience*"[14], that exceeds human capacities to signify as well as human sign systems and semiotics.

In sum, ecophenomenology and, perhaps to a slightly lesser degree, ecosemiotics thus relinquish any assertions of human exceptionality, as each approach calls, instead, for revaluating human-nonhuman relations as horizontal. Undermining the "civilised assumption" that "to speak, or to think in words, is necessarily to step back from the world's presence into a purely human sphere of reflection"[15], they recognise and realise a range of diverse capacities to signify, which engender alternative relations between the human and the nonhuman, including not only animals, but also plants, objects, and artefacts. Ultimately, these alternatives open up new strands within a collective story-telling that promise the possibility for a "renarrativisation"[16] of the hitherto prevalent story of modernity's disenchantment, an "alter-tale"[17] of *The Enchantment of Modern Life* (2001). Put more succinctly, if we choose to acknowledge human and nonhuman capacities to signify as partaking in shared story-telling, then it may well be that this human and nonhuman "[n]arrative agency is the world's reenchanting property"[18].

It is the notion of (re)enchantment[19] that may translate shared human and nonhuman story-telling into a critique of Western-European modernity. Running counter to a dominant narrative of rationality and individuality, enchantment stresses affective relationality. In a nutshell, this affective relationality derives from what Jane Bennett has referred to as the "vitality" of matter.[20] This vitality – or vibrancy – not only denotes material capacities to signify, but foregrounds their (eco)phenomenological potential to induce a sense of wonder and, hence, to affect. In recognising capacities to signify as capacities to affect Bennett shifts awareness from human perceptions of nonhuman articulations to human encounters with nonhuman agencies. Actively engaging with the vitality of their materialisations means "to hone sensory receptivity to the marvellous specificity of things" so as to allow oneself "to be struck and shaken by the extraordinary that lives amid the familiar and the everyday".[21] Even as Bennett retains a human-centred perspective, the enchanted vitality of matter entangles humans and nonhumans in horizontal relations of affecting others and of being affected by others in turn.

This enchantment resonates most profoundly in material ecocriticism's key concept of storied matter. Most notably, this concept correlates the new materialist presumptions of enchanted vibrancy or "thing-power"[22] with ecocritical approaches in literary and cultural studies. Accordingly, "matter is perceived as a site of narrativity [...] where the world reveals its creative becoming, its dynamism, and its reenchantment"[23]. While the notion of geostory has been shown to evoke the comprehensively enmeshed history of the earth, storied matter, in turn, diffracts this history into its multiple, yet still multiply entangled strands. Indeed, storied matter proposes that human and nonhuman agencies come to be articulated in protean configurations of matter and meaning. Their dynamic becoming and affective relating derive from a shared materiality and, subsequently, co-emerge in ongoing processes of materialisation. Translated into the present terminology, this onto-epistemological becoming brings forth human and nonhuman capacities to signify, which partake in the agentic dynamics of shared story-telling. As a conceptual metaphor, story-telling thus evokes human and nonhuman agencies as the threefold configurations of matter's capacities for becoming, signifying, and relating.

Among the manifold efforts at re-thinking narrative agency beyond its prevalent associations with human intentionality and human capacities to signify, storied matter has by now crystallised into a particularly prolific concept. And yet, these animist conceptualisations of storied matter have been criticised not only for their anthropomorphising tendencies, but also for their seemingly all too thorough associations with Western-European notions of story-telling. First and foremost, such criticism points to the contested role of literary studies in contemporary ecocriticism. After all, storied matter appears in the wake of the linguistic turn, which has previously consolidated the binary oppositions of modern thought[24]. Most significantly, at least for the present purposes, it has purported the constitutive power of language and the mind over the body and the physical world. As Karen Barad laments, quite pointedly: "Language matters. Discourse matters. Culture matters. There is an important sense in which the only thing that does not seem to matter any more is matter."[25] Hence, it certainly is an issue of concern when storied matter, albeit drawing on material capacities to signify, relies excessively on literary terminology.

Broadly speaking, storied matter co-occurs along two strands: Firstly, in "the way matter's (or nature's) nonhuman agentic capacities are described and represented in literary texts", and, secondly, in "matter's 'narrative' power of creating configurations of meanings and substances, which enter with human lives into a field of co-emerging interactions".[26] My discussion so far has focused mainly on the latter aspect, on the vibrant dynamics of material becoming and its intrinsic capacities to signify. In the following, I will engage critically with prevailing assumptions of linearity in Western-European narratives, by juxtaposing them with vibrant, i.e. non-linear, alternatives. I argue that storied matter may be rendered most productive when considering that its constitutive matter-flows are non-linear, nomadic or errant, lines of becoming. It is along these lines that storied matter, rather than falling into the trap of anthropomorphism, may actually succeed in revaluating and transforming the idea of narrative and open up new ways of thinking about story-telling in the Anthropocene. Calling for new relations between human and nonhuman agencies, storied matter may thus come to exemplify horizontally and reciprocally entangled trajectories of becoming and relating. After all, story not only affects matter, but matter, in turn, affects story as well.

While the notion of story-telling aptly seconds ecocriticism's grounding in literary and cultural studies, it needs to be expanded, in the present endeavour, so as to accommodate the diverse, often conflicting and disjunctive ways in which nonhuman materialities come to signify. And yet, the Anthropocene's stories have been and will continue to be perpetually confronted with story-telling's firm grounding in human notions of signification and representation. Meeting the valid criticism that ecosemiotics and even ecophenomenology may run in danger of anthropomorphising nonhuman agencies, the notion of material story-telling has become affiliated with new materialist and material-ecocritical approaches that commend self-reflexive anthropomorphism "as a heuristic strategy aimed at reducing the (linguistic, perceptive, and ethical) distance between the human and the nonhuman".[27] It is against this backdrop that the essay at hand seeks to acknowledge and, at the same time, to reach beyond its own human vantage point. After all, and as paradoxical as it may seem, it may be only in due awareness of the "unavoidable feature[s] of our human condition"[28] that we may recognise nonhuman capacities to signify as "meaningfully articulate forms of becoming"[29] in their own right.

In the Anthropocene, then, stories come to matter as they contribute to the intertwined processes of translating human and nonhuman becoming into agentic capacities to signify and into shared articulations of the "ongoing reconfigurings of the world".[30] It may seem that narrative agencies thus revolve around the two pivotal strands of material becoming and material relating. In other words, human and nonhuman agencies hinge upon two crucial modes of planetary existence, namely around errantry and relation[31]. In the following, I aim to explore not only how these modes of planetary existence open up plausible, albeit problematic, trajectories into re-thinking human and nonhuman agencies. Furthermore, I seek to exemplify how they may contribute to expanding storied matter beyond the Western-European premises of the so-called Modern Constitution[32] and into planetary repercussions within an Anthropocenic ecological poetics.

3. Material Becoming: Errantry

The dynamic becoming of storied matter derives from a shared, human and nonhuman, materiality and its ongoing processes of materialisation. In a nutshell, it is by fostering the dynamic property of becoming that materiality may be recognised as matter in movement, in flux, in variation.[33] Furthermore, it is these non-linear dynamics that bring forth and articulate the material capacities to signify that have hitherto been conceived of as human and nonhuman lines of shared story-telling. The present section traces the dynamic entanglements of these lines of story-telling into the narrative fabric of storied matter.

A concise illustration of these dynamics may be discovered in Tim Ingold's model of the meshwork, as it permits correlating lines of story-telling with lines of material becoming. Hence, human or nonhuman capacities to signify may be seen to materialise in a line of story-telling or, in Ingold's terminology: in "a trail along which life is lived".[34] Each of these trails emanates from a material source and, as their articulations materialise, they come to exemplify one of "the multiple pathways of [this material source's] involvement in the world".[35] Accordingly, thus, these trails continuously grow and branch out in their ongoing processes of materialisation and articulation to the extent that they enter into relations with trails emanating from other human or nonhuman material sources. Their reciprocal entanglements come to form "knots in a tissue of knots, whose constituent strands, as they become tied up with other knots, comprise the meshwork".[36] Ultimately, as the meshwork's constitutive articulations continue to prosper through their innate capacities to live, grow and move, the entire meshwork is itself embroiled in ongoing processes of transformation, "continually ravelling here and unravelling there".[37] It is in the protean configurations of multiple and multiply enmeshed material articulations that such matter-flows may come to be recognised as lines of story-telling, which may eventually become enmeshed into an ever-unfolding shared story.

This storied meshwork of human and nonhuman articulations resonates, too, in Olive Senior's poetry cycle *Gardening in the Tropics*.[38] In the opening poem, "Plants", multiple lines of story-telling can be seen to co-emerge: The poem's shared story unfolds on the level of the poetic speaker's and her addressee's human articulations, on the level of plant materialities and their agentic capacities to signify, and, finally, on the level of the poem's particular visual and haptic materiality of ink on paper, words on page. As the scope of the present discussion permits to focus only on the first two levels of material story-telling, it seems all the more worthwhile to include the poem in its full length:

Plants[39]

Plants are deceptive. You see them there
looking as if once rooted they know
their places; not like animals, like us
always running around, leaving traces.

Yet from the way they breed (excuse me!)
and twine, from their exhibitionist
and rather prolific nature, we must infer
a sinister not to say imperialistic

grand design. Perhaps you've regarded,
as beneath your notice, armies of mangrove
on the march, roots in the air, clinging
tendrils anchoring themselves everywhere?

The world is full of shoots bent on conquest,
invasive seedlings seeking wide open spaces,
matériel gathered for explosive dispersal
in capsules and seed cases.

Maybe you haven't quite taken in the
colonizing ambitions of hitchhiking
burrs on your sweater, surf-riding nuts
bobbing on ocean, parachuting seeds and other

airborne traffic dropping in. And what
about those special agents called flowers?
Dressed, perfumed, and made-up for romancing
insects, bats, birds, bees, even you –

don't deny it, my dear, I've seen you
sniff and exclaim. Believe me, Innocent,
that sweet fruit, that berry, is nothing
more than ovary, the instrument to seduce

you into scattering plant progeny. Part of
a vast cosmic program that once set
in motion cannot be undone though we
become plant food and earth wind down.

They'll outlast us, they were always there
one step ahead of us: plants gone to seed,
generating the original profligate,
extravagant, reckless, improvident, weed.

When contemplating these poetic stories with particular focus on the dynamics of material becoming, it is plants that come to enact a secret, even 'deceptive', yet nonetheless superior agency. In fact, the military jargon of invasion and conquest used to express the plants' nonhuman agencies radically alters human-nonhuman relations to the extent that plants covertly eschew their presumed rootedness and pursue, instead, an 'imperialistic / / grand design'. These 'sinister' purposes are not only disguised by the plants' presumably static rootedness, but also by their appearance: While plants are perceived to be '[d]ressed, perfumed, and made-up for romancing', their beauty is merely 'the instrument to seduce / / you into scattering plant progeny'. Hence, in fact, when the plants' nonhuman capacities to signify come into contact with human endeavours to interpret them, the speaker warns, it is humans' stark ignorance of their ontological and epistemological agencies that will effectively upturn human-nonhuman relations.

From a postcolonial perspective, these material stories gain additional weight: Not only do they animate hitherto inert nature into story-telling agencies; what is more, they come to express "processes of translocation in colonial and post-colonial histories [that] bear on and radically transform the materialisation of seemingly "natural" landscapes".[40] These stories may thus be read as a *signifying-back* from colonised Caribbean 'nature' to colonising European 'culture'. Indeed, the material stories of the plants' imperialistic conquest and humanity's 'innocent' ignorance unfold in an affective realm of signification and articulation that exceeds the capacities of human signification and articulation through language. What is more, it is this excess that translates the hierarchies of colonising and colonised agencies into relations between humans and plants. In thus reversing dominant relations in favour of plants and nature, the poem also articulates a critique of Western-European modernity and its constitutive binary oppositions between movement and stasis, culture and nature, humans and their environments.

In sum, these observations have shown material story-telling in its dynamic emergences. What is more, in the Anthropocene, our own – human – lines of story-telling have been shown to co-occur dynamically with the lines of multiple other human and nonhuman agencies. On the one hand, this warrants the conclusion that we need to immerse ourselves into a shared material being in the world, while, on the other hand, we need to acknowledge our decisive influence that has shaped and continues to shape the premises of this being the world. This paradoxical situation can only be solved when we keep moving, following the paths of our lines of material becoming and relating them to the stories we may share with other material agencies. In these entanglements, the dynamics of story-telling exceed linearity, but run in turbulent trajectories. More precisely, they come to be articulated in "a very particular type of multiplicity: non-metric, acentred, rhizomatic multiplicities".[41] It is these 'multiplicities' that not only include human lines of story-telling, but that also call upon us human beings to revaluate our entanglements into this storied matter.

It is the notion of nomadism that may adequately spell out these dynamics of human entanglements in the Anthropocene. Not only does it thrive on the entanglements between human beings and their environments, but it may also provide a useful metaphor for translating material story-telling into a shared human and nonhuman narrative:

> The nomad must be aware of herself as a being that dwells in space, that is dependent upon that space, whose sense of self is built through intersection with a highly differentiated and storied environment. Narratives of identity then grow out of this engagement with local space.[42]

Even as nomadism originates, first and foremost, in theories of human movements across smooth space[43], it has developed into an alternative, i.e. counter-modern, notion for exploring human entanglements with their nonhuman environments beyond mastery and possession.

From a gendered perspective, Rosi Braidotti has adopted Gilles Deleuze and Félix Guattari's *Nomadology* into her "own figuration of a situated, postmodern, culturally differentiated understanding of the subject in general and of the feminist subject in particular".[44] Along these lines, she defines nomadism as "the kind of critical consciousness that resists settling into socially coded modes of thought and behaviour"[45], regardless of whether the people who identify as nomads are "literally nomadic" [46] or travel only in their mind. Indeed, nomadism (sensu Braidotti) seems to disentangle movement from space. As Irene Gedalof criticises, "to put all the emphasis on the going, on the transgression of boundaries, is to sidestep the question of place in the construction of a sense of self".[47]

Hence, it may seem that Braidotti proposes an all too metaphorically inflated appreciation of nomadism: As the conditions of nomadic life materialise chiefly in their overdetermination by environments as well as by political and historical power structures, their ontological and epistemological entanglements may appear quite far removed from the deliberate immersion into a subversive mindset. The nomad, then, "has little in common with the forced, or at least more uncomfortable and complicated, trajectories of migrants, exiles and others who travel without tenure"[48].

And yet, nomadism has been embraced by many Caribbean poets, who have translated nomadism into a particularly localised, decidedly counter-modern, poetics of errance and relation that responds to the particularities of the islands and their long histories of displacement.[49] Allegedly, Western-European modernity has fostered an "arrow-like nomadism" and, therefore, thrives on a linear and "absolute forward projection".[50] Such dynamics are designed to possess territories and, consequently, these dynamics correlate territorial possession with the modern concepts of nation and subjecthood.[51] These trajectories resonate in the lingering trajectories of imperial and colonial relationalities, as they continue to evoke dialectical movements from centre to periphery and from periphery to centre, which have yet to be translated into planetary repercussions beyond peripheries or centres, from any one place to any other.

Quite contrarily, alternative conceptualisations of non-linear or errant nomadism postulate "some specific need to move, in which daring or aggression play no part".[52] Presumably, this errant nomadism constitutes a "not-intolerant form of impossible settlement"[53], which has been taken up again in Eduard Glissant's *Poetics of Relation*[54] and in Kamau Brathwaite's 'tidalectics'[55]. Their conceptualisations of non-linear dynamics privilege a masculine-gendered version of the ongoing story-telling surrounding the middle passage over the feminine-gendered experience of non-linear dwelling in the belly of the slave ship and on the Caribbean islands[56].

Rendering the middle passage in images of giving birth, Grace Nichols' epic poem *i is a long memoried woman* not only introduces a woman's voice into the cultural memory of the middle passage.[57] What is more, she tells a gendered story of material becoming and relating which proceeds, in the speaker's articulations of a woman's slave experience, to intriguingly oscillate in nomadic dwelling:

Web of Kin[58]

[…]

even in dreams I will submerge myself
swimming like one possessed
back and forth across that course
strewing it with sweet smelling
flowers
one for everyone who has made the journey

and at evenings I will recline
hair full of sun
hands full of earth
I will recline on my bed of leaves
bid the young ones enter sit them
all around me

feed them sweet tales of Dahomey

In this brief excerpt, the speaker travels 'back and forth' across the middle journey and, thereby, perpetually moves along non-linear trajectories. All the while, she is 'submerged' in water, 'swimming', rather than being separated from the water by being contained in the slave ship's belly. Her movements are, therefore, thoroughly immersed in and intimately entangled with the nonhuman materiality of the sea and its own tidalectic movements. Similarly, in her island dwelling place, the speaker 'recline[s] on [her] bed of leaves' while she is simultaneously embraced by the nonhuman materialities of the sun and the earth. This, too, is a recurrent scene, 'at evenings', when the speaker gathers 'the young' and 'feeds them sweet tales of Dahomey', of the origins of their diasporic becoming.

This scene evokes nomadic dwelling, not only when the speaker is enmeshed with the nonhuman materialities of her environment (the sea and the island), but, furthermore, when the speaker engages in the dynamics of remembering the middle passage. While she does so through her own dream journeys in the first stanza, the re-telling of this story in the second stanza thrives on the feminine-gendered material dynamics of feeding. As food sustains bodies, the image of nourishment entangles corporeal materialisations with the material stories of cultural memory. In sum, then, the woman speaker's island dwelling is perpetually shaped and re-shaped by nomadic entanglements with other human and nonhuman agencies.

4. Relating Matter: Affect

Material becoming and errant materialisations hinge not only on non-linear dynamics, but also on the affective relationality these nomadic movements engender. As Karen Barad maintains, in her discussion of a quantum physics of shared materiality and touching:

> In an important sense, in a breathtakingly intimate sense, touching, sensing, is what matter does, or rather, what matter is: matter is condensations of response-ability.[59]

It is through recognising this relationality and 'response-ability' that storied matter becomes ecological: Not only are human and nonhuman agencies intrinsically "connected to everything else", as Barry Commoner's much-cited "First Law of Ecology" suggests[60]; but this connectedness calls upon human beings to thoroughly revise the premises – both ontological and epistemological – of our becoming and being in the world as well.

Above all, this ecological relationality thrives on the emphatically plural – relational and relative – assemblages of multiple life forms and their shared story. It translates environment into a notion that is, firstly, "relative […] to the being whose environment it is", while, secondly, it emerges in "a process […] of growth or development" in time, so that, thirdly, it remains utterly distinct from inert and de-historicised nature.[61]

In the light of the present interest in shared story-telling, then, 'environment' becomes a fluid space, an ever-shifting material story of being, knowing and doing into which human and nonhuman, culture and nature, meaning and matter are intimately entangled.

Matter's multiple and multiply entangled capacities to signify elicit pertinent affinities between ecopoetics and the literary genre of ecopoetry, in that "[e]copoetics asks in what respects a poem may be a making (Greek poiesis) of the dwelling-place"[62]. Ecopoetic making, includes and, what is more, correlates place and poetry, ecological relations and poetic significations. Within this ecological poiesis human and nonhuman materialisations become intimately enmeshed through their respective capacities to signify, which immerse them in their singular processes of becoming and in(to) their plural relations with one another. Above all, capacities to signify materialise in the agentic capacities to affect and to be affected in turn.

> Theories of affect [...] name a dynamic that precedes human subjectivity, while signalling the recuperative move in which these intractable forces are recoded as subjective possessions.[63]

In this sense, and in adopting Pieter Vermeulen's above-cited definition of affect in literary works, human story-telling comes to constitute a vital mode of making sense of the difference we encounter in our assemblages with other human or, more so, with nonhuman significations and articulations. This may also link story-telling to its origins in literary studies, i.e. to the notion of literary texts and their significations. After all, literary texts comprise a pool of material (i.e. visual and haptic, acoustic, corporeal, and imaginative) energies, which perpetually materialise and affect us in meaning-making processes.[64]

Literary story-telling co-emerges in each text's materiality (its écriture) and in its ecopoetic, or world-making, capacities to signify and to affect.[65] As Bruno Latour expounds, "[a] work of art engages us [...] If the work needs a subjective interpretation, it is in a very special sense of the adjective: we are subject to it, or rather, we win our subjectivity through it"[66]. These affective dynamics gain particularly relevance in postcolonial ecocriticism. After all, they shed new light upon the multiple and multiply entangled subjectivities that may be brought to materialise in literary texts.

While Derek Walcott's epic poem *Omeros*[67] may provide ample evidence for these affective dynamics and their material stories, they emerge most succinctly in one episode, in which the meandering trails of this poetic odyssey take Walcott's poetic alter ego to London. The speaker's reflections on Britain's imperial history and its underlying monolithic conceptualisations of 'Time' crucially revolve around Big Ben. In its particular nonhuman capacities to signify, this monument articulates a particularly British sense of time, but also materialises a sense of British resilience. In fact, it is this latter mnemonic story-line of Big Ben's materialisation, upon which the speaker reflects and which he, simultaneously, challenges:

> Who decrees a great epoch? The meridian of Greenwich.
> Who doles out our zeal, and in which way lies our
> hope? In the cobbles of sinister Shoreditch,
>
> in the widening rings of Big Ben's iron flower,
> in the barges chained like our islands to the Thames.[68]

By rendering Big Ben's clock face as flower, the passage of time is initially evoked through the material story-telling of this flower's organic growth in 'widening rings'; at the same time, however, this pleasant imagery is intriguingly joined with and, ultimately, undermined by the flower's iron materiality. As iron rings are imagined to spread out from Big Ben, their non-organic flourishing may come to materialise British resilience, but may also allude to the speaker's wretched perception of Great Britain's unrelenting mastery over time and history alike.

Recognising Big Ben as a symbol for London, the materialisation of these 'widening rings' acquires a broader historical, political and cultural-symbolic scope. After all, the metropolis's sustained prosperity hinges on the legacies of British imperialism, which are resumed by the iron chains. As these tie 'barges [...] like our islands to the Thames', they conjure images of slaves' shackles. With the Thames connecting London to the sea, the British Empire could thrive on its seafaring capacities and exploit trade relations across the Black Atlantic, including slave trade. Even at the post-imperial time of the poetic speaker's utterance, the iron flowering of time and its historical chains still bind the Caribbean islands to London. Hence, these material stories are 'chained' to the extent that they disappoint the speaker's 'zeal' as well as his 'hope' for transformation. Besides, they further reveal the lingering memories of this experience as one vital thread in the collective story-telling of Anglophone literatures, which continues to intertwine African, Caribbean and British histories. In fact, as relations of time continue to be determined by their distance or proximity to the standard 'meridian of Greenwich', planetary histories and their significance continue to be proclaimed in relation to London's alleged hold on normativity, too.

Nonetheless, the aesthetic-poetic agency of these material stories does not yield for static interpretations, but always remains on the move, or, more precisely perhaps, in an oscillatory, tidalectic, movement across the meridian. Indeed, the meridian constitutes the central principle of Walcott's poetics:

> The central principle by which such double gestures are performed is the meridian, a cartographic line of mirroring, self-recognition and mimicry that organises Walcott's postcolonial poetic project. An articulation of historical power no less than of contemporary cultural predicaments, the meridian emphasises the ambiguities of a world divided by epic traditions and imperial quests.[69]

Indeed, Walcott's poetry habitually leaves space for such crossings in nomadic dynamics and their affective relations: As Birgit Neumann spells out persuasively, in line with Jim Hannan, with reference to Walcott's undermining of heroic couplets in *Tiepolo's Hound*, this space emerges in the poem's blank lines:

> Prompting readers to continuously move back and forth and to bridge the interstices, the 'crossing couplets' (Hannan 2002, 559) become the crossing condition in a poetic 'multiverse' that thrives on both topographical singularity and transcultural entanglements. The crossing couplet resists the sense of temporal closure and spatial containment that is afforded by the traditional heroic couplet and instead signals an openness, a constantly 'deferred finality' (Hannan 2002:566).[70]

These in-between spaces appear between the triplets of *Omeros* as well, equally opening up sites of rupture and, simultaneously, of dwelling. As the linear reading process is interrupted, the reader is challenged to move into and out of the poem's form, into and out of the poem's materiality, and left in a 'blank' – pro-positional – space.

It may seem, indeed, that the poem itself and the storied matter it articulates remain pro-positional only[71]: Even as its capacities to signify may suggest obstinacy, or at least a certain position, this instance of material story-telling lacks any definite or definitive authority. It remains a preliminary pro-position only, which harbours the prospect of entering into com-positions with other material stories. Accordingly, the above reading of Walcott's *Omeros* has been derived from a pre-figured understanding of Big Ben's materialisation; at the same time, and from its particular grounding in Anglophone literatures, even this brief exploration has significantly re-figured this initial perspective by introducing an additional line of materialisation that articulates the legacies of imperial and colonial histories. Ultimately, then, it is along these errant relationalities that "textual interpretation [becomes] a 'practice of entanglement'"[72] in itself.

5. Storied EcoPoetics

In the Anthropocene, human and nonhuman agencies partake in a shared material story. Indeed, their agentic capacities to signify may be perceived to express "modes of existence"[73] with distinct ontologies and epistemologies. These modes co-occur in their singular dynamics of material becoming and, subsequently, enter into plural affective relations with one another. Thereby, each mode of existence simultaneously affects and is affected by other modes of existence to the extent that they jointly weave a narrative fabric of storied matter.

This storied matter brings forth a vibrant storied ecopoetics, as well. Based on Jane Bennett's definition of ecology as "the study or story (logos) of the place where we live (oikos), or better, the place *that* we live"[74], this ecopoetics answers to the Anthropocene's call for radically altered relations between the human and the nonhuman. Not only does the storied ecopoetics proposed in this essay acknowledge the agentic immersion of humans in the ontological and epistemological configurations constituting 'the place that we live'. But it also suggests a critical re-thinking of poetics in the Anthropocene, which will translate the term's etymological meaning of 'making' into an agentic 'doing' articulated in material capacities to signify.

In expanding story-telling from the human to the nonhuman realm, storied matter also challenges the role of literature. Indeed, storied matter runs counter to binary relations between language and world, as well as between knowledge and the known. Its multiple and multiply diffracted aesthetic agencies challenge modern theories of signification and representation. They reveal how "the asymmetrical faith we place in our access to representations over things is a historically and culturally contingent belief that is part of Western philosophy's legacy and not a logical necessity"[75].

In a nutshell, the 'place *that* we live' comes to be constituted by plural and diverse, relational and processual, as well as spatialised and historicised articulations of this storied matter. Finally, it is storied matter, and particularly its inherent frictions, that bears the potential to revaluate human ways of being, knowing, and doing in the Anthropocene, and, eventually, yield for new perspectives on an ecopoetical becoming of the place that we share.

Notes

[1] Commonwealth Scientific and Industrial Research Organization (CSIRO) et al. "Antropocene Timeline." *Welcome to the Anthropocene*. CSIRO et al, 2012. Web. 09.03.2017 <www.anthropocene.info/anthropocene-timeline.php>

[2] When ecocritical discussions, like the one proposed in this chapter, evoke notions of communality, it seems pivotal to mark the scope of this "we". In my introductory survey of the Anthropocene, I begin by referring to human beings as the new agentic forces in the earth's ecosystems, before I proceed to outline a communality of human and nonhuman agentic forces in the notion of story-telling.

[3] The complex discussions surrounding moral responsibilities in the Anthropocene are further illuminated in Claviez (2006); as well as in Krebs (1999).

[4] Cf. Latour (2014:3).

[5] *Ibid.*, 14.

[6] They thrive, instead, on a different kind of encounter that has often been explored in terms of song, as is also outlined in Jonathan Skinner's thought-provoking contribution to this collection.

[7] I am using "diffracted" in the sense coined by Barad (2007) that has been widely adopted in third-wave ecocritical scholarship.

[8] Wendy Wheeler's contribution to this volume offers a richly detailed survey of biosemiotics and highlights their relation to other pertinent approaches in contemporary critical theory.
[9] Maran (2014a:262).
[10] Cf., for instance, Maran (2014b).
[11] *Ibid.*, 167.
[12] These approaches are pursued not only by Abram (2011). But also by Peterson (2013). As well as Peterson (2001) and Porter Eleanor (1997) and Derrida (2002).
[13] Cf. Abram's title.
[14] Abram (2011:190).
[15] Cf. Abram (2011:190).
[16] Plumwood (2009).
[17] Bennett (2001).
[18] *Ibid.*
[19] While Bennett makes a case for re-acknowledging and re-cognising the already existing enchantment of the world, most ecocritical approaches argue that (Western-European) modernist has deprived the world of its (Romantic) enchantment. There seems to be a notable difference in agency in these perspectives, as enchanted agency resides either in human perception or, in Bennett's sense, in vibrant materiality.
[20] Cf. Bennett (2010).
[21] *Ibid.*, 4.
[22] Cf. Bennett (2010).
[23] Oppermann (2014:31).
[24] Cf. Latour (1993).
[25] Barad (2007:132).
[26] Iovino and Oppermann, eds. (2014:79).
[27] Iovino (2012:142)
[28] Rigby (2004:427).
[29] Oppermann (2014:29).
[30] Barad (2007:141).
[31] Cf. Nancy (2000); also quoted in Kaiser (2014:283).
[32] Cf. Latour (1993).
[33] Cf. Deleuze and Guattari (1986).
[34] Ingold (2011:69).
[35] *Ibid.*, 70.
[36] *Ibid.*
[37] *Ibid.*, 71.
[38] Senior (2005).
[39] Senior (2005: 63-64).
[40] Frenzel and Neumann, "Introduction" (this volume).
[41] Deleuze and Guattari (1986:34).

[42] Porter (1997:9).
[43] *Ibid.*
[44] Braidotti (1994:4).
[45] Braidotti (1994:5).
[46] *Ibid.*
[47] Gedalof (1996:192).
[48] *Ibid.*, 193
[49] Cf. Glissant (1997).
[50] *Ibid.*, 12.
[51] Paul Gilroy has offered insightful connections of the concepts of nationhood and subjectivity with race and has entangled them with imperial and colonial trajectories across the Black Atlantic. Cf. Gilroy (1993).
[52] Glissant (1997:12)
[53] *Ibid.*
[54] *Ibid.*
[55] Cf. Brathwaite (1999).
[56] Cf. DeLoughrey (1998).
[57] Cf. Busia (1994); as well as DeLoughrey (1998).
[58] Nichols (1983:9).
[59] Barad (2012:215).
[60] Cf. Commoner (1971); cf. also Glotfelty and Fromm (1996:xix).
[61] Ingold (2011:79-80) as well as idem (2000:20).
[62] Bate (2000:75).
[63] Vermeulen (2014:122).
[64] Cf. Borsò (2012).
[65] Birgit Neumann's and Jan Rupp's contributions respectively emphasise the Caribbean context.
[66] Latour (2013:241).
[67] Walcott (1990).
[68] *Ibid.*, 196.
[69] Döring (2002:176).
[70] Neumann (2016:448). Cf. also Hannan (2002).
[71] Latour (2004:212).
[72] Iovino and Oppermann, eds. (2014:9)
[73] Cf. Latour (2013)
[74] Bennett (2004:365).
[75] Barad (2007:49).

Works Cited

Abram, David (2011). *Becoming Animal: An Earthly Cosmology*. London: Vintage.

Barad, Karen (2007). *Meeting the Universe Halfway. Quantum Physics and the Entanglement of Matter and Meaning*. Durham: Duke University Press.

--- (2012). "On Touching. The Inhuman That Therefore I Am." *Differences. A Journal of Feminist Cultural Studies* 23.3, 206-223.

Bate, Jonathan (2000). *The Song of the Earth*. London: Picador.

Bennett, Jane (2001). *The Enchantment of Modern Life: Attachments, Crossings, and Ethics*. Princeton, NJ: Princeton University Press.

--- (2004). "The Force of Things. Steps Towards an Ecology of Matter." *Political Theory* 32.3, 347-372.

--- (2010). *Vibrant Matter: A Political Ecology of Things*. Durham: Duke University Press.

Borsò, Vittoria (2012). "Audiovisionen der Schrift an der Grenze des Sagbaren und Sichtbaren: zur Ethik der Materialität." *Poetische Gerechtigkeit*. Eds. Donat, Sebastian, et al. Düsseldorf: Düsseldorf University Press, 163-188.

Braidotti, Rosi (1994). *Nomadic Subjects. Embodiment and Sexual Difference in Contemporary Feminist Theory*. New York: Columbia University Press.

Brathwaite, Kamau (1999). *ConVERSations with Nathaniel Mackey*. Allamuchy, NJ: We Press.

Busia, Abena (1994). "Long Memory and Survival. Dramatizing the Arrivants Trilogy." *World Literature Today* 68.4, 741-746.

Claviez, Thomas (2006). "Ecology as Moral Stand(s). Environmental Ethics, Western Moral Philosophy and the Problem of the Other." *Nature in Literary and Cultural Studies. Transatlantic Conversations on Ecocriticism*. Eds. Gersdorf, Catrin, and Sylvia Mayer. Amsterdam & New York: Rodopi, 435-454.

Commoner, Barry (1971). *The Closing Circle. Nature, Man and Technology*. New York: Alfred A. Knopf.

Commonwealth Scientific and Industrial Research Organization (CSIRO) et al. "Antropocene Timeline." *Welcome to the Anthropocene*. CSIRO et al, 2012. Web. 09. March 2017 <www.anthropocene.info/anthropocene-timeline.php>

Deleuze, Gilles, and Félix Guattari (1986). *Nomadology. The War Machine*. South Paradena, CA: Semiotexte.

DeLoughrey, Elizabeth (1998). "Gendering the Oceanic Voyage. Trespassing the (Black) Atlantic and Caribbean." *Thamyris* 5.2, 205-231.

Derrida, Jacques (2002). "The Animal Therefore I Am (More to Follow)." *Critical Inquiry* 28.2, 369-418.

Döring, Tobias (2002). "Writing Across the Meridian. Epic Echoes in Derek Walcott's Omeros." In: *Caribbean Passages. Intertextuality in a Postcolonial Tradition*. London and New York: Routledge, 169-202.

Gedalof, Irene (1996). "Can Nomads Learn to Count to Four? Rosi Braidotti and the Space for Difference in Feminist Theory." *Women: A Cultural Review* 7.2, 189-201.

Gilroy, Paul (1993). *The Black Atlantic. Modernity and Double Consciousness*. London & New York: Verso.

Glissant, Edouard (1997). *Poetics of Relation*. Ann Arbor: The University of Michigan Press.

Glotfelty, Cheryll, and Harold Fromm (eds.) (1996). *The Ecocriticism Reader. Landmarks in Literary Ecology*. Athens: University of Georgia Press.

Hannan, Jim (2002). "Crossing Couplets: Making Form the Matter of Walcott's 'Tiepolo's Hound'." New Literary History 33.3, 559-579.

Ingold, Tim (2000). *The Perception of the Environment. Essays on Livelihood, Dwelling and Skill*. London & New York: Routledge.

--- (2011). *Being Alive. Essays on Movement, Knowledge and Description*. London & New York: Routledge.

Iovino, Serenella (2012). "Steps to a Material Ecocriticism. The Recent Literature About the 'New Materialisms' and Its Implications for Ecocritical Theory." *Ecozon@* 3.1, 134-145.

---, and Serpil Oppermann (eds.) (2014). *Material Ecocriticism*. Bloomington & Indianapolis: Indiana University Press.

Kaiser, Birgit Mara (2014). "Worlding CompLit. Diffractive Reading with Barad, Glissant and Nancy." *Parallax* 20.3, 274-287.

Krebs, Angelika (1999). *Ethics of Nature*. Berlin & New York: deGruyter.

Latour, Bruno (1993). *We Have Never Been Modern*. Cambridge, MA: Harvard University Press.

--- (2004). "How to Talk About the Body? The Normative Dimension of Science Studies." *Body & Society* 10.2-3, 205-229.

--- (2013). *An Inquiry into Modes of Existence*. An Anthropology of the Moderns. Cambridge, MA & London: Harvard University Press.

--- (2014). "Agency in the Anthropocene." *New Literary History* 45, 1-18.

Maran, Timo (2014a). "Biosemiotic Criticism". *Oxford Handbook of Ecocriticism*. Ed. Greg Garrard. Oxford: Oxford University Press.

--- (2014b). "Semiotization of Matter: A Hybrid Zone between Biosemiotics and Material Ecocriticism". *Material Ecocriticism*. Eds. Serenella Iovino and Serpil Oppermann. Bloomington: Indiana University Press, 141-154.

Nancy, Jean-Luc (2000). *Being Singular Plural*. Stanford: Stanford University Press.

Neumann, Birgit (2016). "Postcolonial Ekphrasis and Counter-Visions in Derek Walcott's Tiepolo's Hound - Contacts, Contests and Translations." *Zeitschrift für Anglistik und Amerikanistik* 64.4, 447-465.

Nichols, Grace (1983). *i is a long-memoried woman*. London: Karnak House.

Oppermann, Serpil (2014). "From Ecological Postmodernism to Material Ecocriticism. Creative Materiality and Narrative Agency." *Material Ecocriticism*. Eds. Iovino, Serenella and Serpil Oppermann. Bloomington: Indiana University Press, 21-36.

Peterson, Anna (2001). *Being Human. Ethics, Environment, and Our Place in the World*. Berkeley & Los Angeles: University of California Press.

--- (2013). *Being Animal. Beasts and Boundaries in Nature Ethics*. New York & Chichester: Columbia University Press.

Plumwood, Val (2009). "Nature in the Active Voice." *Australian Humanities Review* 46, 113-129.

Porter, Eleanor (1997). "Mother Earth and the Wandering Hero. Mapping Gender in Bruce Chatwin's 'The Songlines' and Robyn Davidson's 'Tracks'." *The Journal of Commonwealth Literature* 32.1, 35-46.

Rigby, Kate (2004). "Earth, World, Text. On the (Im)Possibility of Ecopoiesis." *New Literary History* 35.3, 427-442.

Senior, Olive (2005). *Gardening in the Tropics*. Toronto: Insomniac Press.

Vermeulen, Pieter (2014). "Posthuman Affect." *European Journal of English Studies* 18.2, 121-134.

Walcott, Derek (1990). *Omeros*. New York: Farrar, Straus, Giroux.

Wendy Wheeler (London)

A Feeling for Form: Biosemiotics and the Primacy of Aesthetic Knowing (on the Way to Ethics)

1. Literary and Critical Theory and the Occlusion of Biology and Aesthetic Experience

In the late 1970s and 1980s, when 'Continental Theory' began to take hold in universities in the Anglophone world, it joined other related categories in the nascent 'theory revolution' such as 'Marxist theory' and the 'Critical Theory' of the Frankfurt School. Of course the new theory had some disagreements with the old. As well as teaching undergraduates about these new additions, and gauging their place alongside the older ones, courses in Cultural Studies began to develop on the model of content suggested by the work of Richard Hoggart and his then 1964 research fellow, Stuart Hall, at the Birmingham Centre for Cultural Studies at the University of Birmingham in England.[1] This new literary, critical and cultural theory began to flourish also in prestigious MA degrees in British universities such as Sussex, Essex, Southampton and the University of Wales at Cardiff.

In all these places, students learnt about ideology (and post-ideological total 'power-knowledge' systems associated with the work of Michel Foucault) by studying representations of class, women and race along with what were generally thought of as the methodological means for exposing what literary, filmic and other social 'texts' kept hidden. These methodological means, involving what was sometimes called a 'hermeneutics of suspicion', might include Marxist theory (representation as superstructural; material base as occluded) or psychoanalytic theory. In the latter, the representational level was seen as a transformation of deeper repressed meaning structures associated with the unconscious). In the work of the French structuralist, Jacques Lacan, this unconscious was, itself and necessarily, 'structured like a language' since language is a significant part of the environment upon which the human psyche draws in the channelling of instinctual (i.e. human animal) drives. This, of course, was also Freud's essential insight where the dreamwork's tools of condensation and displacement echo the foundational semiotic tropes of metaphor and metonymy, and function as primal modes of transformation in the unconscious. The labour of psycho-analysis (in 'texts' as literature and as well as persons) involved tracing the tropes backwards from manifest to latent content to expose their 'secrets'.

This theme, in turn, recurred in the major semiotic tropes of structuralism. These – the paradigmatic and syntagmatic axes of meaning development – were to be found in the work of Roman Jakobson and in its extension in Claude Lévi-Strauss's structuralist anthropology. In Jakobson's work (and strikingly) this thinking was, in fact, primarily taken from the developmental biology of Karl Ernst von Baer (1792-1876).[2] However, this intellectual and scientific evolutionary source fell into obscurity. This was probably due to an aversion to thinking about biology and the evolutionary inheritance of organisms in a field committed to anthropocentric *tabula rasa* subjectivity within a socio-linguistic constructionist framework. Lévi-Strauss, instead, located his use of the structuralist methodology in the system of differences without positive terms that was associated with the linguistic teaching of Ferdinand de Saussure, and with the synchronic structural aspects of meaning-making. Diachronic or developmental aspects of language and culture formed no part of this Saussurean-derived approach. Later, with Jacques Derrida's critique of the structuralist assumptions of bounded systems of meaning,[3] and his insistence, instead, on the endless and essentially ungrounded 'play of the signifier', post-structuralist Derridean deconstruction came to the theoretical fore. Here the methodological tools included the pulling of an often marginal textual 'thread' whereby the structure of difference breaks down. This kind of difference was an effect of what Derrida, playfully, renamed *différance* – a textual impasse, or aporia, where such *différence* (i.e. in French) was only readily identifiable in writing. The scene of writing is thus the ideal place where sleights of hand, the conjuring of a non-existent stability to meaning, might thus be exposed.

What all these approaches had in common (as family features one might say) was the tacit assumption that the old aesthetic categories by which forms of art had traditionally been judged were simply an historic or ideological foil deployed in the interests of power/knowledge or, in the capitalist era, for the bourgeois befuddlement of readers. Very often, and this was especially true of the categories of interest – class, race and gender – associated with Birmingham cultural studies, what was effectively being championed as the new way of reading wasn't specifically *literary* reading at all (now associated with the old Cambridge fuddy-duddy F. R. Leavis, the unifying enemy)[4] but was more akin to a sociology of literature, with 'high' literature viewed as an 'elitist' part of a much wider 'low' or 'popular' culture. Indeed, students were severely warned off the use of the suspect concept 'aesthetic' at all.

In the mid 1950s, Derrida had spent a year at Harvard, where he read the papers of Charles Sanders Peirce (1839-1914). *Of Grammatology* confirms this influence when Derrida affirms the similarity between his own understanding of the endless movement of the signifier and Peirce's account of the movements of semiosis.[5] Derrida, however, cleaved to the nominalist belief that language is (as he put it) not tied to any kind of experience of a reality beyond the particulars that language itself puts into play at any time and place. Peirce, on the other hand was a realist who believed in universals, and not least in the universal reality of semiotic *relation* itself. Derrida, like Heidegger before him, was also aware of developments in cybernetics[6] and recursivity in systems ('protention' and 'retention' in Derrida's terms)[7] whereby repetition creates habits and the possibility of encoding memory all the way from flesh to computation. The anthropocentric focus, including the closeness to continental philosophy and Saussurean linguistics, meant, however, that wider Peircean and Batesonian concerns with global semiotics, and with organismic biological evolution and social ecologies, were never developed by the most popular post-structuralist theories. Strangely, given its vast importance in our understanding of life, the gaping absence in such literary and critical theory was the theory of evolution. There were some attempts to reduce culture to a gene-centric version of neo-Darwinian evolutionary theory, but these resulted in such impoverished accounts of culture that they were largely stillborn. By the time the Human Genome Project was completed in 2003, whereby it became clear that there was no mechanical one-to-one relation between genes and functions, the reductionist neo-Darwinian account was, itself, already seriously wounded. The more interesting exceptions to this embarrassing ignorance in regard to biological evolution and development, and their impact in terms of cultural evolution, were Gilbert Simondon, Gilles

Deleuze and Félix Guattari. However, and presumably for reasons touched on by Brian Massumi in his consideration of these developments (see quotation below), their work was often incompletely understood and poorly appreciated.

Given the manifest failures of these models of human experience (whether in regards to pleasure, to evolutionary theory, or to political behaviour, among many others), an alternative response might have been to re-think what we meant by 'aesthetic' and 'semiotic' in the first place. But as Massumi has said of 'theory's' encounter with the work of Gilbert Simondon, and of 'information'-based relational ontology in general, ways of thinking remained in place in the 1980s and 1990s which prevented 'theory' from reaching forward into these new forms of informational-relational bio-cultural and non-anthropocentric systems thinking:

> in the 'moment' of 'Theory' in the 1980s and 1990s certain ways of thinking remained in place which meant that Simondon simply couldn't be understood. 'Theory', as Brian Massumi put it, was at that point 'unequal to the question of ontogenesis' (Massumi, 2009: 37), or of how things (in *ens reale* and in *ens rationis*) become. Before Simondon could begin to be properly understood, 'Theory' had to get out of the anthropocentric linguistic constructivist bind it was stuck in. This kind of constructivism did 'not have the resources even to effectively articulate the issue of the nonhuman necessarily raised by ontogenesis' (Massumi, 2009: 37). Apart from anything else, the materialist commitments involved in considering ontological becoming threatened (it was thought) to impose a 'naïve realism', even as the immateriality of information threatened something perhaps worse: i.e. that not all reality, *contra* Marxism, was material. The development of the ecological humanities helped prepare the way out of this impasse by approaching a more complicated realism that was inclined to acknowledge evolution while rejecting the mechanistic reductionism of neo-Darwinian theory. Shaking semiotic theory free of its anthropocentric bias, biosemiotics offered a theoretical resource which made ontogenetic concerns graspable within a semiotic (not semiological) register.[8]

But if Lévi-Strauss's response to the theoretical resources which Roman Jakobson found in developmental biology, and then expressed in his structuralist schema in the 1930s and 1940s, was a partial rejection of biological ontology and relation which continued its life into the 1980s and 90s, the advent of biosemiotic thought in the environmental humanities and ecocriticism now makes an engagement with semiotic and relational ontology – a theory of how bodies, minds, and ecologies take shape and self-articulate – more possible. Interestingly, such questions concerning living forms of in-*form*-ation also return us to the matter of feeling and form raised by aesthetics. In*form*ation, as the word implies, is 'news' (in the sense of communication discussed by Claude Shannon[9]) which shapes its objects. As Simondon, and then Deleuze and Guattari, argued, aesthetic and technical objects, as well as biological organisms and other dependent forms of knowledge, are evolutionary and are shaped by multiple forces. Pascal Chabot writes that, while not suggesting absolute equivalence, Simondon nonetheless affirms that 'The concrete technical object "approximates the mode of existence of natural objects"'.[10] But all such evolutionary forms, both natural and cultural, also shape, in turn, the ecological systems in which they have their effects. For Simondon, as for biosemiotics, the living organism, technical object and aesthetic work are all an effect of natural and/or cultural cybernetic feedback systems.

In other words, where aesthetic objects are concerned, we can think of these as taking their form subject to the same kinds of ecological systems pressures and responses as organisms. And if we think of literary texts (or paintings, sculptures, music, and so on) as organisms, this, of course, has extensive implications for ecocritical reading. We are justified in thinking about a 'natural history' of the text's reception in different social ecologies, and at different times in cultural history. This, in turn, will incline the interested ecocritic towards 'deep mappings'[11] linking natural and social ecologies, and their interwoven mutually shaping relations over time. We will also be concerned with the growth, evolution and development of the interpretive capacities of readers. The life of the text is a living dialogue with its readers whose own development over time feeds back into often deeper understandings of textual life also. Reading, as recursion in time leading to growth in meaning, thus becomes a biosemiotic category. We will be interested not only in the text's adaptive potential in the hands of its readers, but in the reasons for this deep adaptability expressed in the capacities for many, and changing, interpretations and meanings. Here, doubtless, emphasis should fall on the part played by the organism-text's motors of metaphor: its differences and similarities, its adaptive evolutionary potential. Metaphor (iconic semiosis) and metonym (indexical semiosis) should be regarded as the resolutely natural bases of later articulate human uses.

2. Form, In-form-ation, Biosemiotics, Aesthetics

There are many reasons for re-emphasising the importance of the aesthetic dimension, and for its exploration as a part of a wider critical and theoretical understanding; but perhaps the most important, especially with the continuing rise of interest in the environmental humanities and in ecocritical methodologies, lies in the biosemiotic discovery not only that culture is a natural evolutionary development echoing, in human semiosis and mind, the patterns of nature,[12] but also that nature is (*contra* the common scientific metaphor of modernity) not, in fact, a machine but, rather, a self-made, self-unfolding poetry. This important emphasis, showing that organisms (humans in this case) have an evolutionary semiotic affinity, a natural feeling for form, shared with and across the living world, should enable us to effect a deeper exploration of both aesthetic experience and of the ethical feeling that grows from, and depends upon, it. Drawing on the semiotic theory of Charles Sanders Peirce, which has provided substantial philosophical underpinnings for much biosemiotic theory,[13] I propose to offer an outline below of how this is so.

We do not receive the world in unmediated form. We experience the world not as we choose to experience it, but as evolution has sculpted our senses and perceptions to be *able* to experience it. But those abilities themselves remain potential until we live our lives, and learn the business of being and growing. Life is not so much an 'I am' as an 'I can'. We learn to join sense to sense and to differentiate between experienced objects. Studies of people who have been blind since birth, and whose sight is restored, indicate the extent to which our perceiving and organising bodies, environment and memory storage capacities, as well as our enormous creative plasticity, help us to put the world together.[14] What we sense is something real and causally efficacious. But we never get the whole of the object in its infinite reality. This includes not only what it is made of in itself, in every atom and every particle, but also its relation to every other part of the cosmos, and the unknown effects of all these relations. The concepts that we, and some other organisms, extrapolate from our sensual experience are real semiotic, causally efficient, objects even when they are not *things*.[15] In this semiotic (and premodern) sense, ideas are objects (but obviously not things). Equally obviously, as objects of consciousness (and non-consciousness) they have real causal powers. All these objects, both material and extrapolated, are thus potentially received by us and every organism in whose *umwelt* they figure (in whatever capacity) *as signs*: the experience of objects which, in other words, *stand in for* the plenum we are not evolutionarily developed to experience as a part of our *umwelt*.[16] This, of course, is the very definition of a sign: that which *stands in for* something else not present or evident to our sense or senses.

The *umwelt* (essentially the *semiotic* environment in von Uexküll's usage) of each species is not precisely the same (it is, as we say, species-specific).[17] But every organism is made in semiosis, and that life of signs which all inhabit – in nature and in culture – is evolutionary and, itself, tied to the evolutionary life of earth. It is, we might say, a natural constructivism from which none – and certainly not human mind and language – can break wholly free from the embodied and enworlded, semiotic but non-linguistic, life from which it initially emerged.

Even the culture/nature distinction grows increasingly problematic. If by 'culture' we mean the growth of signs in the non-genetic passing of information from one generation to another by learning, we can no longer even make a final distinction between genetic (inherited) and epigenetic (often acquired via micro-organismic symbioses) information. It is clear that the growth of any species is, perhaps, like a dialect, the result of many different factors (familial, cultural, geophysical) working in concert. As an organism, being is doing. The same must be said for living systems as a whole. All function on the model of ecologies in which systems and individuals are potential becomings whose expression is constrained by history and habit, but which always remains, within the logic of the same and of habit, nonetheless open to the adaptive exploration of difference as a response to chance change in the *umwelt*. Where human beings are concerned, social and cultural forms of organisation can extend human semiotic freedom, but they do not escape the formal constraints of its cultural and natural histories. This sense of ontological becomings-in-informational-relation is pursued in the work of Gilbert Simondon and then, after him, by Gilles Deleuze and Félix Guattari who were influenced by Simondon.[18]

There is a constant flow of information – or semiosis as biosemioticians would more accurately say – between organisms and their worlds. These *umwelten*, or signifying worlds, as biologist and first ethologist von Uexküll (1866-1944) described them, constitute cybernetic or cybersemiotic feedback systems for every species.[19] As noted earlier, species do not inhabit semiotically identical worlds. What *means* for one species may not *mean*, or indeed may not even register at all, in the *umwelt* of another organism. Not only that, but meaning is always context dependent. Even our perception of something as apparently simple as colour alters according to what we have learned to expect in terms of different contexts.[20]

3. Discovering Biosemiotics

When people in humanities departments hear the word 'semiotics', they very often think of Saussure, and maybe of Roman Jakobson as a significant founder of structuralism, and of Lévi-Strauss as founder of structuralist anthropology. Saussure's linguistics, however, is both anthropocentric and dyadic. As mentioned above, it focuses on 'differences' and on the dyadic signifier/signified relation in the present moment of any system. It is not interested in philology or the evolutionary history of language or structural evolution. When one of the most important developers of biosemiotic thought, Jesper Hoffmeyer, was working with his then graduate student Claus Emmeche 25 years ago, it became apparent to them that what they were seeing in biology was not mechanism, nor some poorly identified thing called 'information' that was somehow transmitted like packages. What they observed was something much more mysterious, an activity in the life of cells which they recognised as responses which were much more like communications of messages and interpretations.

Early on, they tried to use Saussurean linguistics as a theoretical underpinning, but, being essentially anthropo-psychological and entirely anthropocentric, this theory couldn't offer any help concerning the communicative and interpretative activities of the cell or of non-human organisms. The relations that Hoffmeyer and Emmeche saw at work in biology were biosemiotic but (obviously) not linguistic. They were, thus, not wholly conventional, being primarily based on iconicity (association through similarity, thus what humans call metaphoricity in their own experience) and indexicality (association via what humans similarly call metonymy). The relation between biosemiotic sign use and human language was clear – not least to Jakobson himself.[21] Then Hoffmeyer, at a conference in Germany, ran into the American semiotician and biologist *manqué* Thomas A. Sebeok who told him that he needed to read the American semiotician Charles Sanders Peirce, and then the German-Estonian proto-biosemiotician Jacob von Uexküll. Sebeok was a Professor at Indiana University and, more pertinently, had been a graduate student of Roman Jakobson in New York. I shall return to Jakobson, whose intellectual history is poorly known among the post-1970s 'theory' generation, in a moment.

Sebeok's advice to Hoffmeyer, of course, was sound. The biosemiotic endeavour thus became, for most biosemioticians, underpinned by the semiotic philosophy of the scientist, logician and founder of American Pragmatism, Charles Sander Peirce, much aided by the ethnology of von Uexküll and the semiotics of Juri Lotman who, as Departmental Chair, had influenced the development of a similar biosemiotic endeavour at the University of Tartu. Lotman's Chair eventually fell to Kalevi Kull, currently Professor of Biosemiotics at Tartu where the biosemiotic tradition also continues to grow and develop.[22]

4. The Peircean Framework: Premodern Semiotics

Peirce wanted to know how we know things, and he asked himself some searching questions. He began with the seemingly most straightforward questions about how we know about the world to which our senses introduce us. He realised that our senses do not reveal to us unmediated data, but that mind is a tool for organising meaning from experience. That means any object of experience presents itself to us as something which is never fully known as it is in every aspect. That – the desire to know more than appears in common sense – is, of course, what drives religion, philosophy, science and the spirit of inquiry.

So, as outlined above, Peirce differentiated between the 'object' (whether as material thing or immaterial idea) which generates what presents itself to our senses (or, by abstraction, to our imagination) and that aspect which 'stands in for it' in the form of a sign. The latter he recognised as the sign-vehicle. He called this not the representation (which might imply something complete and accurate) but, rather, the 'representamen'. But, beyond the significant object and the representamen (or sign vehicle), there is a third aspect to the triadic sign relation, and that is the sense, or meaning, which any organism makes of the object in its form as representamen. This, we might call, in our human way, an interpretation. But Peirce understood rightly that an 'interpretation' is not necessarily mental, but rather resides in the change, or difference, it brings about in the understanding, and thus the life, of the organism. This is what the object-representamen sign relation *means*. This, the full total of any sign relation's effects, *is* its *meaning*.[23] To mark this difference, Peirce called this third aspect of the triadic sign relation the 'interpretant'. To use Gregory Bateson's well-known definition of information, the interpretant is the result of information: 'a difference which makes a difference'.[24] Bateson had read Peirce, of course. But we must ask ourselves 'What *is* information?'. In living things, the answer can only be that information is much better understood as semiosis – a move mainstream biology has yet to make – although it is moving closer. Every organism is entirely dependent upon information as semiosis. The *Innenwelt* of cells, chemical messengers and neural circuits is given life by the carrying of information as biosemiosis. The immune system is precisely a profoundly complex system of information and memory. DNA is a cellular library. Itself inert, DNA is summoned and read by the cell. The *umwelt* is also animated by biosemiosis. It is what affords the organism the capacity for making assessments about how to go about living in a potentially changeable world.[25]

We might wonder why biology has been so slow to make this move from an ill-defined concept of information to the more detailed one of semiosis. Two things have figured importantly here. The first is the dominance of the machine metaphor over the past 400 years. The second is that European science, from its seventeenth century beginnings, as a defining fruit of early modernity, has been committed to material explanations only. There are good reasons for this in post-Reformation thought – not least the circumvention of the explanatory limits of societies shackled to the explanatory primacy of religious views. But the typically nominalist preoccupation with distinct material things, at the expense of a realism of relations as the medieval Latins understood them, has meant that information has been bound to present a problem. This is because information is not itself a material *thing* at all. It is the effect of *relations between objects*. Information always concerns *relation* in its transmission of news of difference. As Norbert Wiener noted nearly seventy years ago in his book *Cybernetics*, 'information is information, not matter or energy'.[26] In other words, while communications requires material codes and channels, relation *itself* is immaterial. Obviously, this is a distinct problem for a solely materialist worldview. Acknowledging the reality of an ontology of relation is possibly the greatest challenge to science in the twenty-first century.

The machine assumption is, in its own way, similarly problematic. In a world characterised as much by chance unpredictability as by habit, life forms which behave entirely mechanically could never survive. Organisms *must* have flexibility and choice in regard to their inputs. No machine can, not even a computer, of its own accord and without instruction from an external intelligence, self-organise in this manner. Organisms must also be able to discriminate, because the same sign vehicle may *mean* quite differently in different contexts. We recognise this easily in our own cultural contexts of semiosis. Signs and meanings are context dependent. But the same is true for natural semiosis – i.e. biosemiosis – also. An identical gene sequence, for instance, can mean quite different things to the cell under different conditions. James Shapiro, discussed at more length below, calls these 'coincident messages'.

5. Natural Aesthetics

These capacities – the ability to have 'a sense of aboutness', to make discriminations pertinent to survival, and to possess a flexibility in regard to interpretation and meaning – are best designated by the word 'semiosis' – from the Gk. *semeion*, for sign. This applies to all living organisms – from bacteria, cells in bodies, plants, fungi, and nonhuman and human animals. Biosemioticians think that one definition of life may well be 'that which is semiotic'. Here is an example, from the molecular biologist James A. Shapiro discussing the cell:

> cells do not act blindly. We know from physiology and biochemistry and molecular biology that cells are full of receptors. They monitor what goes on outside. They monitor what goes on inside. And they're continually taking in that information and using it to adjust their actions, their biochemistry, their metabolism, the cell cycle, etc., so that things come out right. That's why I use the word cognitive to apply to cells, meaning

> they do things based on knowledge of what's happening around them and inside of them. Without that knowledge and the systems to use that knowledge they couldn't proliferate and survive as efficiently as they do.[27]

Shapiro is not a self-identified biosemiotician, but he is certainly travelling the same path – along with many other biologists – towards this revolution in our understanding. He has realised that all forms of life have cognitive capacities, and deal in meanings. As many people have recognised, this also means that there is a continuation of patterns and behaviours from evolutionary nature to evolutionary culture: patterns repeated with subtle differences over time and in the *Innenwelten* and *umwelten* of organisms. This means that a feeling for form and pattern – what we humans would call aesthetics – is there in life long before us, and indeed from the beginning.

In a newspaper article entitled 'DNA as Poetry: Multiple Messages in a Single Sequence', Shapiro, whose most recent book is *Evolution: A View from the Twenty-First Century*, points out that what he calls 'coincident messages,' that is, multiple messages written within the same DNA coding sequence, cause tremendous problems for a mechanistic account of biological functions.[28] We understand perfectly well that the same words in human languages can have different meanings according to the contextual interpretation. It appears that DNA code, like human language, is, indeed, not a mechanical but a semiotic, and thus interpretive, phenomenon. Cells and bodies and organisms have learned to use these memory codes, along with non-genetic information, to make many complex and beautiful meanings. Altogether this has painted a much more complex picture of biological life and development, and aided the advance of evolutionary developmental (Evo-Devo) and complex development systems biology.[29] With this, the gradual decline of Neo-Darwinism begins, and a far more nuanced account of evolution and development, one that bridges the nature-culture divide, has started. Biosemiotics is, of course, a part of that new conceptual architecture.

Both Gregory Bateson and Denis Noble have talked about understanding the driver of evolutionary change as the play of similarity and difference, or habit and chance as Peirce puts it, as forms of natural metaphor. Noble describes evolution as nature switching from one metaphor to another.[30] Bateson talks about metaphor, an important part of Peircean logic which the latter called abduction. As in metaphor, abductive logic means the carrying of meaning (and biological function) from one site to another one. This means that abductive logic – the nonconscious play of musement which generates every new idea – builds, like languages, via metaphor and has an evolutionary history just as bodies do, that is drawn from many layers, and twists and turns, of metaphoric and metonymic development. The growth of metaphor and metonym, as in Jakobson's two axes schema,[31] grows the semantic chain that constitutes the basis of a narrative. We can, thus, call these movements natural stories. Here is Gregory Bateson, from *Mind and Nature: A Necessary Unity*, quoted by Jesper Hoffmeyer:

> [...] whatever the word "story" means ... the fact of thinking in stories does not isolate human beings as something separate from the starfish and the sea anemones, the coconut palms and the primroses. Rather, if the world be connected...then *thinking in terms of stories* must be shared by all mind or minds whether ours or those of redwood forests and sea anemones. Context and relevance must be characteristic not only of all so-called behavior (those stories that are projected out into action), but also of all those internal stories, the sequences of the building up of the sea anemone. Its embryology must be somehow made of the stuff of stories. And behind that, again, the evolutionary process through millions of generations whereby the sea anemone, like you and me, came to be – that process, too, must be the stuff of stories.[32]

The basic phenomena as patterns which shine forth for cognition (phenomenon, Gk. *phainesthai* – that which shines forth), therefore, must be patterns of difference and (it follows) repetition (similarity). Based upon the primary experience of iconic signs, such patterns are lived forms of analogy, including the sufficiently analogous similarity and difference that the humanities identify as metaphor.[33] In his book on metaphor, for example, Paul Ricoeur writes, about linguistic metaphor, words that we can easily translate into an evolutionary biological form whether in terms of codes or in terms of morphology:

> Can one not say that the strategy of language at work in metaphor consists in obliterating the logical and established frontiers of language, in order to bring to light new resemblances the previous classification kept us from seeing? In other words, the power of metaphor would be to break an old

> categorization, in order to establish new logical frontiers on the ruins of their forerunners.[34]

As with biosemioticians after him, Gregory Bateson recognised that there must exist a necessary unity between mind and nature.[35] If that is the case, and the idea of natural metaphor is right, then mind and nature are joined by patterns which are much more like poetry (which, like all literature, is semiotically recursive) than linear mechanical procedures. The more general form of semiotic organisation in which the book of nature is written (and that includes human bodies and minds, of course) is not deductive logic, but the much more widely applicable natural forms that Bateson called 'syllogisms in grass'. It turns out that nature's logic is informing, relational, poetic and full of meanings – semiotic, in other words.

Thus, the human inclination for poetry does not derive from anthroposemiosis but lives and extends in the human imagination because it belongs to the more general biosemiosis of nature. Fittingly, Samuel Beckett, citing Vico, argued that poetry does not spring in the first place from elevated and sophisticated minds but from man in his most primitive state and early uses of (i.e. spoken) language:

> Poetry, he says, was born of curiosity, daughter of ignorance. The first men had to create matter by the force of their imagination, and 'poet' means 'creator`. Poetry was the first operation of the human mind, and without it thought could not exist. Barbarians, incapable of analysis and abstraction, must use their fantasy to explain what their reason cannot comprehend. Before articulation comes song; before abstract terms, metaphors. The figurative character of the oldest poetry must be regarded, not as sophisticated confectionery, but as evidence of a poverty stricken vocabulary and of a disability to achieve abstraction. Poetry is essentially the antithesis of Metaphysics: Metaphysics purge the mind of the senses and cultivate the disembodiment of the spiritual; Poetry is all passion and feeling and animates the inanimate; Metaphysics are most perfect when most concerned with universals; Poetry, when most concerned with particulars. Poets are the sense, philosophers the intelligence of humanity. Considering the Scholastics' axiom: '*niente è nell' intelleto che prima non sia nel senso*', it follows that poetry is a prime condition of philosophy and

civilization. The primitive animistic movement was a manifestation of the '*forma poetica dell spirito*.'[36]

Reminding us of the many remaining mysteries of biosemiosis and biological meaning-making, James A. Shapiro writes, 'At a time when we pride ourselves for being able to read DNA sequences with increasing speed, it is salutary to keep in mind that we are still far from knowing how to interpret the complex overlapping meanings contained in the genomic texts we store in our databases. DNA, like poetry, often has to be read in several ways'.[37] Bateson says similarly:

> whether you approve or disapprove of poetry, dream and psychosis, the generalisation remains that biological data make sense – are connected together – by syllogisms in grass. The whole of animal behaviour, the whole of repetitive anatomy, and the whole of biological evolution – each of these vast realms is within itself linked together by syllogisms in grass, whether the logicians like it or not.[38]

But as we know, evolution builds upon anterior developments. And that must mean not only that there is a place in scientific thinking for the creativity of metaphor as a real semiotically causal force of evolutionary change, but also that scientific logic itself depends, as Peirce claimed it did, upon the abductive, feelingful and aesthetic, insights – born of "*Il Lume Naturale*", the fit between human mind and natural mind – that metaphor inscribes in nature and in culture.[39]

The human animal is an evolutionary and meaning-concerned part of an evolutionary and meaning-concerned living world. Nature-culture is clearly a continuum in which culture is an evolutionary development of nature in humans (how could it be otherwise?), and to some extent in some other animals also. But many, if not all, the things which we think of as 'culture' long pre-existed – at least in some form – humans. The aesthetic dimension studied by much of the humanities is one such example.

We are made in the present of patterns and relations, natural and cultural, which precede us and which turn up again and again in the world. In being, and becoming aware of, these patterns, organisms find meanings. This logic of pattern, which is the species recognition of a natural logic to phenomena, an order to the world, is essentially repetition and difference (including mimicry).[40] Patterns repeat on the basis of similarity (visual or haptic or chemical or neurochemical, and so on), but that similarity is capable of containing aspects of difference. Organisms build their ontological forms and maps in their encounters with the world they live in. Both form and context act as constraints on ontological expression. In humans, these forms are expressed not only in evolutionary bio-ontology, and in the form and growth of flesh and cognition, but also in the forms and content, the rhythms and the tropes, of the stories human animals tell.

The most straightforward way of understanding the logic these processes obey is to recognise that they are essentially living metaphors, as Gregory Bateson suggested. Strung together like beads on the necklace of habit and chance, they form biosemiotic stories.[41] From an evolutionary perspective, this means not only that we can derive insights about the present from the past (biologically and culturally), but also that we can derive insights into cultural patterns from biological patterns. We can even derive insights about biological expressions and behaviours from cultural ones. And of course molecular biologists trying to understand the workings of DNA molecules have, indeed, been obliged to borrow their lexicon from the languages of semiotics (codes, expressions, reading, transcriptions, translations, interpretations, and so on). Much of our own human behaviour is driven by imperatives which long preceded *Homo sapiens*. We can see these at work throughout nature (see my account of François Jacob's discussion of nature as a tinkerer). We can thus extrapolate backwards and outwards from our own natural behaviour to the behaviour of other nonhuman parts of nature. Like small societies, bacteria interpret conditions and make decisions through what is aptly called quorum sensing. Similarly, recent research on viral macrophages indicates that they, too, communicate across the generations, like humans, by 'writing' chemical messages which are read by their descendants.[42]

6. New Ways of Thinking: Reconceptualising Minds, Selves and Knowing

The culture/nature distinction grows increasingly irrelevant. A biosemiotically informed critical theory of subjects, society and culture might well help us to move beyond the problems which have driven critical theory in the humanities for the past 35 to 40 years. That formation was largely dominated by two sources: a Marxist theory of false consciousness critical of Enlightenment reason and claims to truth, and the 'post-modern' theory which says that all meanings are made by humans and that human meanings are just a ceaseless circulation of signifiers unanchored from bodies and Earth. The biosemiotic realisation that meaning-making belongs to all living things, and that human meaning-making, although distinctive of *Homo sapiens*, has its roots in the common descent of non-human semiotic life, indicates that reality is *not* 'constructed in human language'. It is experienced in sign relations that are anchored in bodies and in the shared Earth. All other organisms make meanings too, and human life is lived among, and dependent upon, those meanings. We humans are part of a world – in flesh and in imagination – that all life weaves together. Organisms continually both shape and are shaped by the embodied and enminded semiotic relations which both scaffold matter and energy, and also constitute life and meaning on this planet.

The modern sciences and humanities have both tended toward inadequate models of mind and subjectivity. Computational models produce the problem of mechanistic genetic determinism versus free will. On the humanities side, *tabula rasa* models have produced a socio-linguistically deterministic model of human selves that is both biologically and semiotically shallow. Critical theory in the humanities has tended to reject scientific accounts as reductive, and as especially simplistic in their gene-based attempts to explain cultural experience and meaning-making.

Contemporary ideas of 'mind' and 'meaning' both require expansion. Mind does not require a brain: 'Brains, of course, lend tremendously increased power to the cognitive regime of a species but the brain in itself is just a tool for the semiotic body, not an independent organ of semiosis. There is no semiosis without a body, but plenty of semiosis without brains'.[43] From a biosemiotic point of view, and like the sign itself, mind must be composed of three necessary aspects: a semiotically active body in a semiotically active world and some form of (conscious or nonconscious) system capable of memory. DNA fulfils the latter function in important ways. Its processes, along with evolutionarily and developmentally subsequent ones in organisms, appear to depend upon the ability to register forms of similarity and difference.[44] This 'difference which makes a difference' is also the basis of metaphor and of what

Charles Peirce described as abductive guessing. It is what lead Bateson to the insight that all of nature depends on this form of logic:

> It becomes evident that metaphor is not just pretty poetry, it is not either good or bad logic, but is in fact the logic upon which the biological world has been built, the main characteristic and organizing glue of this world of mental process that I have been trying to sketch for you.[45]

In addition, brains are developmentally specialised and enfolded skin. We can thus surmise that the forms of encoding found in complex molecular systems within the primal membranes by which selves are primarily constituted are subsequently evolved in the sensual relations between bodies and environments, and that these form the basis of phenomenologically enhanced mind in evolved animals. Eventually, human capacities for abstraction, representation and formal logic build upon these semiotic processes. However, the active bases upon which such subsequent levels depend remain essentially aesthetic forms which are more like natural metaphors, poems and music than they are like machines. The understanding that the forms, structures and processes of life begin in sensation and feelings which are essentially aesthetic is a very good reason for a biosemiotic science to value the humanities. As Bateson wrote:

> On the whole, it was not the crudest, the simplest, the most animalistic and primitive aspects of the human species that were reflected in the natural phenomena. It was, rather, the more complex, the aesthetic, the intricate, and the elegant aspects of people that reflected nature. It was not my greed, my purposiveness, my so-called 'animal', so-called 'instincts', and so forth that I was recognising on the other side of that mirror, over there in 'nature'. Rather, I was seeing there the roots of human symmetry, beauty and ugliness, aesthetics, the human being's very aliveness and little bit of wisdom. His wisdom, his bodily grace, and even his habit of making beautiful objects are just as 'animal' as his cruelty. After all, the very word 'animal' means 'endowed with mind or spirit (animus)'.[46]

7. Conclusion: Aesthetics on the Way to Ethics with Biosemiotics

Finally, there's the matter of ethics. This cannot be framed primarily in terms of law at all. In Peirce's schema, this would be putting the cart before the horse. According to Peircean categories, the order of being is aesthetics as (the universe of) Firstness, which is pure feeling (intuition and the logic of abduction). From this springs (the universe of) Secondness from which ethics springs as the realm of resistance and counter resistance, the struggle of enworlded and bounded being, the testing of being and of forms and behaviours which are tolerable to any being and those which are not (the logic of induction). Thirdly comes the taking and establishing of habits (in the universe of Thirdness) in which law-like behaviours shore up being, the possibility of continuation and communication, encoding and the function of memory and repetition (the logic of deduction). Law is one way of describing habit, but it may not be the most helpful one, not least because habits of communication grow organically, while modern (at least) ideas of law, as regards ethics, can simply be imposed – supposedly rationally, as though conscious reasoning is all there is to be said about knowing.

Human abstract thought is a wonderful thing, but sometimes it simply runs amok because it forgets that it is tied, by the chains of semiosis to all our (and other organisms') other semiotic relations – aesthetics, ethics, habit – in an emergent process. These are not relativistic processes untied from the Earth and a matter of choice merely. They are linked by chains of semiosis right back from abstract concepts to bodies and earthly being. The loss of these vital environmental *umwelt* connections in our thinking breaks the semiotic links between past, present and future, and gradually undoes being. When meaning breaks apart in this way, we are witnessing the semiocide that signals ecocidal fragmentation.[47] Ivar Puura, who invented the term semiocide to describe these destructive processes, wrote:

> The diversity of nature is overwhelming. Every living creature, being part of a greater whole, carries in itself memories of billions of years of evolution and embodies its own long and largely still unknown story of origin. By wholesale replacement of primeval nature with artificial environments, it is not only nature in the biological sense that is lost. At the hands of humans, millions of stories with billions of relations and

> variations perish. The rich signscape of nature is replaced by something much poorer. It is not an exaggeration to call this process semiocide.
> I understand semiocide to be a situation in which signs and stories that are significant for someone are destroyed because of someone else's malevolence or carelessness, thereby stealing a part of the former's identity.[48]

And of course, all those biosemiotic signs and stories are significant for the organisms that live in them. Thus, neglect and destruction of the forms of aesthetic being in the nature that we embody in flesh and in mind, and have grown from, lead directly to the destruction of human habits of memory and ethical life also.

Notes

[1] Famous for his foundational work in cultural studies, Stuart Hall became Director of the Birmingham Centre for Cultural Studies in 1968.
[2] See Sériot (2014); Wheeler (2016).
[3] See Derrida (1978 [1967]).
[4] See Eagleton (1983).
[5] Derrida (1978 [1967]:49); see Wheeler (2016).
[6] Wheeler (2016:175-177).
[7] *Ibid.*, 176-177.
[8] *Ibid.*, 206.
[9] Shannon (1948a:I); Shannon (1948b:II).
[10] Chabot (2003:17).
[11] The term 'deep mapping' originates with William Least Heat-Moon. See Least Heat-Moon (1991).
[12] See Bateson (2002 [1979]).
[13] See Hoffmeyer (2008a).
[14] See Magee and Milligan (1998).
[15] For the useful distinction between objects and things in semiotic thinking, see Deely (2009); Deely (2015).
[16] See Uexküll (1957).
[17] See Uexküll (2001).
[18] See Wheeler (2016).
[19] See Brier (2008).

[20] See Beau Lotto, "Optical Illusions Show How We See." https://www.ted.com/talks/beau_lotto_optical_illusions_show_how_we_see. Web. 4 February 2017.

[21] Wheeler (2016:148).

[22] See Favareau (2010).

[23] Peirce (1878). Also in CP 5: 388-410. 293. This is what Peirce called the pragmatic maxim: 'It appears, then, that the rule for attaining the third grade of clearness of apprehension is as follows: Consider what effects, that might conceivably have practical bearings, we conceive the object of our conception to have. Then, our conception of these effects is the whole of our conception of the object.' (Peirce on p. 293 of "How to Make Our Ideas Clear", *Popular Science Monthly*, 1878, v. 12, 286-302. Reprinted widely, including *Collected Papers of Charles Sanders Peirce* (CP) v. 5, paragraphs 388-410.) I follow the convention here of citing Peirce's writing in the *Collected Papers* as CP following by the section number and paragraph number, and in *The Essential Peirce* as EP followed by the volume number (1 or 2).

[24] Bateson (1972:459).

[25] See Wheeler (2016).

[26] See Wiener (1965 [1948]).

[27] Mazur (2015:15).

[28] See Shapiro (2011); Shapiro (2012).

[29] See Sapp (2003); Gilbert and Epel (2009); Pigliucci and Müller, eds. (2010).

[30] Noble (2006:103-104); see Noble (2017).

[31] Jakobson (1960:358).

[32] See Hoffmeyer (2008b:2).

[33] See Ricoeur, P. (2003 [1975 *La Métaphore Vive*]).

[34] Ricoeur (2003:233).

[35] See Bateson (2002).

[36] Beckett (1976).

[37] See Shapiro (2012); see also Lin, Kheradpour, et al. (2011).

[38] Bateson and Bateson (1988:27).

[39] See Peirce (1891).

[40] See Maran (2017).

[41] See Wheeler (2016).

[42] See Calloway (2017).

[43] See Hoffmeyer (2015).

[44] See Wagner (2014).

[45] Bateson and Bateson (1988:28).

[46] Bateson (2002:4-5).

[47] See Puura (2013); also Maran (2013).

[48] Puura (2013:152).

Works Cited

Bateson, Gregory (1972). *Steps to an Ecology of Mind*. Chicago, IL: University of Chicago Press.

--- (2002 [1979]). *Mind and Nature: A Necessary Unity*. Cresskill, NJ: Hampton Press.

---, and Mary Catherine Bateson. (1988). *Angels Fear: Towards and Epistemology of the Sacred*. New York: Bantam Books.

Beckett, Samuel (1976). "Dante ... Bruno. Vico ... Joyce." *A Samuel Beckett Reader: I Can't Go On, I'll Go On*. Ed. Richard W. Seaver. New York: Grove Press.

Brier, Søren (2008). *Cybersemiotics: Why Information Is Not Enough!* Toronto: University of Toronto Press.

Calloway, Ewen (2017). "Do You Speak Virus? Phages Caught Sending Chemical Messages: A Virus that Infects Bacteria Listens to Messages from its Relatives when Deciding how to Attack its Hosts." *Nature* 18 January 2017, n.p.

Chabot, Pascal (2003). *The Philosophy of Simondon: Between Technology and Individuation*. London: Bloomsbury.

Deely, John (2009). *Purely Objective Reality*. Berlin and New York: Mouton de Gruyter.

--- (2015). "Objective Reality and the Physical World: Relation as Key to Understanding Semiosis." *Green Letters: Studies in Ecocriticism* – Special Issue on Biosemiotics and Culture. Eds. Wendy Wheeler, and L. Westling. 19.3, 267-279.

Derrida, Jacques (1978 [1967]). *Writing and Difference*. London: Routledge & Kegan Paul.

Eagleton, Terry (1983). *Literary Theory: An Introduction*. Oxford: Blackwell.

Favareau, Donald (2010). "Introduction: An Evolutionary History of Biosemiotics." *Essential Readings in Biosemiotics: Anthology and Commentary*. Ed. Donald Favareau. Dordrecht: Springer.

Gilbert, Scott F., and David Epel (2009). *Ecological Developmental Biology: Integrating Epigenetics, Medicine, and Evolution*. Sunderland, MA: Sinauer Associates.

Hoffmeyer, Jesper (2008a). *Biosemiotics: An Examination into the Signs of Life and the Life of Signs*. Ed. Donald Favareau. Scranton, PA: University of Scranton Press.

--- (2008b). "Introduction: Bateson the Precursor." *A Legacy for Living Systems: Gregory Bateson as Precursor to Biosemiotics*. Ed. Jesper Hoffmeyer. Dordrecht: Springer.

--- (2015). "Semiotic Individuation and Ernst Cassirer's Challenge." *Progress in Biophysics and Molecular Biology*. 119.3, 607-615.

Jakobson, Roman (1960). "Concluding Statement: Linguistics and Poetics." *Style in Language*. Ed. T. A. Sebeok. Cambridge MA: MIT Press.

Kull, Kalevi (2001). "Jakob von Uexküll: An Introduction." *Semiotica* 134, 1-59.

Least Heat-Moon, William (1991). *PrairyErth (A Deep Map)*. London: André Deutsch Ltd.

Lin, Michael F., et al. (2011). "Locating Protein-Coding Sequences under Selection for Additional, Overlapping Functions in 29 Mammalian Genomes." *Genome Res* 21.11, 1916-1928.

Magee, Bryan, and Martin Milligan (1998). *Sight Unseen*. London: Phoenix.

Maran, Timo (2013). "Enchantment of the Past and Semiocide. Remembering Ivar Puura." *Sign Systems Studies* 41.1, 146-149.

--- (2017). "Mimicry and Meaning: Structure and Semiotics of Biological Mimicry." *Biosemiotics Series*. Vol 16. Berlin: Springer.

Massumi, Brian (2009). "'Technical Mentality' Revisited: Brian Massumi on Gilbert Simondon. With A. De Boever, A. Murray and J. Roffe." *Parrhesia* 7, 36-45.

Mazur, Suzan (2015). *The Paradigm Shifters: Overthrowing 'the Hegemony of the Culture of Darwin'*. New Work: Caswell Books.

Noble, Denis (2006). *The Music of Life: Biology Beyond Genes*. Oxford: Oxford University Press.

--- (2017). *Dance to the Tune of Life: Biological Relativity*. Cambridge: Cambridge University Press.

Peirce, Charles S. (1878). "How to Make Our Ideas Clear." *Popular Science Monthly* 12, 286-302.

Pigliucci, Massimo, and Gerd B. Müller (eds.) (2010). *Evolution: The Extended Synthesis*. Cambridge, MA: MIT Press.

Puura, Ivar (2013). "Nature in Our Memory." *Sign Systems Studies* 41.1, 150-153.

Ricoeur, Paul (2003 [1975 *La Métaphore Vive*]). *The Rule of Metaphor: The Creation of Meaning in Language*. London: Routledge.

Sapp, Jan (2003). *Genesis: The Evolution of Biology*. Oxford: Oxford University Press.

Sériot, Patrick (2014). *Structure and the Whole: East, West and Non-Darwinian Biology in the Origins of Structural Linguistics*. Berlin: Walter de Gruyter.

Shannon, Claude E. (1948a). "A Mathematical Theory of Communication. Part One." *The Bell System Technical Journal* 27, 379-423.

--- (1948b). "A Mathematical Theory of Communication. Part Two." *The Bell System Technical Journal* 27, 623-656.

Shapiro, James A. (2011). *Evolution: A View from the Twenty-First Century*. Upper Saddle River, NJ: FT Press Science.

--- (2012). "DNA as Poetry: Multiple Messages in a Single Sequence." *The Huffington Post*. 24 January. Web. 14 March 2016 <www.huffingtonpost.com/james-a-shapiro/dna-as-poetry-multiple-me_b_1229190.html>.

Uexküll, Jakob von (1957) "A Stroll through the Worlds of Animals and Men: A Picture Book of Invisible Worlds." *Instinctive Behavior: The Development of a Modern Concept*. Ed. C. H. Schiller. New York: International Universities Press.

Wagner, Andreas (2014). *Arrival of the Fittest: Solving Evolution's Greatest Puzzle*. New York: Current.

Wiener, Norbert (1965 [1948]). *Cybernetics: or Control and Communication in the Animal and the Machine*. Cambridge, MA: The MIT Press.

Wheeler, Wendy (2016). *Expecting the Earth: Life/Culture/Biosemiotics*. London: Lawrence & Wishart.

Timo Müller (Regensburg)

The Road in the Garden: Pastoral Environments in the Post-War Caribbean Novel

1. Introduction

In *Caribbean Discourse* (1981), perhaps the richest discussion of Caribbean ecologies, Édouard Glissant repeatedly turns to a space few would regard as part of the natural environment: the road. While in the United States and Europe the road is typically associated with concrete and car travel, Glissant conceives it as a natural space that invites close observation and contemplation. Like Derek Walcott, who opens his early poem "Tales of the Island" (1962) on a "marl-white road" in SaiLucia, Glissant notes "the white dust that, in certain roads of our towns, at the edge of barely constructed slopes, suggests so much care and neatness".[1] For both writers, as for many of their Caribbean peers, the road is distinctly a part of nature, which provides the material elements – the marl, or dust – and the sensual impressions that make up the experience of the road.

For Glissant, however, the unity between the natural and cultural spheres is disappearing under the regime of global capitalism. Today, he claims, there

> barely remains along the roads, as far as smells go, the sugary blanket of hog plums in whose wake you can get lost, or, in some places along the Route de la Trace, the delicate smell of wild lilies beckoning. The land has lost its smells [...]. The flowers that grow today are cultivated for export. Sculptured, spotless, striking in precision and quality. But they are heavy also, full, lasting. You can keep them for two weeks in a vase.[2]

The Caribbean environment has been transformed by those forces of capitalist standardization, technological modernization, and social reorganization that the West calls progress. Glissant's ambivalence about the road and the flowers is representative of his general attitude toward this transformation. He acknowledges the results of progress around him but points out what has been lost: not "a vanishing idyll" but a "fragile and fragrant" land that "demanded in the past daily care from the community that acted on its own".[3] Like the flower, he suggests, Caribbean nature has become an object for consumption abroad. It does not afford him the sensual impressions he remembers from his youth, nor does it sustain the kind of agrarian communality he ascribes to the previous generation.

That generation witnessed the beginnings of the transformation Glissant diagnoses, and among its many responses are two novels that will be the topic of this essay. Both of these novels were published by influential writers of the post-war generation, and both negotiate the advent of techno-capitalist progress by tracing the impact of road building on rural communities. Sam Selvon's *A Brighter Sun* (1952) and Earl Lovelaces' *The Schoolmaster* (1968) depict the construction of asphalt roads as the intrusion of modern technology into a pastoral scene – of *The Machine in the Garden*, as Leo Marx put it in his classic study of nineteenth-century American literature. We will see, however, that they differ from Western conceptions of the pastoral in key respects. They understand the natural and social environments of the pastoral community to be dynamic, not static, which makes the introduction of modern technology a gradual, ambivalent process rather than an unforeseen catastrophe. While Marx's argument is limited to the United States, moreover, the novels under discussion here address the imperialist dimension of road building and its role in the capitalist exploitation of the land (which Selvon, for one, traces explicitly to the United States). In tracing these ambivalences and revisions, the essay proposes a more nuanced understanding of environmental concerns in the Caribbean. A brief survey of environmentalist approaches to the region shows that such nuance has often been lacking: observers have tended to privilege either natural or cultural factors, running the risk of reducing Caribbean culture to nature or vice versa.

2. Ecocriticism and the Caribbean

The academic field of ecocriticism has experienced a transformation around the turn of the twenty-first century, when scholars began to foreground locally specific environments and conditions. This shift of focus extended the ecocritical project in several respects: from recovery of nature to analysis of its cultural negotiation; from environmental protection to environmental justice; from the affluent West to its former colonies with their different, sometimes directly opposed concerns; and from literary texts to a variety of genres and media. All of these extensions complicated the conception of 'nature' underlying the ecocritical project, stressing the social construction and instrumentalization of nature as well as the interrelatedness of natural and cultural environments. Ecocritical work on the Caribbean played a key role in these developments. The region was one of the first outside the United States and Britain to appear on the ecocritical radar, as the discussion of Aimé Césaire and Edward Kamau Brathwaite in Jonathan Bate's classic *The Song of the Earth* (2000)[4] attests. Its eventful history, which had left its traces in the landscape and the population alike, made it difficult for scholars to ignore issues such as environmental justice, postcolonial power structures, and the cultural transformation of nature. Moreover, the centrality of the natural environment to Caribbean life and thought inspired a rich variety of proto-ecocritical commentary from writers and historians of the region.

Antonio Benítez-Rojo's *The Repeating Island* (1989), for example, argues from a poststructuralist perspective that Caribbean people are "not terrestrial but aquatic" because their maritime environment impels them "toward travel, toward exploration, toward the search for fluvial and marine routes".[5] Aimé Césaire and the Créolité movement, on the other hand, drew on the Caribbean landscape to distinguish their notion of *négritude* from the ideology of technological domination over nature that they saw represented in the European city. These early theorists share a somewhat reductive approach in that the natural environment appears in their texts primarily as a figuration of socio-historical developments and is often idealized. It was the publication of *Caribbean Literature and the Environment: Between Nature and Culture*, a collection of essays edited by Elizabeth DeLoughrey, Renée Gosson, and George Handley in 2005 that inaugurated a theoretically informed, self-reflexive ecocriticism in Caribbean studies. In their introductory remarks, the editors position the collection in the field of postcolonial ecocriticism, from which they adopt a concern with imperialist appropriations of the environment, with the commodification of local natures for tourist consumption, and with the privileging of affluent white people in much traditional ecocriticism and environmental activism.[6] The subtitle of the collection, moreover, indicates a shift of focus from the recovery of unspoiled, precolonial nature to the sociocultural developments that have shaped Caribbean landscapes more recently.

In these respects the volume illustrates the increasing theoretical sophistication of Caribbean ecocriticism, as do more recent publications by Lorna Burns and Lizabeth Paravisini-Gebert.[7] Yet the shift toward sociocultural analysis in *Caribbean Literature and the Environment* risks another kind of reductivism that acknowledges the importance of nature primarily insofar as nature can be enlisted for an anticolonial agenda. The editors note, for example, that Caribbean writers and intellectuals "have defended the role of literature in forging an environmental imagination in the Caribbean and in prioritizing spatial/natural relations. [...] Precisely because literature's rhetorical stance is one of imagined relations, it is well suited to the task of responding to History's presumed absence in the region".[8] The project of forging an environmental imagination, in this view, is valuable not for environmental reasons but because it counteracts imperialist stereotypes about the region. The editors hesitate to pursue classic environmental concerns, as their introductory remarks suggest, because this might be regarded as imposing a metropolitan agenda and thus as yet another colonizing move.[9] A closer look at theoretical and literary texts from the region shows, however, that writers have long been preoccupied with environmental issues without falling into the extremes of either idealizing a precolonial natural state or adopting Western templates to the detriment of local concerns.

Glissant's theoretical essays are an instructive example of this ambivalent environmentalism.[10] The interplay of landscape and language is a recurrent motif in *Caribbean Discourse*, which resolves the nature/history opposition by reading nature as imbued with "intermingled histories"[11] and vice versa. Glissant calls for a "poetics of the landscape"[12], an ambiguous concept that evokes both the inspirational force and the legibility of the natural environment – or in Western terms, both Romantic and postmodernist ideas about nature. Landscapes have an inherent "creative energy", he claims, but they are also texts that require interpretation: his home island of Martinique, for example, "is like an anthology of landscapes".[13] Any "aesthetics of the earth", he adds in *Poetics of Relation* (1990), begins with a "passion for the land where one lives" but needs to avoid the "obsolete mysticism" of environmental essentialism.[14] In a similar vein, Glissant stresses the ambivalence of modernization in a colonized region like the Caribbean. He speaks of the colonization experience as an "irruption into modernity"[15] which destroys local traditions but sets free creative forces at the same time. "We do not have a literary tradition that has slowly matured: ours was a brutal emergence that I think is an advantage and not a failing."[16] Recent scholarship on Caribbean modernity has supported this view, noting the "complex interactions, negotiations, and transformations"[17] the region underwent and rejecting schematic conceptions of modernity as either oppressive or liberating. Rather than adopting or dismissing Western environmentalist ideas outright, many Caribbean writers and theorists negotiate regionally specific environmental experiences that may or may not partake of these ideas.

The adaptation of the pastoral in Caribbean literature is an instructive example of this hybrid environmentalism. An idealizing depiction of rural life, pastoral as a genre and mode classically revolves around the loves and sorrows of musical shepherds. Like some early ecocritics, it tends to idealize life in nature by ascribing to it virtues such as simplicity, innocence, and an organic connection with the land.[18] This idealizing tendency has been criticized from various angles, including social, postcolonial, and environmental ones. The social critique of pastoral, articulated most influentially by Raymond Williams[19], faults it for colluding with the ruling classes in obscuring the harshness of rural labor. Postcolonial critics have rejected pastoral as an instrument of cultural imperialism in that it presented a distinctly European landscape as ideal, which in colonial contexts fostered the perception of local landscapes as exotic and excluded natives from representations of their own homelands.[20] From an environmentalist point of view, pastoral was criticized as objectifying nature for human pleasure rather than valorizing it for its own sake.[21]

These problems notwithstanding, a number of scholars have revalorized pastoral in environmental and postcolonial contexts. Two foundational works of ecocriticism, Lawrence Buell's *The Environmental Imagination* (1995) and Bate's *The Song of the Earth*, can be read as environmentalist defenses of pastoral against the anthropocentrism of its social critique. Glen Love, another early ecocritic, recommended pastoral as a template for contemporary environmental thought in that it traditionally explored human anxieties over threats to natural environments.[22] In a more positive vein Greg Garrard proposed rethinking pastoral as an enabling alternative to the poststructuralist "hermeneutics of suspicion".[23] Terry Gifford recovered pastoral by distinguishing conventional pastoral from 'post-pastoral', a modified variety aware "of the conventional illusions upon which Arcadia is premised, but which finds a language to outflank those dangers with a vision of accommodated humans, at home in the very world they thought themselves alienated from by their possession of language".[24]

In postcolonial studies, the debate around pastoral has created a tension between writers' continuing use of pastoral elements and scholars' ideological reservations about this practice. Confronted with the productivity of pastoral in the works of Aimé Césaire, George Lamming, V. S. Naipaul, Derek Walcott, and other influential writers, scholars of Caribbean literature have offered various explanations for this persistence.[25] Some regard it as an unfortunate remnant of colonial ideology consciously or unconsciously perpetuated by postcolonial writers.[26] Others dismiss it as a minor phenomenon that was eventually outgrown and is of merely historical interest.[27] Graham Huggan and Helen Tiffin, in *Postcolonial Ecocriticism*, adopt Gifford's strategy and conceptualize Caribbean pastoral as a post-pastoral that focuses on concerns shared by postcolonial scholars: "on the idea of land as collective resource, not individual luxury; on the idea of a transnational, not western-globalist, environmental ethic; and on the idea of an 'imagining of survival'".[28] What most scholarly explanations have in common is that they acknowledge the influence of pastoral but emphasize those aspects of pastoral that writers criticize or reject, rather than those they adopt and rework.[29]

Nuanced discussions of postcolonial pastoral are rare in scholarship. Buell's *The Environmental Imagination* includes a section on "indigenes' pastoral" that reads negritude as a "pastoral mode".[30] Not only does negritude evoke "a traditional, holistic, nonmetropolitan, nature-attuned myth of Africanicity in reaction to and critique of a more urbanized, 'artificial' European order", Buell points out, but it does so "from the standpoint of one who has experienced exile and wishes to return".[31]

Insightful as it is, this reading remains aloof of the local landscape, which goes unmentioned in Buell's discussion of Césaire, Walcott, and other postcolonial writers.[32] Erin Somerville, in "The Problem with Culture: Sam Selvon's Postcolonial Pastoral", contends that it is the "American-centric"[33] perspective of conventional ecocriticism that keeps Buell from recognizing the interplay of nature and culture in postcolonial pastoral. After tracing Selvon's evocation and ultimate rejection of traditional pastoral in *A Brighter Sun*, Somerville identifies creolization and "nature-based nationalism" as motifs that connect the natural and cultural environments depicted in the novel.[34] Graham Huggan's revalorization of pastoral in the context of postcolonial ecocriticism shares this concern with the sociocultural shaping of nature on both the material and the discursive levels. Through a close reading of Naipaul's *The Enigma of Arrival*, Huggan argues that a critically revised conception of pastoral might enhance awareness of issues of agency, control, and proprietorship in postcolonial countries.[35] This is borne out by Lovelace's *The Schoolmaster*, which Chris Campbell convincingly reads as a revised pastoral.[36] Arguably, however, Lovelace and Selvon base their revisions not primarily on classic pastoral but on Leo Marx's account of the intrusion of modern technology into a pastorally conceived American landscape.

Marx's *The Machine in the Garden* (1964) is a study of the pastoral tradition in the literature of the United States. Marx acknowledges the problems of pastoral, especially its escapist and idealizing tendencies, but argues that the major nineteenth-century American writers developed a more "complex" variant of the genre that foregrounds the tension between "rural peace" and "urban power", "simplicity" and "sophistication".[37] Complex pastoral has a broader significance in American culture, he argues, in that it responds to the colonization and industrialization of the land. The characteristic manifestation of this response is a motif Marx finds in many canonic writers of the nineteenth century: the intrusion of technology into a peaceful natural scene, of the machine into the garden. The motif captures the ambivalent feelings engendered by the encounter between rural life and technological progress as "tension replaces repose" and the intrusion of the machine "arouses a sense of dislocation, conflict, and anxiety".[38]

The motif that signals the advent of modernity in United States literature, Marx argues, is the sudden appearance of the railroad in a natural scenery enjoyed by the solitary writer. *A Brighter Sun* and *The Schoolmaster* dramatize the intrusion of modern technology into a pastoral landscape as well, but instead of the railroad they depict the introduction of asphalt roads in rural Caribbean communities.[39]

Both novels depict these communities in clearly pastoral terms. In *A Brighter Sun* the road is literally built through 'gardens', as the villagers call the small plots they farm on the back of their homes. The novel associates these gardens with biblical paradise in several ways. All the villagers seem to live off the fat of the land, and some can grow fruit almost magically, which occludes the hardships of peasant life. For the protagonist of the novel, a young man named Tiger, the clearing of the gardens takes on mythical dimensions.

> A tractor levelled down the beds on which he had planted lettuce at one time; he saw earth where melongene and tomatoes grew change shape, scooped up into the air and flung to one side. And he thought how after one time, is another. In one week the landscape was showing the colour of the naked brown earth and the deep impressions of the tractors. (146)[40]

As a result of this existential upheaval, some of the villagers are deprived of their livelihood and exposed to premature death, while others embrace the opportunities to be gained from their enlightened state.

The first group is represented by Sookdeo, the most accomplished farmer in the community, who cannot adapt to the new conditions because he has lost his connection to the land. Sookdeo is the most explicitly pastoral character in the novel, Erin Somerville points out, in that he extends his idealized view of farming to the colonial plantation system. His death thus "symbolises the death of the colonial pastoral"[41] and suggests that progress is inevitable and ambivalent at the same time. The beneficial side of progress is stressed by Tiger, who "wanted things to be different" and "had no intention of continuing to farm the land" (118-119). While some critics read him as a quasi-pastoral figure, stressing his "sincerity" and "naiveté", Tiger consistently rejects pastoral idealization by stressing the "hard work" of farming and by forcefully reversing the

Edenic view of the land: "to hell with the garden!" (158; 108).[42] While the novel describes rural Trinidad in pastoral terms, then, it undermines any idealizing tendency. For Tiger as for the country he represents, progress means new opportunities but also the persistence of old prejudices.

Similarly, *The Schoolmaster* depicts a pastoral community whose inhabitants take varying stances on political and technological progress. Pastoral is evoked by pointed allusions like the flute-playing of Pedro, a young farmworker who completes with the eponymous teacher for the hand of the village beauty, Christiana Dandrade, and by the archaizing sketches of the village and its natural environment that open many of the chapters. "Time goes slowly in Kumaca, and events are significant" (91), one of these sketches begins, stressing the premodern, idyllic character of village life. The pastoral view is most strongly endorsed by the priest, Father Vincent, who perceives the village as an unspoiled natural idyll and advises the inhabitants against establishing a school on the grounds that it would mean "a complete break away from your traditional ways" (34). Another, more realistic endorsement comes from Consantine Patron, a wealthy farmer who does not idyllicize the past but wants to uphold traditional customs (102). The novel pits these pastoral characters against the forces of socio-economic progress personified in the shopkeeper, Dardain, and the schoolmaster, Winston Warwick. Not only is the schoolmaster described as machinelike in his collected, uncompromising ambition, but he allies with the shopkeeper to speed up the construction of an asphalt road to the village. The shopkeeper in turn introduces strategies of capitalist appropriation when he secretively buys up the land along the likely route of the road and secures the schoolmaster's assistance in retaining that route.

While the construction process itself remains marginal to *The Schoolmaster*, the environmental destruction and exploitation it entails is foreshadowed by a powerful scene in the priest's imagination:

> It was very green, the country. That was because of the high forest and the hills, and the rainfall these attracted. Perhaps when the road came in from Valencia, forestry would become an industry. They would cut out much of the valuable timber. Tractors would come up, and men with axes and canthooks and saws, and trucks with winches would come up to reel up the logs and transport them. Then there would not be so much greenness, and not so much rain, and the parrots would cross in another sky. (184)

This imagined scene is the strongest ecological statement in the novel, and it uses the contrastive motifs Marx identifies in *The Machine and the Garden*. The clear stances the characters take have led some scholars to confuse one of the characters' views with that of the novel as a whole.[43] On closer inspection, however, the novel endorses neither the pastoral nor the progressive point of view. It dramatizes the collision of these views triggered by the arrival of the schoolmaster and his road-building project. The representative figures in that sense are neither the priest nor the schoolmaster but two villagers caught up in the ambivalences of progress: Paulaine Dandrade, a wealthy farmer who brings the schoolmaster to the village and endorses the road project in hopes of improving the village's chances in the capitalist marketplace, and Pedro Assivero, who is firmly rooted in the village's pastoral tradition yet interested in the economic opportunities afforded by the road building project.[44]

To the extent that these novels can be described as pastoral, they are what Marx would call complex pastorals in that they foreground the historicity of the pastoral landscape. Against the conventional view of pastoral as timeless and static, Marx argues, complex pastoral texts "expose the pastoral ideal to the pressure of change – to an encroaching world of power and complexity", thus creating a "sense of history as an unpredictable, irreversible sequence of unique events".[45] In contrast to the American writers in Marx's study, however, Lovelace and Selvon neither condemn nor celebrate the transformation of the pastoral land. They depict change as inevitable and focus on its consequences for local nature and culture. In *The Schoolmaster* the desire for change and progress comes out of the rural community itself, as we have seen, in that many of the villagers expect economic advantages from the school and the road. Moreover, the novel indicates at several points that the pastoral state is itself the product of history – more specifically, of a history of continual struggles for economic dominance. When Pedro's father, a gambler and alcoholic, speaks with the wealthiest farmers of the village they indulge him "because they knew that he had had some good cocks and that they had aided greatly in his fall. They waited in silence, intently, and with some sadness that neither of them wanted to show" (105). Far from a timeless idyll, this pastoral community is the scene of power struggles as fierce and consequential as those of the capitalist economy that is making its way toward the village.

Lovelace further undermines idealizing views of the pastoral state by pointing to the stultifying effect of the community's traditional customs. Pedro Assivero, the supposed pastoral hero of the novel, plans to confine his beloved Christiana to the home after their marriage:

> "When we are married she will have things at home to do, Robert."
> "It will not be good for the school. And it will be hard for her not to take the examination after taking lessons from the schoolmaster."
> Pedro said, "That is how things are, Robert." (95)

While her progressive father, a widower, has allowed Christiana to attend school in spite of her role as substitute mistress of the family, Pedro plans to revoke this opportunity because it does not accord with traditional custom. Christiana's intellectual talents, which have secured her the position of assistant schoolteacher, threaten to be wasted and any progress in education and self-determination checked. The scene acquires a broader resonance through Christiana's synecdochal function. A figuration for the village as a whole, she is suspended between the impersonal, ruthless progress embodied by the schoolmaster and Pedro's promise of emotional warmth and harmonious sociality. While the novel ultimately sides with Pedro by contrasting his respectful love of Christiana with the schoolmaster's sexual violence, this scene serves as an arresting reminder that the harmony of pastoral society comes at the cost of personal freedom and opportunity.

While Lovelace exposes the power dynamics within pastoral society, Selvon destabilizes pastoral conventions by drawing attention to the historicity of the landscape. The construction of the road in *A Brighter Sun* does not amount to the destruction of nature by culture but transforms a landscape that has been shaped by nature-culture interaction all along. Where the American writers in Marx's study stand aghast at the intrusion of the machine into the garden, the local community in Selvon's novel regards the road as part of the environment. After all, the very materials that make up the road come from that environment: "Boulders and gravel from the Laventille Quarry and other sites were brought in by trucks. Where the land was soft stones were laid two feet deep. Then gravel stones consisting chiefly of different kinds of quartz, obtained from river beds in the Northern Range, were laid" (178). "The asphalt came from the famous Pitch Lake in La Brea, a southern district" (197). In attending to the material history of the road, the locals incorporate the road into an environmental memory that blurs the distinction between 'natural' and manmade parts of the landscape.

Selvon further destabilizes pastoral conventions through the leitmotif of surveying. This motif recalls Glissant's 'poetics of the landscape' in that it emphasizes the legibility of the natural environment. Where Glissant foregrounds the cultural and environmental sensitivity to be gained from reading the land, however, Selvon stresses the analogies between surveying and the colonizer's acquisitive gaze.[46] For Tiger the position of assistant surveyor is primarily a means of acquiring power: "The job of going ahead and feeling out the land gave him a feeling of importance. He knew he was doing something much bigger than just manual labour" (157). Tiger effectively derives social power from his ability to make the land readable and thus exploitable by a capitalist economy. For Western philosophers like Adorno and Horkheimer, this would be an obvious case of "instrumental" power that combines social and environmental subordination.[47] There is a slight but momentous difference, however, between this point of view and Tiger's. Instead of using his surveying skill to overcome his dependence on and attain domination over nature, Tiger conceives it as contributing to a collective environmental imagination that includes both the road and the landscape through which it is built. He imagines himself sharing his knowledge of the land in colloquial talk with people from other villages:

> Tiger help to build that road. Look at all them cars and jeeps and trucks passing. You see there, right by where that jeep slowing down now? I remember, when we was building the road, it had a tree right there, it so hard to come out we had to use dynamite and blow it up. (123)

While Tiger's work does support the Americans' military and economic appropriation of the land, the novel's critique of pastoral conventions questions this exploitative approach. In foregrounding the multilayered history of the landscape the novel maintains a politically informed environmentalism that avoids reducing culture to nature or vice versa.

Selvon and Lovelace take a similarly nuanced position on the social transformations of which the road is both a trigger and a manifestation. For Marx, writing on the nineteenth-century United States, the sudden appearance of technology in the pastoral scene represents the unfortunate yet irrevocable progress of capitalist modernity.[48] The Caribbean, by contrast, had experienced its "irruption into modernity" much earlier: From the sixteenth century onward European colonization had wiped out the native population and instituted key structures of capitalist domination such as slavery, plantation labor, and a lopsided trade system.[49] From a Caribbean perspective, then, the American experience of modernity is both belated and partial. It occludes the United States' participation in and extension of such exploitative structures – supported not least by the pastoral idealization of the new continent that Marx and others have revealed. Against this background, it is hardly surprising that the arrival of the road in the mid-twentieth-century Caribbean communities depicted by Selvon and Lovelace is neither sudden nor catastrophic.

4. Revising Pastoral Conventions

This is partly because road building takes time and is preceded by an intricate process of planning and petitioning. More fundamentally, the arrival of the road transforms the local economy by encouraging construction and service activity to complement the traditional emphasis on farming. Tiger embraces the opportunity to switch to construction work and tells his wife to sell lunch to the road workers. While this transition toward the secondary and tertiary sectors leaves some villagers destitute, the novel points to the benefits as well and implicitly endorses Tiger's development by paralleling his economic progress with his increasing education. *The Schoolmaster* offers a very similar perspective on this transition. It traces the transition of power from the landowners (Dandrade, Patron) to those in the tertiary sector (Dardain, Warwick) triggered by the construction of the road. More explicitly than *A Brighter Sun*, it shows that the uneducated (such as Benn, the donkey-cart driver) stand to lose their jobs and that the new economy encourages abusive, ruthless behavior such as the bargain between Dardain and Francis Assivero: the shopkeeper threatens to ruin Pedro's father unless he calls off the wedding of Pedro and Christiana. Nevertheless, Lovelace too depicts the disappearance of the old agrarian system as inevitable. None other than Benn provides the conclusive statement on the transition: "There is no need to be sad because of the road. It had to happen. Sometime it would have to be open" (186). Both novels thus remain ambivalent on economic and technological modernization. Since they do not idealize the earlier pastoral state, they succeed in tracing the intricacies and nuances of change and show that modernization is a slow, gradual process rather than a sudden intrusion.

Another important difference to Marx's account of pastoral and modernity is the critical perspective Selvon and Lovelace cast on the United States' role in the expansion of global capitalism. Where Marx's writers are safely ensconced in the landscape, social structure, and intellectual community of an emerging world power, Caribbean writers hold a more volatile position as their land and community are under latent threat by American military, economic, and cultural imperialism. Written in the transition period from British to American dominance, *A Brighter Sun* explicitly addresses the impact of the United States on Trinidad: the construction of the road is an American military project devised during World War II. The Americans already have a military base on the island, which pays the highest wages and attracts the best workers in the area, draining communal structures. "From de time people hear bout Yankee work", Tiger's neighbor Rita remembers, "dey leaving everyting else, post office and treasury and government work, because dey getting more money dan de government cud pay" (135). Many of Tiger's acquaintances work on the base (Joe), start imitating the Americans (Bunsee), or even plan to emigrate to the United States (Boysie). The military, economic, and cultural dimensions of American imperialism are thus already in place, and Tiger experiences them directly once the road project begins.

The American officers in charge, including Tiger's boss on the surveying crew, act from a position of almost god-like power. "Everyone was waiting for the Americans to come and measure out the land" (118), the narrator reports fatalistically. "Tiger had a premonition his garden would go" (118). They expect the locals to be of service and do their bidding even if it goes against entrenched customs, of which they are ignorant anyway. When Tiger invites his supervisors home for dinner, their "philosophy of dominating everything" comes to the fore, and they act in a manner scholars have described as "condescending" and "patronizing".[50] On the other hand, the Americans bring beneficial economic impulses to the island. Rita, one of the more authorial voices in the novel, welcomes the new, highly paid jobs and stresses the advantages of the American model over the British colonial one: "American people not cheap like British people" (135). The historical background of the plot indicates, however, that these impulses will be short-lived and determined by the Americans' interest rather than the locals'. The island will remain economically dependent on the United States, and when the finished road is named the "Churchill-Roosevelt Highway" (197) the implication is that one model of domination has simply been replaced with another.

Perhaps the most pervasive manifestation of Americans' covert imperialism is the immediate influence they attain over local culture. When the officers arrive to survey the route of the road, Tiger imagines "a long, pretty road, not like those stupid roads in Barataria where you 'stumped' your toe all the time, but a real road, built by the Americans" (122). Not only do Americans set the standards by which local culture is measured and found deficient, in other words, but they define what is "real" (their world) and what is not (the locals' world). Reflecting on his stereotypes about the island, one of Tiger's American supervisors says, "I expected [...] natives creeping through the bush with bows and arrows! Instead, what do I see? A modern city streaming with American cars" (175). Modernity is equated with Americanness here, so that the island is prevented by definition from modernizing on its own terms. The Americans' cultural imperialism also shows in their ignorance of local ways, their stereotyping, their tendency to homogenize the local workers (they call them "John" regardless of their actual names), and their propagation of individualism over custom.[51]

> "Let me tell you something about customs, John" – Larry leaned over the table and wagged a knife in Tiger's face – "most of it is just plain dumb. A man hasn't got to live like that, John. A man must choose what he should do and what he shouldn't do, not be forced into anything just because it is a custom or a tradition. You mustn't let things rule you, John, you must rule things." (171-172)

The scene captures the ambivalence of the Americans' role in the novel. On the one hand, the knife-wagging makes Tiger's supervisor appear rude and even threatening. The gesture transfers these attributes to the American ideals Larry propagates – freedom, progress, self-reliance. These ideals threaten the local community in that they impose the capitalist principles of economic primacy and unrestrained competition. On the other hand, Tiger is receptive to Larry's advice not least because he shares his ideals. From the beginning of the novel he has sought independence from his family, social and educational progress, and an active, autonomous role in public life. The novel endorses his development on the whole, for example by pointing out that his mental independence leads him to reject racial prejudice and stereotyping. In between the poles of a conventional life ruled by local custom and unquestioning assimilation to the American way of life, Tiger develops a culturally hybrid identity that the novel holds up as a promising direction for the country he represents.

Lovelace negotiates the problems of colonization and cultural imperialism on a more allegorical level. The changes in the village are not the consequence of overt American or British intervention; in fact, the only white character in the novel, Father Vincent, comes from a former British colony as well (Ireland) and tries to shield the villagers from the effects of modernization. Yet the novel can be read as dramatizing the colonial mindset in its various facets and consequences. Father Vincent imposes a colonial narrative on the villagers, for example, in that he regards them as childlike, innocent, and ultimately naïve in their desire for progress. This is not only a factual misjudgment, as we have seen, but one reminiscent of the European colonial strategy of muting native voices that might contradict the colonizers' predefined stereotypes. The priest takes on the "white man's burden"[52], J. Dillon Brown notes, of self-appointed stewardship of an allegedly backward people. By foregrounding the priest's stereotypical notions of rural innocence and harmony, the novel points to the frequent use of pastoral for self-servingly beneficent representations of colonial exploitation.[53]

The schoolmaster, though ostensibly the priest's antagonist in his push for modernization, holds a remarkably similar view of the villagers. He too regards them as naïve and childlike – literally turning them into schoolchildren through his singing school – and assumes the role of benevolent yet self-serving guarantor of their welfare. In a further parallel, he draws on religious vocabulary to style himself as a representative of higher powers, and implicitly even as the god-like creator of the modernized village.

> This was his world. It was no mere inclination to remain, it was a duty. If he left, what would become of the villagers, the council, the school, the road, the many projects that he had in his brain. It was a duty. He would not run away. […] This village was his. And he felt now not only as if he

> had discovered Kumaca, but had had it willed to him by some Sovereign of The Backward Regions. (154)

The schoolmaster's gaze is that of the colonizer who appropriates religious and political structures to secure his power over the native. By implying that the villagers are unable to govern themselves he cloaks his exploitative, self-glorifying stance in the language of benevolent progress. In establishing colonial linguistic structures, Campbell points out, the schoolmaster goes so far as to reintroduce "the terminology of colonial administration" as he encourages the villagers to address him as "governor" and "ruler".[54]

Following Campbell, the novel can thus be read as revising the pastoral model along the lines of Gifford's post-pastoral. It complicates pastoral "notions of retreat, return, renewal and regeneration" by stressing the power hierarchies that have evolved under colonization: religious subordination (embodied in the priest's paternalism), economic exploitation (embodied in the shopkeeper) and "sexual and political domination" (embodied in the schoolmaster).[55] The very use of pastoral elements shows Lovelace's awareness of environmental issues as they contribute to his exploration of the nature-culture relationship under the sign of colonialism. Much the same can be said of Selvon's *A Brighter Sun*: both writers combine environmentalist with postcolonial concerns, and they do so by appropriating, questioning, and modifying the pastoral tradition. They present rural Caribbean landscapes as beautiful, agrarian, and communal, but not as ahistorical idylls. On the contrary, they dramatize the exposure of the rural sphere to the forces of technological exploitation and point up the imperialist dimension of these forces. Yet they avoid the extremes, often found in scholarly discussions of the Caribbean environment, of an idealizing conservationism or a reduction of nature to its political significance. In their novels, as in Walcott and Glissant, the road and the garden do not destroy but transform each other. From an ecocritical point of view, literary texts do not merely reflect this process of transformation but negotiate the underlying cultural values and epistemological parameters.

Notes

[1] Walcott (1986:22); Glissant (1989:241).
[2] Glissant (1989:51-52, trans. amended).
[3] *Ibid.*, 52.
[4] Bate (2000:79-89).
[5] Benítez-Rojo (1992:11).
[6] On postcolonial ecocriticism see DeLoughrey and Handley (2011); Bartosch (2013); Huggan and Tiffin (2015).
[7] Burns (2008); Paravisini-Gebert (2011).
[8] DeLoughrey, Gosson and Handley (eds.) (2005:13).
[9] The essays collected in *"What Is the Earthly Paradise?" Ecocritical Responses to the Caribbean*, a more recent collection edited by Chis Campbell and Erin Somerville, avoid this problem by focusing on cultural conceptions and representations of nature entirely.
[10] See Mardorossian (2013).
[11] Glissant (1989:154).
[12] *Ibid.*, 146.
[13] *Ibid.*, 146; 159.
[14] Glissant, (2010:147-148).
[15] Glissant (1989:100).
[16] *Ibid.*, 146.
[17] Fumagalli (2009:1-4).
[18] Abrams (1999:202-203); Baldick (1990:162); Empson (1935:25). As these scholars and others point out, pastoral operates on the level of genre, mode, and motif. The novels under discussion here are not pastorals in themselves but, as will be seen in the following, allude to the conventions of the genre and mode by including pastoral motifs.
[19] Raymond (1973).
[20] Coetzee (1988:4-6); Tiffin (2005:200); Williamson (2012:578); cf. Burns (2008); Huggan and Tiffin (2015:99-100); Tobin (2005).
[21] Garrard (2012:64-65); Buell (1995:3); cf. Gifford (2013:23).
[22] Love (1992:198-201).
[23] Garrard (1996:454; cf. 464-465).
[24] Gifford (1999:149).
[25] On these writers see Buell (1995:64-67); Huggan (2007:76); O'Brien (2001:4); Huggan and Tiffin (2015:126-134).
[26] Brown (1984:65-66); Nixon (1992:161-162).
[27] DeLoughrey (2011:269).

[28] Huggan and Tiffin (2015:134).
[29] See also Huggan and Tiffin (2015:127); Williamson (1973:579).
[30] Buell (1995:62; 64).
[31] *Ibid.*; Casteel (2007:109) gestures in the same direction.
[32] *Ibid.*, 64-67.
[33] Somerville (2007:98).
[34] *Ibid.*, 88; 96-97.
[35] Huggan (2007:83). A slightly revised version of this essay appears in Huggan and Tiffin (2015:126-134).
[36] Campbell (2008:67-68).
[37] Marx (1964:5-7) for the escapist and idealizing tendencies; 19 for the distinction of simple and complex pastoral.
[38] *Ibid.*, 16; cf. 354.
[39] Birbalsingh (1977). Birbalsingh's critique of the dominance of "pictorial" elements and local color in *A Brighter Sun* can be read as a critique of pastoral as well (9-15).
[40] Selvon (1989); Lovelace (1998). Further references to both of these editions will be included in the text.
[41] Somerville (2007:91). The pastoral dimension of the novel is also noted in passing by Ramchand (1976:64). On a related note Wyke (1991:62) points out that Tiger occasionally perceives the landscape in terms familiar from British Romanticism.
[42] Birbalsingh (1977:8) on Tiger's continuing attachment to the land see Barratt, Harold (1981:333-335); on the ambivalences in his response to the advent of progress see Ramchand (1976:69-70).
[43] Ekpa (1990:70-73) and Sunitha (1989:80) endorse Dandrade's view; Sunitha, (1989:131) then switches to the priest's view.
[44] See also Brown, (2008:45-46).
[45] Marx (1964:24,31).
[46] On the analogies between surveying and colonial appropriation in the novel see also Looker (1996:34).
[47] Adorno and Horkheimer (1979:44 and passim). For a similarly critical reading of Tiger see Gikandi (1992:121-122). While Gikandi rightly stresses the ideological dimension of Tiger's acquisition of knowledge and power, he disregards the benefits Tiger, and by implication all (post)colonial societies, draws from this knowledge when he begins to form a political consciousness toward the end of the novel.
[48] Marx (1964:26-27).
[49] Glissant (1989:146).
[50] Barratt (1981:332); Macdonald (1979:209).
[51] On their remaining stereotypes see Barratt (1981:332).
[52] Brown (2008:46).

[53] See also Campbell (2008:65).
[54] *Ibid.*, 67.
[55] *Ibid.*, 66-67.

Works Cited

Abrams, M. H. (1999). *A Glossary of Literary Terms*. 7th ed. Fort Worth: Harcourt Brace.

Adorno, Theodor W., and Max Horkheimer (1979). *Dialectic of Enlightenment*. London: Verso.

Baldick, Chris (1990). *The Concise Oxford Dictionary of Literary Terms*. Oxford: Oxford University Press.

Barratt, Harold (1981). "Dialect, Maturity, and the Land in Sam Selvon's *A Brighter Sun*: A Reply." *English Studies in Canada* 7.1, 329-337.

Bartosch, Roman (2013). *EnvironMentality: Ecocriticism and the Event of Postcolonial Fiction*. Amsterdam: Rodopi.

Bate, Jonathan (2000). *The Song of the Earth*. London: Picador.

Benítez-Rojo, Antonio (1992). *The Repeating Island: The Caribbean and the Postmodern Perspective*. Durham: Duke University Press.

Birbalsingh, Frank (1977). "Sam Selvon and the West Indian Literary Renaissance." *Ariel* 7.3, 5-22.

Brown, J. Dillon (2008). "Nostalgia for the Future: The Novels of Earl Lovelace." *Caribbean Literature After Independence: The Case of Earl Lovelace*. Ed. Bill Schwarz. London: Institute of the Study of the Americas, 41-60.

Brown, Lloyd W. (1984). *West Indian Poetry*. 2nd ed. London: Heinemann.

Buell, Lawrence (1995). *The Environmental Imagination: Thoreau, Nature Writing, and the Formation of American Culture*. Cambridge, MA: Harvard University Press.

Burns, Lorna (2008). "Landscape and Genre in the Caribbean Canon: Creolizing the Poetics of Place and Paradise." *Journal of West Indian Literature* 17.1, 20-41.

Campbell, Chris (2008). "Illusions of Paradise and Progress: An Ecocritical Perspective on Earl Lovelace." *Caribbean Literature After Independence: The Case of Earl Lovelace*. Ed. Bill Schwarz. London: Institute of the Study of the Americas, 61-75.

Casteel, Sarah Phillips (2007). *Second Arrivals: Landscape and Belonging in Contemporary Writing of the Americas*. Charlottesville: University of Virginia Press.

Coetzee, J. M. (1988). *White Writing: On the Culture of Letters in South Africa*. New Haven: Yale University Press.

DeLoughrey, Elizabeth (2011). "Ecocriticism: The Politics of Place." *The Routledge Companion to Anglophone Caribbean Literature*. Eds. Michael A. Bucknor and Alison Dowell. London: Routledge, 265-275.

--- (2005). "Introduction." *Caribbean Literature and the Environment: Between Nature and Culture*. Eds. E. D., Renée Gosson, and George Handley. Charlottesville: University of Virginia Press, 1-30.

---, Renée Gosson, and George Handley (eds.) (2005). *Caribbean Literature and the Environment: Between Nature and Culture*. Charlottesville: University of Virginia Press.

---, and George Handley (eds.) (2011). *Postcolonial Ecologies: Literatures of the Environment*. Oxford: Oxford University Press.

Ekpa, Anthonia A. (1990). "A Redefinition of the Ideal Caribbean Identity: An Aesthetic Evaluation of Earl Lovelace's *The School Master* [sic] and *The Dragon Can't Dance*." *Literature and Black Aesthetics*. Eds. Dele Orisawayi et al. Ibadan: Heinemann, 67-84.

Empson, William (1935). *Some Versions of Pastoral: A Study of the Pastoral Form in Literature*. Harmondsworth: Penguin.

Fumagalli, Maria Cristina (2009). *Caribbean Perspectives on Modernity: Returning Medusa's Gaze*. Charlottesville: University of Virginia Press.

Garrard, Greg (2012). *Ecocriticism*. 2nd ed. London: Routledge.

--- (1996). "Radical Pastoral?" *Studies in Romanticism* 35.3, 449-465.

Gifford, Terry (1999). *Pastoral*. London: Routledge.

--- (2013). "Pastoral, Anti-Pastoral, and Post-Pastoral." *The Cambridge Companion to Literature and the Environment*. Ed. Louise Westling. Cambridge: Cambridge University Press, 17-30.

Gikandi, Simon (1992). *Writing in Limbo: Modernism and Caribbean Literature*. Ithaca: Cornell University Press.

Glissant, Édouard (1989). *Caribbean Discourse: Selected Essays*. Charlottesville: University Press of Virginia.

--- (2010). *Poetics of Relation*. Ann Arbor: University of Michigan Press.

Huggan, Graham (2007). "Hating Nature Properly: Naipaul and the Pastoral." *"What is the Earthly Paradise?" Ecocritical Responses to the Caribbean*. Eds. Chris Campbell and Erin Somerville. Newcastle: Cambridge Scholars, 74-84.

Huggan, Graham, and Helen Tiffin (2015). *Postcolonial Ecocriticism: Literature, Animals, Environment*. 2nd ed. London: Routledge.

Looker, Mark (1996). *Atlantic Passages: History, Community, and Language in the Fiction of Sam Selvon*. New York: Peter Lang.

Love, Glen A. (1992). "*Et in Arcadia Ego*: Pastoral Theory Meets Ecocriticism." *Western American Literature* 27.3, 195-207.

Lovelace, Earl (1998). *The Schoolmaster*. London: Faber and Faber.

Macdonald, Bruce F. (1979). "Language and Consciousness in Samuel Selvon's *A Brighter Sun*." *English Studies in Canada* 5.1, 202-215.

Mardorossian, Carine (2013). "'Poetics of the Landscape': Édouard Glissant's Creolized Ecologies. *Callaloo* 36.4, 983-994.

Marx, Leo (1964). *The Machine in the Garden: Technology and the Pastoral Ideal in America*. New York: Oxford University Press.

Nixon, Rob (1992). *London Calling: V. S. Naipaul, Postcolonial Mandarin*. New York: Oxford University Press.

O'Brien, Susie (2001). "Articulating a World of Difference: Ecocriticism, Postcolonialism and Globalization." *Canadian Literature* 170/171, 140-158.

Paravisini-Gebert, Lizabeth (2011). "Deforestation and the Yearning for Lost Landscapes in Caribbean Literatures." *Postcolonial Ecologies: Literatures of the Environment*. Eds. Elizabeth DeLoughrey and George B. Handley. Oxford: Oxford University Press, 99-116.

Ramchand, Kenneth (1976). *An Introduction to the Study of West Indian Literature*. Kingston: Nelson Caribbean.

Raymond, Williams (1973). *The Country and the City*. London: Chatto & Windus.

Selvon, Sam (1989). *A Brighter Sun*. Harlow: Longman.

Somerville, Erin (2007). "The Problem with Culture: Sam Selvon's Postcolonial Pastoral." *"What is the Earthly Paradise?" Ecocritical Responses to the Caribbean*. Eds. Chris Campbell and Erin Somerville. Newcastle: Cambridge Scholars, 85-100.

Sunitha, K. T. (1989). "The Discovery of Selfhood in the Fiction of Earl Lovelace." *Subjects Worthy Fame: Essays in Commonwealth Literature*. Ed. A. L. McLeod. New Delhi: Sterling, 123-132.

Tiffin, Helen (2005). "'Man Fitting the Landscape': Nature, Culture, and Colonialism." *Caribbean Literature and the Environment: Between Nature and Culture*. Eds. Elizabeth DeLoughrey, Renée Gosson and George Handley. Charlottesville: University of Virginia Press, 199-212.

Tobin, Beth Fowkes (2005). *Colonizing Nature: The Tropics in British Arts and Letters, 1760-1820*. Philadelphia: University of Pennsylvania Press.

Walcott, Derek (1986). *Collected Poems 1948-1984*. New York: Farrar, Straus and Giroux.

Williamson, Karina (2012). "'From Arcadia to Bunyah': Mutation and Diversity in the Pastoral Mode." *A Companion to Poetic Genre*. Ed. Erik Martiny. Malden: Wiley Blackwell, 568-583.

Wyke, Clement H. (1991). *Sam Selvon's Dialectal Style and Fictional Strategy*. Vancouver: University of British Columbia Press.

Jan Rupp (Frankfurt am Main)

Geopoetics of Matter and Memory in M. NourbeSe Philip's *Zong!*

1. Introduction: Dynamic Materiality in Caribbean Writing

Geopoetics has been a fruitful concept for discussing Caribbean literature, as a body of writing both shaped by and shaping geography. Emphasizing the textuality of geography on the one hand and the extent to which authors have reworked the materiality of Caribbean environments on the other, the concept appropriately situates their texts as writing about as well as of the region. Given this defining inscription and creative impact of Caribbean landscapes, one might even go so far as to say that "if the large body of work that can be called Caribbean literature has anything in common (and this is an extremely heterogeneous field) it is its strong focus on materiality" – a "focus [that] arises out of both the history and the geography of the islands"[1].

From the joint perspective of material and postcolonial ecocriticism as delineated by Birgit Neumann and Sonja Frenzel in their introduction to this special issue, Caribbean geopoetics throws into relief a multiplicity of material-aesthetic entanglements in place of the nature/culture binary, and it equally debunks the fantasy of nature being outside of history as per European imaginaries of the Caribbean[2]. As such, geopoetics provides a shared rubric for various attempts, among others by 'founding fathers' of postcolonial Caribbean literatures like Éduoard Glissant and Edward Kamau Brathwaite, to turn to the land as a way of decolonizing tradition, of articulating new poetic idioms in tune with the region's local experience, and of working through collective historical memories and traumas.[3] This double focus on matter and memory[4] has served to reconstitute the Caribbean as an inevitably diverse but relational and unitary cultural space.[5]

Following the central premises of third-wave approaches in (material) ecocritism, the Caribbean is a space made up by invariably dynamic, overarching material-cum-semiotic environments, which emerge and are co-produced between aesthetic practices and the worlds these represent. Representation, in this connection, needs to be understood not only in a strong sense of (shaping, transforming) aesthetic mediation. As a result, literature is also a fundamental part, and 'representative' in a material sense, of the environments it engages with, rather than merely reflecting represented objects beyond the text. Material-aesthetic configurations, from this perspective, connote a "dynamic notion of materiality"[6] that is constantly in motion. This dynamics can be assessed, among others, by "the concept of material networks" such as "Bruno Latour's [...] actor-network theory, where it is the interaction between a series of human and non-human 'actants' (animals, solid objects, etc.) that is understood as agentic".[7] Materiality, thus, no longer comes down on one side of a static nature/culture divide, but it continuously evolves as "moving matter"[8] from a set of agencies across human and non-human material networks.

Precisely in this sense of devolved agency, the Guadeloupian author Daniel Maximin has theorized Caribbean geopoetics as 'fruit of the cyclone'. In his critical study, *Les fruits du cyclone. Une géopoétique de la Caraïbe* (2006), Maximin reiterates a focus on materiality and the geophysical, but productively blurs boundaries between them and poietic aspects of creation, depicting nature-culture relations as closely intertwined.[9] Already in the title of Maximin's book, the cyclone cuts across the nature/culture divide to inform or even constitute a Caribbean geopoetics. Conventionally seen as a destructive force, the storm here is understood as bearing fruit to suggest that nature shapes or even brings about culture and poetic forms. At the same time, of course, depicting the cyclone in this way is a tropological meditation on nature on Maximin's part. This kind of investment is well known, if one thinks of the larger, almost proverbial associations of "the islands' dramatic geomorphology and their discursive enmeshment with notions both of paradise and hell".[10] In a nutshell, Maximin's title expresses the way in which nature and culture are dialectically related in Caribbean writing, as a poetics informed by and informing the perception and experience of geography.

Storms are arguably the most iconic image in Caribbean geopoetics, referencing as they do the region's erratic, cyclical, and violent earth forces, as well as the ways in which these have been taken up in writing to enquire into their constitutive role as a social and "political ecology"[11] in the region. In Maximin's account, the cyclone is an element of cataclysmic, but resistant human-world relations which undermine central dichotomies of the European geographical and geopolitical imagination. As against "on-going efforts to control 'nature'", Maximin's geopoetics seeks to "destabilise existing boundaries, to rethink alliances and to resituate ourselves"[12] – as 'fruit' of the cyclone.

In my chapter, I will take this focus on matter and the geophysical as a point of departure to review some prominent tropes and topoi in recent geopoetic writing about and of the Caribbean, eventually zooming in on a reading of M. NourbeSe Philip's *Zong!* (2008). Philip's collection of poems revisits an infamous event in the history of the trans-Atlantic slave trade, to engage with the sea as a memory site and a liquid grave of the dead of the Middle Passage. Intertextually, the poems resonate with a large number of writings which have returned to the black Atlantic as a witness of history[13], reclaiming it as a site of commemorative dwelling and thereby revising its stereotypical role in the European imagination, where it tends to figure as a space merely of (neo-)imperial transit. While invoking this tradition, however, Philip takes a different approach in her use of concrete poetry as opposed to earlier texts which have launched counter-narratives to represent the sea and mnemonic meanings stored in it. As much as retrieving alternative archives of memory, *Zong!* deconstructs language to conjure up an "affective memory"[14] of sound, moan, and shout as approximating the existential horror and anguish of slaves thrown overboard on the Middle Passage – an infamous though common practice at the time to claim compensation for lost human 'cargo' when food and water supplies ran low, or when slaves in poor health conditions did not look to sell well on plantations of the New World at the journey's end.

This affective memory of horror and pain emerges from an encounter with the sea as a material space, and it likewise involves the physicality of words as 'linguistic matter' beyond their capacity to 'mean'. Exploiting as well the page's visual materiality and arranging her poems in varying shapes, Philip creates an unsettling water space for the reader to not only re-member but almost relive the black Atlantic in her poems' echoes of drowning bodies and voices. In the final instance, Philip's foregrounding of linguistic and corporeal materiality is motivated by an ethics of memory, by a desire for this memory to speak to historical realities and experiences. Thus, she deliberately pushes the boundaries of aesthetic mediation and dynamic materialization, producing a poetic seascape that grapples with the (un-)representability of atrocious events.

2. Geopoetics in/of the Caribbean

It bears repeating that geopoetics carries a particular critical inflection in the Caribbean context, as will become clear by comparison with the Franco-Scottish poet Kenneth White, who coined the term 'geopoetics'. White also founded the so-called International Institute of Geopoetics in 1989, whose manifesto highlights the growing sense of environmental crisis in the latter half of the 20th century and calls for poetry, as well as for ways of living more broadly, to reconnect with nature.[15] To a large extent, geopoetics emerges as a critique of civilization for White, as in his poem "City", in which modern urban life appears under the double sign of human and natural degeneracy:

> City the anonymous slavery that
> rots the mind and makes offal
> of dreams and the frenzied rootless
> urge to escape from this swamp
> of carrion life.[16]

Interestingly, the city not only evokes associations of estranged and morally corrupt humanity ("anonymous slavery"), it is also a place of rotting nature and all-pervasive death ("offal of dreams", "swamp of carrion life"). Implicitly, White paints the counter-image of an untouched, pure and unchanging nature, to which the "frenzied rootless urge to escape" wishes desperately to return. This is the idealized alternative to civilized modernity reminiscent of thinkers – and founding figures for US-based, first-wave ecocriticism – like Henry David Thoreau, whom White references in his "inaugural text"[17].

To be sure, it is not indispensable to refer to White at this point, because geopoetics has been picked up in a number of different ways, and it is not a school or movement with White as an originary figure.[18] Moreover, "ecocriticism covers the same field as geopoetics but with much more concern for theory".[19] These "[t]wo […] authoritative literary and global approaches" similarly focus on the "intertwining of the biosphere, poetry, and poetics". While geopoetics might be seen to "offe[r] a hodgepodge of ideas, without the systematic theoretical framework it might have aspired to provide", one of its advantages, for present purposes, is the fact that its prefix 'geo' makes the approach's "global range" explicit.[20] Literary environments in Caribbean writing are often conceived in precisely such overarching terms of 'geo'-poetics – in terms of hurricanes as geophysical forces, for example, or in terms of the sea, the beach, the volcano and the archipelago as elements of the region's particular topography and geomorphology. There is also a sense in which Caribbean engagements with the geophysical tend to direct attention to larger global and international constellations. In a decidedly postcolonial vein, geopoetic explorations here frequently respond to and contradict claims of (neo-)imperial European geopolitics and the geographical imagination underlying it. As Maximin states: "La Caraïbe oppose aux politiques de l'espace une poétique de l'espace."[21] As against the Caribbean's insularity and fragmentation, which for long served as pretext and geopolitical rationale of colonial conquest, foreign intervention, and the alleged impossibility of self-government, Maximin stresses the region as "espace de relation", to be retrieved in and through the poetic imagination: "[u]n espace où les dynamiques entre rêves et réalités, entre espoirs et désespoirs, entre centre et périphérie, sont toujours à l'œuvre".[22] This explains the currency of geopoetics in a book like Maximin's, although the approach generally covers a similar ground as ecocritical readings, with both focusing on the interplay between biosphere, literature, and human-environment relationships more broadly.

Another purpose of referencing Kenneth White's work and European intellectual traditions of thinking about poetics and the environment is to pinpoint an important difference with postcolonial ecocritical projects. While both Caribbean and European geopoetics seek to cross nature/culture binaries, many examples of the latter tend to idealize and essentialize nature, as in White's poem "City", in which a mythic idea of primal origins is presented as desirable alternative to city life. By contrast, nature in the Caribbean plays a more active part as opposed to White's European pastoral imagination. It is neither a backdrop to human happenings nor a place of refuge from civilization, but a key historical figure, as Maximin calls it: "La nature dans la Caraïbe n'est pas un décor, c'est un personnage central de son histoire."[23] A major 'person' in Caribbean history and memory, nature is, by extension, a central (f)actor within the region's literature as well. In this image and personification of nature as an active historical and mnemonic force, human-nature relationships and the devolved agencies of material-aesthetic environments are quintessentially expressed.

Throughout his study, Maximin fundamentally reconceives conventional environmental thinking to define a Caribbean geopoetics. Among other familiar tropes, he rejects sensationalizing representations of natural disaster in the region[24], such as regularly employed by media coverage of the hurricane season. Cataclysms like hurricanes do expose man's vulnerability, but in Maximin's view they should also be reimagined as an element of resistance against outside economic and political interests. Just as popular colonial trading posts like Port Royal in Jamaica were repeatedly washed away by tsunamis and hurricanes in the past – by the "foaming, rabid maw of the tidal wave swallowing Port Royal"[25] as remembered in Derek Walcott's "The Sea is History", for example – economic and touristic projects in the region today are confronted by a similarly unruly nature. In effect, Maximin envisions a new sense of alliance between humanity and Caribbean erratic nature against European colonial and neo-imperial intervention. Moreover, geophysical forces and meteorological conditions are shown to have thoroughly shaped a wide range of cultural practices, apart from literature also music, dance, architecture and even cooking. Given this reciprocal intermingling of the material and the cultural, it is in and through these geopoetic practices and discourses that the complexity of human-world relations is recognized and explored. The image of humanity as fruit of the cyclone and the idea of nature as a central figure in history are part and parcel of this discursive enmeshment of nature.

Maximin's conception of Caribbean geopoetics is informed by an inevitably complex relation between nature and aesthetic practices, including nature's "alterity"[26] as a threat that cannot be entirely contained. It is a poetics which offers a more holistic view than traditional pastoral and geopolitical imaginaries. It also contains a more ethical view of human-world relations, because it pinpoints man's general relationality with nature, as well as connections across human and non-human spheres, for which destructive earth forces are a shared alterity. The human abode of the typical "case antillaise", whose "matériaux utilisés marquent son inscription dans l'environnement naturel"[27], is subject to devastating tidal waves and tropical storms just like the underwater life of coastal areas. Not least, Maximin formulates a geopoetics of the Caribbean specifically

– a new, alter/native aesthetics and ethics that is enabled by the region's particular environmental experience of erratic, cyclical nature. It is launched from there as a postcolonial corrective to the European geographical imagination and international geopolitics at large.

Moving on to take a closer look at the way in which this postcolonial concern with matter and memory manifests itself in literature, images of the storm – "almost over-determined as a figure within the formation of Caribbean geopoetics"[28] – no doubt loom large. From countless texts dealing with the devastation wrought by hurricanes to others in which they are depicted as allies or even friends, storms are over-determined precisely because they have been discursively enmeshed in multiple ways. In Grace Nichols's much-anthologized poem "Hurricane Hits England", for example, the hurricane is a "back-home cousin"[29], visiting the speaker in her diasporic British migrant setting. It is conspicuously over-determined as both "fearful and reassuring"[30], and as a distinct marker of Caribbean identity and island experience. It is through Nichols's poem and similar writings, inspired by the hurricane, that geophysical forces like it take on multi-faceted meanings as part of material-aesthetic environments, which replace the dualistic idea of textual representation and inert nature outside of the text by an insight into dynamic materializations and shared agencies across human and non-human spheres.

However, storms are by no means the only element of Caribbean geopoetic writing, but part of a wider range of tropes and topoi. Following Édouard Glissant's characterization of Caribbean literature as a "language of landscape"[31], Sarah Phillips Casteel has detailed a large number of such topoi in a "lexicon of the Caribbean spatial imaginary"[32], including such diverse examples as the tropical garden, the sea, the beach, the hinterland, and the archipelago as a whole. Characteristically, all these topoi – as orienting coordinates within the literary imagination – do not merely reflect but continuously co-produce their geophysical reference points in the complex sense of material-semiotic environments. As polyvalent images, they figure and re-member the natural world in multiple ways. In so doing, Caribbean geopoetic tropes and topoi frequently go against one-sided representations and take on earlier historical traces inscribed therein, such as colonial (and touristic) fantasies of the tropical garden as a paradise or garden Eden. Similarly, the archipelago has been read in a number of ways, in terms of fragmentation and fragmented culture, but also in terms of (submarine) unity. The island, too, represents a world unto itself in many texts, or it may stand for some larger connectivity.

Collectively, these topoi in what is an agentic and performative rather than merely representational 'lexicon' of landscape demonstrate the extent to which Caribbean writing is informed by geography – and to which how intensely the islands' materiality, in turn, is invested with literature and tropological inscription. The result is an aesthetics and ethics of multivalent meanings and multiple material-semiotic environments, which are repeatedly reconstituted in dialogue with memories attached to earlier figurations. Alongside cultural practices such as architecture, music and dance, literature has an important role to play for Caribbean geopoetics with its potential to explore, enrich and critically reflect on nature-culture relations. This goes particularly for those environments of tropes and topoi in which the connection between memory and physical as well as aesthetic materiality is particularly pronounced. From those topoi, the Atlantic sea and the Middle Passage as commemorative sites of slavery's traumatic history are arguably the most prominent example.

3. Matter and Memory in *Zong!*

On the cover *of Zong!*, the sea's centrality for Caribbean geopoetics and Philip's characteristic entanglement of physical and aesthetic materiality in her collection of poems are conspicuously signposted. Against a backdrop of floating waves, a piece of human bone extends vertically from top to bottom. Cutting across (and forming a cross with) the skeletal fragment is the work's title, which makes the topos of the sea as a liquid grave of the Middle Passage complete. As readers familiar with black Atlantic writing will be readily aware, *Zong!* is a reference to the infamous 18th-century slave ship *Zong*, with a slight but significant variation indicated by the title's concluding exclamation mark. This exclamation mark signals the performative dimension of Philip's work, its foregrounding of sound and the spoken word, and its generic affinity with the genre of (anti-)elegy and lamentation[33]. These formal characteristics are a measure of how *Zong!* draws on but also defamiliarizes extant memories of the black Atlantic. While Philip builds on "the concept of the ocean as guardian of the African slave population who perished midway across the Atlantic"[34], as found in many other texts of Caribbean seascape poetry, it presents a very different notion and material-aesthetic version of this aquatic memory.[35] Philip's poetry cycle is indeed placed in a tradition of recovering the (his)tory of the *Zong*, but it is acutely aware of the "labors of narration in the face of events whose tailoring into a story neglects losses and lives crucial to the counter-memory of the event".[36] In James E. Young's sense of counter-memory, *Zong!* challenges not only the official historical record, but also familiar forms of re-membering in the black Atlantic tradition.[37]

In 1781, the *Zong* departed from Africa's Gold Coast with more slaves than the vessel could reasonably hold.[38] Having taken much longer than the usual journey across the Atlantic, it overshot its destination in Jamaica to exacerbate the situation on board even more. As a solution to diminishing supplies and infectious diseases spreading, the ship's captain decided to throw more than 130 sick and frail slaves overboard, so as to ensure that the healthy and strong who remained would fetch a good price on New World slave markets.[39] Part of his calculation was a regulation in maritime law at the time, which allowed the ship's owners to claim compensation for human 'cargo' lost at sea. When they did, and the insurance company refused to pay, the ensuing court case in 1783 attracted great public attention in British society and catalyzed the growing movement for the abolition of the slave trade. Retrospectively, the *Zong* has been interpreted as the single most important event in the European slave trade's history, which would lead to the end of slavery eventually but continue to haunt its aftermath. In Ian Baucom's study *Specters of the Atlantic: Finance Capital, Slavery, and the Philosophy of History* (2005), the *Zong* case is seen to epitomize slavery's capitalist underpinnings and immoral character, and it is a central point of reference for his analysis of "notions of justice and value that emerge from a contemporary politics of black Atlantic remembrance".[40] Similarly, the *Zong* is a key and core example for James Walvin's writings on the history of the slave trade, in *Black Ivory: A History of British Slavery* (1992), for example, or, even more prominently, in his latest book *The Zong: A Massacre, the Law and the End of Slavery* (2011).

Thus, quoting the ship's name alone on the cover of Philip's collection of poems is enough to conjure up the *Zong*'s original story as well as its various fictional and non-fictional retellings over the past couple of decades. "You have heard this story before", Erin M. Fehskens remarks in her discussion of Philip's collection, and "[y]ou will hear this story again and again", pointing out the recursive, almost ritualistic nature by which this particular as much as emblematic story has been revisited and commemorated.[41] Fehskens even uses a generic term, "*Zong* literature"[42], to subsume under it David Dabydeen's long-poem *Turner* (1994) or novels like Barry Unsworth's *Sugar and Rum* and Fred D'Aguiar's *Feeding the Ghosts* (1997). Together with founding Caribbean texts like Walcott's poem "The Sea is History" (1979), these earlier works have typically launched counter-narratives to represent the Atlantic and reveal commemorative messages stored in it, thereby revising European views of the sea as a 'non-place' devoid of meaning and history.

Published one year after the bicentenary of the abolition of the slave trade in 2007, Philip's cycle of poems clearly adds to the extant body of '*Zong* literature' and builds on the dynamics of material-aesthetic representation in previous texts. Yet, if the *Zong* had become a central symbol and story content of black Atlantic remembrance in 2007, when a replica of the ship took part in a bicentenary parade on London's Thames, Philip's *Zong!* draws on and departs from this commemorative mode at the same time. Her titular reference to the ship's name – a "mistranscription"[43] of the vessel's earlier Dutch name *Zorg* (meaning 'care'), and a most cynical slippage considering the *Zong*'s fateful journey after it had been taken over by its new, Liverpool-based owners – at once invokes and modifies the familiar narrative, for the poems do little in the way of telling a story. In fact, the only other reference to more conventional ways of storytelling comes in the subtitle ("As told to the author by Setaey Adamu Boateng"), by which Philip extends authorship to share it with an imaginary "ancestral voice".[44] Other than this, however, *Zong!* has been read, paradoxically, as employing as well as rejecting narrative, including by Philip herself in "Notanda", her essay in which she reflects on the writing of her poems and which forms part of her collection. In "Notanda", she variously describes the *Zong* massacre as a "story that cannot but must be told" and characterizes her project, ambivalently, as one of "not-telling"[45]. If "the *Zong* literature of the 1990s works in ekphrastic, lyric, and novelistic modes out of an effort to invent lost subjectivities or characters, *Zong!* displays "Philip's profoundly anti-narrative sensibility in this work"[46].

In creating her poems, Philip takes quite a different approach from narrative in her use of concrete language poetry. In an overtly deconstructive vein, she draws on the legal decision *Gregson v. Gilbert*, which is so named after the ship's owners and their insurers respectively and remains one of the few original accounts of the *Zong* to have survived. While Philip reproduces this legal text from the court case's appellate hearing in full at the end of her collection, in her poems she substantially mines, reorganizes and picks the decision's wording apart. Shocked at the mind set conveyed, such as the judge's comparison of slaves to horses[47], and yet realising that this is the language through which the horrors of *Zong* have been made possible and been handed down, Philip uses only these words to reimagine the victims' suffering – from a text whose "very name, legal shorthand for the litigating parties, expunges the victims' lives from the official record"[48], to reimagine the victim's suffering. Throughout her collection, she critically inspects and fragments language in place of a coherent story, stripping it down to letters, morphemes and sounds, and arranging these fragments in floating shapes on the page. Highly sceptical of legal decision's semantic content and underlying world-view, Philip foregrounds the materiality of language – such as its sonic dimension as indicated by the exclamation mark in the collection's title – to recapture the situation on board the *Zong*. In line with insights into the primacy of the signifier as argued by Jacques Derrida and other poststructuralist thinkers, linguistic materials are exposed to suggest how language shapes and creates material conditions rather than merely reflecting them. Moreover, to speak with Gilles Deleuze and Félix Guattari, language in *Zong!* is a social and material-semiotic "assemblage of enunciation"[49], which is enacted in pragmatic situations and makes itself felt on the body – constituting, aboard the Zong, the corporeal reality of the slaves' suffering. As a case in point, the collection's opening poem picks apart the phrase 'want of water' – the reason given by the ship's captain's for his decisions to throw slaves overboard, as documented in *Gregson v. Gilbert*. In Philip's poem, the phrase's component but dismembered parts are scattered across the page – drifting letters capturing the sound, and tracing the movement, of and drowning bodies and voices.

Throughout, this foregrounding and constant recombination of linguistic material enters into dialogue with other types of moving matter, most obviously when fragments of speech disintegrate, but do take on new (visual) meaning through the floating seascapes they come to compose. At no point does Philip's deconstructionist approach turn into self-serving linguistic word-play, it is always directed at probing a new aesthetics and ethics of re-membering the *Zong*. This engagement and reciprocal cross-inflection of poetry and historical as well as physical realities is also reflected in the six subsections of Philip's collection, the Latin-titled "Os" (bone), "Sal" (salt), "Ventus" (wind), "Ratio" (reason), "Ferrum" (iron) and "Ebora" – Yoruba for underwater spirits – respectively. All these different "bodily, meteorological, legal, and cultural aspects"[50] co-produce, and come together in, Philip's material-aesthetic representation of the *Zong* massacre. In a linguistic 'colonization in reverse', she challenges the 'ratio' of *Gregson v. Gilbert*, "underscores the lacunae in the foundational text"[51] and 'mutilates' its legal wording as a way of recreating the manner in which Africans were treated and randomly selected for transportation. The general principle of composition is creating what she calls a liberating "semantic mayhem"[52], which seeks to capture a sense of horror and despair at the only seeming order and rationality of 18th-century legal discourse, with its dehumanization of Africans in considering them as property, chattel and 'cargo'. As Philip elaborates in "Notanda": "In *Zong!*, the African, transformed into a thing by the law, is re-transformed, miraculously, back into a human. Through oath and through moan, through mutter, chant and babble, through babble and curse, through chortle and ululation"[53].

In "Os", *Zong!* starts with a sequence of 26 poems, which are so numbered: "Zong! #1", "Zong! #2", "Zong! #3", and so forth. Given that 26 is also the number of letters in the alphabet, the fact that Philip assembles just this number of poems in the first part of her collection already signals her highly self-reflexive use of language, by which *Zong!* takes an extremely multi-faceted and innovative approach to Caribbean seascape poetry. With its influences from concrete and visual poetry, the collection capitalizes on the physicality of the signifier to both problematize habitual and develop new forms of representation. Words are scattered across the page and cluster in varying ways, closely involving the reader to make sense of highly disparate and irregular patterns. Philip deliberately seems to push the limits of (conventional, narrative) representation, while remaining steadfastly concerned to unearth a memory of slavery from what she calls the "bone beds of the sea"[54]. The one regular, recurring element in the first 26 poems is a list of African names in an ongoing footnote. Symbolically, this footnote 'names' and commemorates the forgotten and unrepresented Africans on board the *Zong*, who in historical texts, such as the *Gregson v. Gilbert* document, only appear under the default identification 'Negro'.

The poems' diverging visual patterns and "convoluted optics"[55] frequently suggest a floating movement of letters and words, which resemble the wayward and shifting nature of memory. Indeed, the sea and its material-aesthetic representation are explicitly compared to memory, because just as "the ocean appears to be the same yet is constantly in motion, affected by tidal movements, so too this memory appears stationary but is shifting always".[56] The sea is a substantial creative principle for Philip, as she suspends linguistic structure ("having cut myself off from the comfort and predictability of my own language – my own meaning"[57]) and gives herself up to a journey that equals the situation of being at sea, with no language system to hold on to.

Importantly, this situation is replicated for the reader, who is often left guessing as to how to connect words and how to bridge the spaces between them, or even whether to read from left to right or from the top down: "Philip utilizes a multitude of formal techniques to destabilize the reader" in "her most formally innovative text".[58] In this way, the image of the sea and the memory-work it depicts are not only metaphorical, but also material and very real in the "discomfort and disturbance created"[59] both in the writing and in the reading process: "The reader is often figuratively immersed under the flood of language in the text, only occasionally grasping a life-raft of meaning, and thus vicariously experiencing the dislocation of the slaves on board the *Zong*."[60] By foregrounding the physicality of language and by distorting it, Philip indeed provides her poetry with a strong experiential dimension, appealing to as well as relying on the reader's immersion.

Comparing Philip's poetry cycle to earlier black Atlantic writing as well as to different modes of collective memory, Jenny Sharpe has persuasively argued that *Zong!* seeks to "evoke intuitive response rather than thought and contemplation" by presenting a "more visceral form of memory than storytelling".[61] As against the notion of the archive, with its western provenance, its reliance on writing and scripture, and its canonical authority that both excludes subaltern memories and therefore becomes a site of contestation,[62] Sharpe emphasizes affect as an alternative mode of memory. While there is no shared definition of the concept, as Sharpe points out, its focus on aspects of the body and materiality make affect studies a useful point of reference when discussing "forms of representation that do not necessarily conform to a western logic of language and writing"[63]. Affect no doubt lends itself well to works like *Zong!*, with its strong concern for the corporeal repercussion and environmental circumstances of slave suffering. In Sharpe's understanding, however, affect is not limited to the body, as in Brian Massumi's influential distinction between bodily sensations (affect) and socially co-construed emotions or feelings, which Sharpe cites.[64] Rather, her "interest in the term [affect] has to do with its ability to address both the body and the mind, reason and the passions"[65].

Even though suspending linguistic meaning on the page to create affective potentials can hardly match the slaves' experience on board the *Zong*, Philip does indeed seem to aim for what Sharpe calls affective memory as much as for a story to reintegrate into "archival memory".[66] As Almas Khan concurs, "*Zong!* is an experiential text in that it is felt more readily than it is described linguistically"[67]. It bears emphasis, however, that this mode of affective memory is not necessarily placed in opposition to the archive, or to storytelling, for that matter. Nor does affect, in Sharpe's understanding, equate with one side of the "dualism between body and mind" – "a philosophical tradition that is not universal, being spread across the globe primarily through European colonization"[68]. Instead of falling back on binary oppositions such as mind and body, it is worth remembering the conjunction "and" in the title of Sharpe's article ("The Archive and Affective Memory M. NourbeSe Philip's *Zong!*"). Philip's collection of poems is arguably best located somewhere in-between archive and affect, because it lays claim to both. Its emphasis on affective memory needs to be seen as relative to previous texts in the tradition of '*Zong* literature'. *Zong!* employs "a non-narrative form that is frequently embedded in narrative projects to illuminate its contradictions and gesture towards a different mode of representation"[69]. Indeed, Philip's poetry presents a counter-memorial impulse placed within the tradition of earlier black Atlantic writing, rather than outside of it. This intermediate position is reflected by Philip's paradoxical attitude towards storytelling. After all, her poems, however non-narrative, rely on (the reader actualizing) intertextual references to the *Zong*'s story, and the author's own narrative reflection in her essay forms an integral part of her book-length collection, just as critics will use "Notanda" as a non-fictional narrative and important paratext to frame Philip's poetry.

Apart from text's visual patterns and deconstruction of meaning, affective memory is evoked in *Zong!* by the materiality of language as sound and by various musical influences which the collection displays.

As Philip isolates words and breaks them down to morphological and phonological units, she creates a "language of pure sound fragmented and broken by history"[70]. In "Notanda", she draws an analogy between her composition and the fugue, highlighting the contrapuntal, counter-memorial and polyvocal character of her poems. Via her use of North American "language poetry"[71] comes another line of influence in this genre's association with the aleatoric music of composers like John Cage. Cage's principle of random, indeterminate composition and performance is appropriated in Philip's text, and made explicit in her widely differing public readings in which she uses varying tempi and takes different selective itineraries through the labyrinthine patterns of her text. Just as authorship becomes collaborative in *Zong!*, there is a sense in which the texts produced take on a life of their own. Philip repeatedly speaks of "the poem I want to write and the poem that must write itself"[72]. Her combinatory matrix furnished from the *Gregson v. Gilbert* document is not unlike the musical score typically devised by indeterminate music.

These musical borrowings clearly add to the importance of phonic aspects in her poetry and stress its performative quality. The fact that the poems serve as scripts for (changing) performance(s) highlights the extent to which *Zong!* reconstructs an embodied memory from the sea, conjured up by "rituals of ancestry".[73] A general feature of Caribbean writing, this ritualistic nature of performing collective memories of the Middle Passage constitutes a special potential for Philip's poetry, too, as she suggests with another pair of floating signifiers or phonemes – "*Zong!* is Song!"[74]. If the aspect of ritual and performativity has been recognized as a key element of black Atlantic literatures,[75] Philip clearly corroborates this view, whether through the mantra-like repetition of words or through her description of the act of writing as a kind of ritual.[76] At the same time, there is no better example than her poetry – relying on the layout of the page from which it derives its specific phonic quality – to contradict any one-sided identification of Caribbean literary traditions with either the written or the spoken word.

The phonic, physical and material dimension of language significantly expands affective memory's experiential quality of, shifting attention from the question of "[w]hat did, in fact, happen on the *Zong*?" to the question of "what it must have been like for those Africans on board the *Zong*"[77]. In foregrounding the 'sound matter' of words, Philip eventually approximates a primordial state of "pure utterance", in which the agony of slavery is expressed. It is a painful but empowering state of "pre-literacy", which dismantles the contaminating presence of the colonizer's language.[78] By reducing language to its visual and phonic materiality, Philip eventually resolves her paradox, namely, that the *Zong*'s story must be told by not telling it. Focusing on the visual and phonic materiality of words, this is the language through which the horror on board the *Zong* can, not be 'told', but articulated and offered to memory.

As much as imaginatively recounting historical incidents, Philip arrives at a different answer to what happened on the *Zong*. As she suggests in her essay: "Could it be that language happened?"[79] By way of answering this rhetorical question, she retrieves an embodied, resonant, material memory. Her account of the writing of *Zong!*, which involved several crossings of the Atlantic along triangular routes to the slave ports of Ghana and Liverpool, is testament to the significance of engaging with the sea as a mnemonic site and material-aesthetic practice. The outcome is a memory of the bones, cries, and wails of the Middle Passage, evoked by the physical matter of language. This and Philip's multiple references to material traces of the sea – salt, wind, the movement of water and the seabed as a liquid grave – configure memory as a multi-sensory experience to be gleaned not just from stories, but form immersing oneself in material-aesthetic environments, movements and sounds of floating signifiers and phonemes.

4. Conclusion

To a considerable extent, then, memory and the literary sea environment are reconstructed and conveyed in *Zong!* through a 'geopoetics' of floating signifiers, spatial fragmentation and the sound quality of the text. As much as retrieving silences of (counter-)archival memory as narrative, Philip conjures up an affective memory of sound, moan, and shout, which goes beyond 'meaning' to rely on the materiality of language. Her paradoxical recourse to and departure from narrative might be seen as ambivalent, privileging self-reflexive linguistic experiment instead of feeding much-needed subaltern stories back into the archive. Yet her innovative creation of literary sea environments is effective as well as affective. By translating the physical materiality of water and sea onto the page, it offers a viable and ethically valuable memory of lived experience, and provides a pertinent twist on questions around materiality, culture and representation in Caribbean writing.

As Philip's formally innovative collection of poems, Maximin's central image of the storm, and the idea of writing as fruit of geophysical forces show, boundaries between the material and the symbolical become productively blurred in Caribbean geopoetics. In works like *Zong!*, this goes vice versa for language and symbolical representations, too. Caribbean geopoetics consists not in stable ways of representing an outside materiality, but is the product of ever-shifting "dynamic processes of materialization"[80], which may involve the matter and physicality of language as well. Literary environments informed and constituted by Caribbean geopoetics are thus revealed as multiple material-aesthetic interactions which go both ways. In so doing, they thoroughly revise attempts to essentialize or dominate nature in pastoral imaginaries and European geopolitics.

Notes

[1] Noxolo and Preziuso (2012:123).

[2] Cf. Deloughrey Gosson and Handley (eds.) (2005).

[3] On the "liberationist" aspects of developing new literary languages in tune with the Caribbean's regional experience and ancestral memory cf. Neumann (2016) and Brathwaite (1984) for the concept of 'nation language'. Cf. also Glissant (1999 [1989]:11): "Our landscape is its own monument: its meaning can only be traced on the underside. It is all history" (cited in the introduction to DeLoughrey et al. 2005).

[4] The phrase 'matter and memory' features prominently in Henri Bergson's 1896 book *Matière et mémoire. Essai sur la relation du corps à l'esprit*. Responding to new scientific findings at the time, Bergson rejects the theory that memory is primarily physical, located in a particular part of the brain. By contrast, he emphasizes the spiritual nature of certain memories, which cannot be reduced to the body. While I do not draw on Bergson's study here, the sense in which memory for him straddles the mind/body divide chimes with the material-aesthetic entanglements of Caribbean geopetics as explored in the present chapter.

[5] Cf. Glissant (1997) and Braithwaite's oft-quoted statement that the Caribbean archipelago's "unity is submarine" in Brathwaite (1974:64).

[6] Noxolo and Preziuso (2012:121).

[7] *Ibid.*, 121-122. Further on actor-network theory cf. Latour (2005).
[8] Cf. Noxolo and Preziuso (2012).
[9] Cf. Last (2015) and Deckard (2016).
[10] Noxolo and Preziuso (2012:123).
[11] Cf. Deckard (2016).
[12] Last (2015:57).
[13] Cf. Eckstein (2006). On the 'black Atlantic' cf. also Gilroy (1993).
[14] Cf. Sharpe (2013).
[15] Cf. White (1989).
[16] White (1963:65).
[17] Cf. White (1989).
[18] Cf., e.g., Mitchell (ed.) (2000); Balasopoulos (2008); Leer (2009) and Poddar (2013).
[19] Westphal (2011:xi).
[20] *Ibid.*
[21] Maximin (2006:108).
[22] *Ibid.*, 107, 108.
[23] *Ibid.*, 81.
[24] Cf. Last (2015).
[25] Walcott (1984 [1979]:365).
[26] Cf. Last (2015:60).
[27] Maximin (2006:46).
[28] Deckard (2016:4).
[29] Nichols (1996:34).
[30] *Ibid.*
[31] Glissant (1999 [1989]:145).
[32] Cf. Casteel (2011).
[33] Cf. Khan (2015).
[34] Tynan, Maeve (2010:150).
[35] Cf. Neumann and Rupp (2016), on which I build in my analysis of Philip's *Zong!*.
[36] Fehskens (2012:409).
[37] In the context of Holocaust remembrance, Young (2010:360) describes as counter-memory or counter-monuments the work of architects and memory practitioners who "reject the traditional forms and reasons for public memorial art, those spaces that either console viewers or redeem such tragic events […]. Instead of searing memory into public consciousness, they fear, conventional memorials seal memory off from awareness altogether". A similar example of black Atlantic counter-memory in this sense can be found in Bernardine Evaristo's novel *Blonde Roots* (2008), which revisits the history of slavery by satirically reversing the roles of (white) slaves and (black) slave owners.

[38] Cf. Walvin (2011:27), who describes the *Zong* as "an unusual vessel for the 1780s. At 110 tons, she was relatively small, and when she finally set out on her Atlantic crossing, [...] she was carrying 459 people. [...] the *Zong* was more crowded than most slave ships of the period. A typical British slave ship of that size and at that time would only have carried around 193 Africans."
[39] Like their total number on the *Zong*, the number of Africans thrown overboard differs in historical records as well as fictional rewritings of the case. Walvin (2011), 1, gives it as "132 Africans", while Philip puts their number at 150. Cf. Philip (2008:191). Cf. also Fehskens (2012:407): "Of the 470 or 442 or 440 slaves, either 150, 133, 132, or 123 were thrown in the Atlantic." Fehskens reviews various "sources detailing the *Zong*'s journey" and chooses "not to resolve the inconsistencies because they reveal a loss in miscalculations and misrecordings in addition to the tremendous loss of life occasioned by Collingwood's decision" (*Ibid.*, 423).
[40] Baucom (2001:63).
[41] Fehskens (2012:407, 408). Cf. also Corio (2014:330): "The story of the *Zong* tends to repeat itself, to multiply, to accumulate and to recur."
[42] Fehskens (2012:423).
[43] Khan (2015:5).
[44] *Ibid.*, 19.
[45] Philip (2008:196). Cf. also Corio's title (2014) and Austen (2011:64): "Philip grounds her project at the site of paradox, acknowledging both the necessity and impossibility of her task".
[46] Fehskens (2012:423, 413).
[47] Cf. Walvin (2011:153).
[48] Kahn (2015:6).
[49] Deleuze and Guattari (1987 [1980]:83).
[50] Fehskens (2012:412).
[51] Khan (2015:6).
[52] Philip (2008:193).
[53] *Ibid.*, 196.
[54] *Ibid.*, 203.
[55] Khan (2015:17).
[56] Philip (2008:201).
[57] *Ibid.*, 190.
[58] Khan (2015:17, 14).
[59] Philip (2008:198).
[60] Khan (2015:19).
[61] Sharpe (2013:1).
[62] For the notion of archive vs. non-western forms of memory cf. also Taylor, Diana (2003). *The Archive and the Repertoire: Performing Cultural Memory in the Americas*. Durham: Duke University Press.

[63] *Ibid.*, 5.
[64] In his notes on the translation of Deleuze and Guattari's *A Thousand Plateaus*, Massumi distinguishes affect from "personal feeling (*sentiment* in Deleuze and Guattari)". Cf. Deleuze and Guattari (1987 [1980]:xvi). By contrast, affect is "a prepersonal intensity corresponding to the passage from one state of the body to another" (*Ibid.*). Cf. also Massumi (2002:27-28), as referred to by Sharpe (2013:5).
[65] Sharpe (2013:5).
[66] *Ibid.*, 1.
[67] Khan (2015:19).
[68] Sharpe (2013:5).
[69] Fehskens (2012:409).
[70] Philip (2008:205).
[71] *Ibid.*, 197.
[72] *Ibid.*, 199.
[73] Dabydeen (1990:13).
[74] Philip (2008:207).
[75] Cf. Stein (2004:10).
[76] Cf. Philip (2008:193).
[77] *Ibid.*, 196, 198.
[78] *Ibid.*, 207, 206.
[79] *Ibid.*, 206.
[80] Noxolo and Preziuso (2012:127).

Works Cited

Austen, Veronica J. (2011). "*Zong!*'s "Should we?": Questioning the Ethical Representation of Trauma." *English Studies in Canada* 37.3-4, 63-81.

Balasopoulos, Antonis (2008). "Nesologies: Island Form and Postcolonial Geopoetics." *Postcolonial Studies* 11.1, 9-26.

Baucom, Ian (2001). "Specters of the Atlantic." *South Atlantic Quarterly* 100.1, 61-82.

Baucom, Ian (2005). *Specters of the Atlantic: Finance Capital, Slavery, and the Philosophy of History*. Durham, NC: Duke University Press.

Brathwaite, Edward Kamau (1974). *Contradictory Omens: Cultural Diversity and Integration in the Caribbean*. Mona: Savacou Publications.

--- (1984). *A History of the Voice: The Development of National Language in Anglophone Caribbean Poetry*. London: New Beacon Books.

Casteel, Sarah Phillips (2011). "The Language of Landscape: A Lexicon of the Caribbean Spatial Imaginary." *The Routledge Companion to Anglophone Caribbean Literature*. Ed. Michael Bucknor, and Alison Donnell. London: Routledge, 480-489.

Corio, Alessandra (2014). "Anagrams of Annihilation: The (Im)possible Writing of the Middle Passage in NourbeSe Philip and Édouard Glissant." *International Journal of Francophone Studies* 17.3-4, 327-348.

Dabydeen, David (1990). "On Not Being Milton: Nigger Talk in England Today." *The State of the Language*. Ed. Christopher Ricks, and Leonard Michaels. London: Faber & Faber, 3-14.

Deckard, Sharae (2016). "The Political Ecology of Storms in Caribbean Literature." *The Caribbean: Aesthetics, World-Ecology, Politics*. Ed. Chris Campbell and Michael Niblett. Liverpool: Liverpool University Press, 25-45.

Deleuze, Gilles, and Félix Guattari (1987 [1980]). *A Thousand Plateaus: Capitalism and Schizophrenia*. Minneapolis: University of Minnesota Press.

DeLoughrey, Elizabeth, Renée K. Gosson and George Handley (eds.) (2005). *Caribbean Literature and the Environment: Between Nature and Culture*. Charlottesville: University of Virginia Press.

Eckstein, Lars (2006). *Re-membering the Black Atlantic: On the Poetics and Politics of Literary Memory*. Amsterdam: Rodopi.

Fehskens, Erin M. (2012). "Accounts Unpaid, Accounts Untold: M. NourbeSe Philip's *Zong!* and the Catalogue." *Callaloo* 35.2, 407-424.

Gilroy, Paul (1993). *The Black Atlantic: Modernity and Double Consciousness*. London: Verso.

Glissant, Édouard (1997). *Poetics of Relation*. Ann Arbor: University of Michigan Press.

--- (1999 [1989]). *Caribbean Discourse: Selected Essays*. Transl. J. Michael Dash. Charlottesville: University Press of Virginia.

Khan, Almas (2015). "Poetic Justice: Slavery, Law, and the (Anti-)Elegiac Form in M. NourbeSe Philip's *Zong!*" *Cambridge Journal of Postcolonial Literary Inquiry* 2.1, 5-32.

Latour, Bruno (2005). *Reassembling the Social: An Introduction to Actor-Network-Theory*. Oxford: Oxford University Press.

Last, Angela (2015). "Fruit of the Cyclone: Undoing Geopolitics through Geopoetics." *Geoforum* 64, 56-64.

Leer, Martin (2009) "'Dry and Upside Down' on Telegraph Wire: The Geopoetics of the Line in Australian Poetry." *The Journal of the European Association of Studies on Australia* 1, 73-89.

Massumi, Brian (2002). *Parables for the Virtual*. Durham, NC: Duke University Press.

Maximin, Daniel (2006). *Les fruits du cyclone. Une géopoétique de la Caraïbe*. Paris: Editions Seuil.

Mitchell, W. J. T. (ed.) (2000). *Geopoetics*. Special Issue *Critical Inquiry* 26.2.
Neumann, Birgit (2016). "Liberationist Political Poetics." *Cambridge Companion to British Black and Asian Literature (1945-2010)*. Ed. Deirdre Osborne. Cambridge: Cambridge University Press, 59-76.
---, and Jan Rupp (2016). "Sea Passages: Cultural Flows in Caribbean Poetry." *Atlantic Studies: Global Currents* 13.4, 472-490.
Nichols, Grace (1996). "Hurricane Hits England." *Sunris*. London: Virago, 34-35.
Noxolo, Patricia, and Marika Preziuso (2012). "Moving Matter: Language in Caribbean Literature as Translation between Dynamic Forms of Matter." *Interventions: International Journal of Postcolonial Studies* 14.1, 120-135.
Philip, M. NourbeSe (2008). *Zong!* Middletown: Wesleyan University Press.
Poddar, Namrata (2013). "Postcolonial Ecocriticism, Island Tourism and a Geopoetics of the Beach." *International Journal of Francophone Studies* 16.1-2, 51-71.
Sharpe, Jenny (2013). "The Archive and Affective Memory in M. NourbeSe Philip's *Zong!*" *Interventions: International Journal of Postcolonial Studies*, 1-18.
Stein, Mark (2004). *Black British Literature: Novels of Transformation*. Columbus: Ohio State University Press.
Talyor, Diana (2003). *The Archive and the Repertoire: Performing Cultural Memory in the Americas*. Durham: Duke University Press.
Tynan, Maeve (2010). "Polyps, Plankton, and Passages: Mythopoeic Islands and Long-Memoried Seas." *Space and Culture* 13, 144-153.
Walcott, Derek (1984 [1979]). "The Sea Is History." *Collected Poems, 1948-1984*. London: Faber & Faber, 364-368.
Walvin, James (1992). *Black Ivory: A History of British Slavery*. London: HarperCollins.
Walvin, James (2011). *The Zong: A Massacre, The Law and the End of Slavery*. New Haven and London: Yale University Press.
Westphal, Bertrand (2011). "Foreword." *Geocritical Explorations: Space, Place, and Mapping in Literary and Cultural Studies*. Ed. Robert Tally Jr. London: Palgrave Macmillan, ix-xvi.
White, Kenneth (1963). *Wild Coal.* Paris: Club des Étudiants d'Anglais de la Sorbonne.
White, Kenneth (1989). "Inaugural Text." Presentation of the Institute for Geopoetics. Web. 16 February 2017. http://institut-geopoetique.org/en/presentation-of-the-institute.
Young, James E. (2010). "The Texture of Memory: Holocaust Memorials in History." *A Companion to Cultural Memory Studies*. Ed. Astrid Erll and Ansgar Nünning. Berlin and New York: de Gruyter, 357-365.

John Thieme (East Anglia)

Therianthropes Past and Future: Transformative Figures in Colonial and Postcolonial Writing

Writing animals has never been an easy proposition for human beings. As Nigel Rothfels puts it:

> [T]here is an inescapable difference between what an animal *is* and what people *think* an animal is. In the end, an animal or species is as much a constellation of ideas (for example, vicious, noble, intelligent, cruel, caring, brave) as anything else.[1]

Human attempts to capture animality in words vary considerably, moving along a continuum that has anthropocentric sentimentalism at one end and feral otherness at the other.[2] That said, both extremes, along with the numerous intermediate positions between them, run the risk of representing animals in a manner that has affinities with colonial appropriations of exotic or savage alterity, as well as other elitist discourses that assume the right to speak for excluded subalterns. Arguably a discursive practice analogous to the capture and display of animals in imperial zoos is involved, since human accounts of animal alterity are acts of rhetorical captivation that mirror the transportation of creatures from around the globe to zoos in the imperial 'centre' for the public at home to gaze at,[3] and animals have no recourse to writing back.

Contemporary zoos, with their emphasis on conservation and breeding, which can help to secure the future of endangered species, are often a far cry from zoos that incarcerated animals for the entertainment of spectators during the heyday of Western imperialism, but the issue of how to arrive at non-intrusive procedures for promoting animal welfare remains acute in the continuing Age of the Anthropocene,[4] if only because *homo sapiens* still sees itself as having an exclusive right to determine the management of the planet. And again, the ethical issues surrounding zoological practices are mirrored by the discursive challenge of how to write animals.

Animals do not write literary texts and so how can their subaltern situation be articulated with a degree of ethical responsibility? In this essay, I suggest that *one* potentially productive strategy for countering the human appropriation of the animal is a focus on the figure of the therianthrope. It is potentially productive since the very notion of therianthropy blurs the boundaries between the human and the animal and consequently can work as a figurative means for contesting humanity's assumption that it has an innate right to manage the lives of other species. The central problem remains, since therianthropes themselves are still being represented by human agency, but the challenge to a belief in human uniqueness – a belief that historically has affinities with the European annexation of territories inhabited by supposedly less advanced peoples and today continues to find parallels in perverted iterations of American exceptionalism – goes some way to eroding the inequities involved in animal rights debates conducted within Anthropocene frameworks that perpetuate the notion of human exclusiveness.

With this agenda in mind, I begin by briefly reviewing a selection of works that depict therianthropes across the centuries, particularly looking at representations of such figures in late colonial texts, and then focus more closely on the use of therianthropic tropes in two novels that engage with more recent American economies, economies that bring or threaten environmental damage to 'other' communities: Indra Sinha's Man Booker-shortlisted *Animal's People*[5] and Margaret Atwood's second novel, *Surfacing*[6]. Published several decades apart, these two novels not only share a concern with neo-colonial American interventions, but also, like many of the earlier texts to which I refer, ask questions about the nature of what it is to be human and, exploring a human/animal continuum, evince a preference for the animal end of this continuum.

I have devoted a chapter of my recent book, *Postcolonial Geographies*, to therianthropes. Focussing particularly on what I refer to as "Paper Tigers",[7] I discuss R. K. Narayan's *A Tiger for Malgudi*[8], Witi Ihimaera's *The Whale Rider*[9] and Barbara Gowdy's *The White Bone*[10], with a particular focus on the animal side of the therianthropic continuum. Here, in discussing *Surfacing* and *Animal's People*, I am looking at texts with a slightly different emphasis, texts, where the protagonists are humans with therianthropic leanings and whose personal situations are indices of larger cultural issues. In different ways, the protagonists of both novels aspire to animality. In so doing they interrogate the Anthropocene and in each case an assumption of animal identity offers refuge from globalizing American imperialism, albeit in very different ways: in Sinha's case, as an individual response to a fictionalized version of the aftermath of the Bhopal gas leak disaster of 1984, in which the eponymous narrator, the self-styled Animal, who opens his account with the words "I used to be human once"[11], is a four-footed survivor of what is repeatedly referred to as "that night"[12]; in Atwood's case, as a response to the perceived Americanization of Canadian wilderness, a topic that is treated with some irony, but remains part of the novel's serious agenda. Atwood's post-millennial *MaddAddam* trilogy[13] offers a more obvious comparison with the apocalyptic horror of *Animal's People*, since it depicts a dystopian future that speaks to the global present, a future in which remnants of humanity struggle for survival in a world largely destroyed by a man-made plague and inhabited by human-engineered mutant creatures, but I have chosen to discuss *Surfacing* because it offers an alternative to the Anthropocene that engages with the notion of a return to prehuman animality rather than posthuman mutations.

The therianthrope is, of course, an age-old figure in myth and legend – to be seen across the centuries in manifestations that often associate animal-human hybrids with some kind of monstrosity or menace to civilized humanity. The minotaur and the siren in Greek mythology, the lycanthrope and the vampire in more modern representations: such figures transgress the human-animal binary in ways that frequently seem to threaten the human. But this is only half the story: in the medieval era the unicorn was seen as a type of Christ; in Hindu mythology therianthropes such as Ganesh and Hanuman bring humanity and animality together in more positive, often collaborative, incarnations; and in West African and Afro-Caribbean tale-telling the figure of Anancy the spiderman, trickster though he is, is a conduit for transforming experience, a source of sustenance and resistance. In short, then, while Jungian-inspired commentators such as Joseph Campbell[14] have found reassuring similarities in supposedly universal archetypes around the globe and across the centuries, a short genealogy of therianthropes suggests the opposite. Such figures carry very different associations depending on the cultures and communities that have created them and the periods to which they belong and these varied provenances became more overt in the Age of the Anthropocene, at a time when Western mercantilist exploitation was rewriting the conduct books of what constituted ethical behaviour, particularly with regard to relationships with non-Western peoples.

Therianthropes were nothing new in Western European culture prior to this. Medieval *mappae mundi*, such as the Hereford and Ebstorf world maps, contain many such figures, ranging from unicorns, which as I have said carry positive associations, to cynocephali (men with dog heads), which, like werewolves, represent the demonic side of interspecies syntheses. But around the beginnings of the so-called Age of the Enlightenment interest in animal-human hybrids assumes a new urgency. Swift's two contrasted species of human-animal hybrids in the fourth book of *Gulliver's Travels*[15] open up a dialogue on what constitutes humanity, with Gulliver finding the bestial Yahoos much closer to the human end of the therianthropic continuum than the idealized equine Houyhnhnms, and the effect of his seeing the Yahoos as humanoid inevitably undermines the notion that *homo sapiens* is a discrete species, categorically different from other animals. Swift's interrogative stance is, of course, pre-Darwinian, but it resonates with post-Darwinian representations of the therianthrope, where such hybrids abound, for example in the body shared by Dr Jekyll and Mr Hyde and in H. G. Wells's *Island of Dr Moreau*[16], where the vivisectionist of the title attempts to endow animals with human attributes, but only succeeds in creating Yahoo-like Beast People. Arguably it is no coincidence that Wells's novel is set on a remote island. It contains echoes of *Robinson Crusoe* and *The Tempest*, as well as Gulliver's final voyage, and it lends itself to interpretation as colonial allegory, since Moreau assumes the Prospero-like role of trying to domesticate and humanize feral otherness – the animals on which he conducts his experiment have been brought from Africa and, like the inmates of nineteenth-century zoos, they are subject to his imperialistic human control.

In Wells's fable the Beast People and the threat they represent to the Anthropocene have to be destroyed and the narrator, Edward Prendick, returns home, like Gulliver and the Ancient Mariner, who comes back from a voyage in which animality in the form of the albatross has been killed, a sadder and a wiser man, no longer a believer in human reason. So, at least from one point of view, the Aristotelian belief that humans are a unique species, because they are rational animals has been seriously interrogated. In other classic post-Darwinian texts that lend themselves to colonial readings the therianthrope is less threatening and the challenge to human exclusiveness more easily managed. In one of the late colonial period's most interesting versions of the therianthrope, the figure is a male child socialized among animals who must be reclaimed into the human order, thereby implicitly reaffirming the superiority of the Anthropocene. In *The Jungle Books*[17], Mowgli is raised by wolves in a community that mimics Anglo-Indian society in its adherence to the Law of the Jungle, codes transgressed only by the tiger Shere Khan, who in this reading embodies an extra-colonial India that defies the rule of the Raj[18]. All the other animals play their part in maintaining the civil order of Jungle society and Mowgli man-cub though he is, ultimately has to be reabsorbed into human (which in this case equates with colonial) society. *Tarzan of the Apes* may have been the creation of an American author,[19] but the novel traces a similar trajectory, when the hero assumes his inheritance at the top of the English social hierarchy as the aristocrat Lord Greystoke.

In *Heart of Darkness*, Kurtz's scrawled words at the end of his report for "The International Society for the Suppression of Savage Customs", "Exterminate all the brutes!"[20], most obviously refers to his demented inversion of his earlier colonial idealism, which culminates in the heads on stakes around the Inner Station. However, given his obsession with ivory, it could equally well refer to his attitude to elephants, who as Graham Huggan and Helen Tiffin point out[21], are an absence in the text in a way that even Conrad's shadowy Africans, flitting denizens of the forest, are not. So the elephants have been textually exterminated. As ever Conrad hovers on the edge of a critique of colonialism and while Kurtz embodies its perversion, Marlow's attitude to his encounter with the interior is altogether more ambivalent, not least because he realizes that the boundaries between the supposedly human and the supposedly animal have been blurred. And from this point of view the ambiguity surrounding the identity of the "brutes" is telling, since, while they could be either humans or elephants, it raises the possibility that they might, through the mediation of Kurtz's crazed mind, be a trope for the challenge that post-Darwinian therianthropic thinking represents to traditional conceptions of human superiority.

In each of these cases, then, although attitudes towards the therianthrope vary, the figure is linked with colonial as well as Darwinian-inspired debates about what constitutes the human and in English fiction this continues well into the twentieth century, at least as far as William

Golding's end-of-Empire novel *Lord of the Flies.*[22] *Lord of the Flies* has widely been seen as dealing with a more universal situation,[23] a group of boys reverting to savagery when they are marooned on a desert island. However, this narrative of degeneration is entwined with a rewriting of R. M. Ballantyne's *Coral Island*, itself a juvenile equivalent of *Robinson Crusoe*, built on a bedrock of imperialist and Christian values, and so it seems mistaken to resist reading it, at least on one level, as a late colonial allegory.

As mentioned above, although Indra Sinha's *Animal's People* and Margaret Atwood's *Surfacing* belong to different periods – they were published forty-five years apart – they share a concern with neo-colonial American interventions into 'other' countries, and beyond this they also ask fundamental questions about the nature of what it is to be human and, exploring relationships between humans and animals, evince a preference for animal identity.

Sinha's protagonist Animal is a survivor of a toxic gas leak disaster in the town of Khaufpur, a fictional surrogate for Bhopal.[24] Six years old on "that night", he was crippled by the disaster, which twisted his spine and left him unable to stand upright. Subsequently he has learnt to walk on all fours. Taunted by a fellow-boy with being a "jungli Jaanvar"[25], a wild animal, he comes to espouse this identity as a positive and, although he privately wishes to be able to walk upright, particularly because it will enable him to fulfil his strong sexual urges, the mantra he recites to the external world is that he does not want to be human. So his condition provides the focus for the novel's debate about what it is to be human and what it is to be animal. Others tell him he is really human, but he rejects this on the grounds that to accept himself as such would be to see himself as an aberration. As an animal, he says, he is "four-footed and free [...] whole, my own proper shape, just a different kind of animal"[26]. So his identification with animals involves more than making a virtue out of necessity: it gives him a claim to uniqueness. He looks through a book that depicts all the animals of India, and finds none that resemble him, before shortly afterwards categorizing himself as "the bat-eared ape that climbs only in the dark of night"[27].

Physiologically, he is closer to the human end of the therianthropic continuum, but he affiliates himself with the animal, particularly seeing himself as existing outside the parameters of humanity, because he has no religious or communal affiliation, doubts whether he is trustworthy[28] and in any case feels that as an animal he is not "subject to the laws of men"[29]. So, in this elective version of self, he is exempt from ethical and spiritual norms, a posthuman product of the catastrophe that the American Kampani's (Company's) factory has visited on his people. The novel is called *Animal's People* and this seems appropriate, because while Animal's own "story sung by an ulcer"[30] is to the fore, he speaks on behalf of a subaltern community who find themselves powerless against the neo-colonial Kampani, which, for most of the novel, acting like latter-day absentee imperialist landlords, refuses even to send representatives to India to face the charges against it.

On that night the people of Khaufpur were choked by poison. Now, Animal says, "it's words that are choking us"[31] and his narrative, which is presented as an oral account recorded on a series of tapes, offers a grass-roots alternative to versions controlled by a multinational corporation, in collusion with local politicians. The idea of telling his story to a tape recorder has been given him by an Australian journalist whose overtures to put his story in a book he rejects – he views journalists as vultures – but whose suggestion he adopts, while claiming ownership of his people's story by using his own tape machine and imagining himself speaking his narrative to a single auditor, whom he names "Eyes". His rejection of the journalist's mediation enables Sinha to foreground the problem of the external commodification of subaltern experience for global consumption, but of course leaves him open to the charge of acting as just such a spokesman for the dispossessed. Arguably he avoids complicity in such appropriation through the effectiveness of his ventriloquization of the highly individual voice of Animal. At the very least this provides a persuasive strategy for articulating the subaltern side of the story.

Animal's name Jaanvar means "one who lives"[32] and despite his sense of trauma he is an embodiment of pragmatic survival. Other inhabitants of Khaufpur have not been so lucky and their fate is exemplified by a foetus, Khã-in-the-Jar, a dicephalic parapagus (two-headed conjoined twin), who has been preserved in liquid in a jar and who begs Animal to free him. Like such figures in late colonial writing, Khã can be seen as a trope for human potential denied life by oppressive external forces. For example, in the plays of African and Caribbean dramatists of the independence generation, there is the recurrent figure of the half-born subject that seems to relate to the stifling of independent consciousness in the colonial era: Wole Soyinka introduces the character of a "half-child", based on the traditional Yoruba figure of the *abiku*,[33] into his play *A Dance of the Forests* (first performed at the time of Nigerian Independence in 1960) in a manner that suggests the earlier suppression of an embryonic independent consciousness. Prior to this, Derek Walcott had concluded his play *Ti-Jean and His Brothers*[34] (1957), which has attracted interpretation as an allegory of the development of a postcolonial sensibility,[35] with the coming into life of a *bolom*, or unborn foetus. Both figures are drawn from folk myths and are open to multiple allegorical interpretations, but they particularly lend themselves to being read as tropes for the emergence of a postcolonial consciousness at the time of Independence. There is no such hope for Sinha's Khã-in-the-Jar, a more deformed version of life aborted before birth. He is described as "a half-rotted relic of that night"[36] and ultimately when Animal endeavours to save him from a marauding mob, he drops Khã's jar and his remains spill out. One possible interpretation of this is that the consequences of a neo-colonial ecological disaster, such as Khaufpur/Bhopal has suffered, are irreversible. The effects of the Kampani's actions continue and, although the novel itself is a postcolonial protest against such environmental destruction and lack of accountability, it offers no real hope of restitution.

The night of the disaster represents the end of the world as they have known it for Animal's people. Quite apart from the destruction it has caused, it means that the name of their city, like that of Bhopal and places such as Chernobyl and Three Mile Island, becomes synonymous with the tragedy it has suffered. The catastrophe also has an ongoing psychological impact on the survivors, which Sinha particularly personifies in the character of an elderly French nun, Ma Franci. On that night, she loses her sanity and her ability to speak or understand languages other than French, but subsequently becomes a voice of reason in madness. She likens what she calls the Apokalis to the Last Judgement of the Book of Revelations and, when news of the destruction of the World Trade Centre reaches Khaufpur, sees this as a manifestation of the Armageddon that the world is facing, predicting that the Apokalis will end as it has begun in Khaufpur. There are, however, also non-Christian provenances for the notion of Apokalis in the text: Animal points out that Ma Franci's version of the word contains letters that spell out Kali and the land on which the Kampani's factory stands has formerly been known as "Kali's ground"[37]; and after that night the derelict remains of the site are plagued with cobras, snakes associated with Siva whose dance betokens the end of the world.

So Christian and Hindu versions of the end of the world are fused, with both holding out the possibility that there may be some kind of rebirth after this cataclysm. Siva is a god of procreation as well as destruction; the Christian account of apocalypse is linked with the second coming. Ma Franci predicts this is imminent and her prophecy is in one respect at least fulfilled, when, towards the end of the novel, a riot against the Kampani brings a second night of terror, which she refers to as "Qayamat, the [Islamic] end of all things".[38]

At this point, Animal takes a large amount of the poisonous intoxicant datura, a plant used in small amounts in rituals and prayers to Siva. He retreats from society into the seemingly extra-social space of a forest, where he experiences a series of nightmarish hallucinations before appropriately being found and brought back to society by an animal, the dog Jara that has been his companion throughout most of the novel. Animal's time in the forest brings the novel's dialogue about what constitutes humanity and what comprises animality to a climax. As before he sees himself as a unique one-creature species, claiming he's "not just any animal", but "THE ANIMAL"[39] and in his hallucinatory trance, he hears a voice asking him "WHAT IS A MAN?".[40] He enters the forest, saying he will discover his "true state, die or live, animal returning to its truly [sic] home"[41], but initially finds it devoid of other animals, an environment of parched earth and little vegetation. Supposedly extra-social Nature, it is clear, is not immune to the ecologically destructive impact of human behaviour. There *seems* to be no possibility of existing completely outside the dystopian human world of Khaufpur, but then in the middle of his delirious personal apocalypse, Animal envisages himself dying and being reborn into a new life in a paradise populated by animals and two-legged figures with horns and tails that are "neither men nor animals, or else they are both".[42] So paradise is therianthropic – the confluence of the human and the animal offers the visionary possibility of a transformative response to the trauma initiated by the ecological disaster that the Kampani has caused.

The end of the novel sees Animal, returned to society, being told that a possibility that has been mooted for much of the narrative – that he may be able to go to America for an operation that will cure his condition – is now a reality. However, he appears to be on the point of rejecting this opportunity, preferring to retain his uniqueness and remain closer to the animal end of the therianthropic continuum. He says that as an upright human he "would be one of millions, not even a healthy one at that".[43] But this four legs good, two legs bad conclusion is far from simply affirmative, because he sees the plight of his people, the poor, as ongoing. His final words are "We are the people of the Apokalis. Tomorrow there will be more of us".[44] The novel rejects the Anthropocene callousness of corporate capitalism, but remains far from sanguine about attempts to counter its hegemony.

Atwood's *Surfacing* may seem remote from *Animal's People*. It is not set against the background of a mega-disaster, though the characters inveigh against American incursions into Canadian wilderness space, and initially it seems to be an altogether more personal story. An unnamed narrator/protagonist, who is a commercial artist, travels from the city back to the Quebec woods and a lake where she spent much of her childhood. She returns, with three friends, in search of her father who has gone missing. It gradually becomes clear, though, that the quest for her father is not the only quest being undertaken. The dissociated and unreliable narrator has repressed crucial aspects of her past and, although she is not consciously aware of it at the outset, she is embarking on a journey into self, for which her father's disappearance has been the catalyst.

This may, then, seem a world away from *Animal's People*, but the two novels share numerous elements, among them a concern with the Anthropocene, a narrator/protagonist who identifies with animals, the use of the trope of an unborn child, an encounter with wilderness space that initiates the narrator into a new phase of awareness and a hostility to American neo-colonial interventions: Atwood's small group of characters envisage the U.S. invading Canada for its water and more generally feel that Uncle Sam is taking over the Canadian psyche like an invasion by "creatures from outer space, body snatchers".[45] Read today, *Surfacing* is in some respects very much a novel of its period: its characters are influenced, in varying degrees, by the hippie philosophy of the late 1960s and early 1970s, and its feminism, progressive though it was when the novel appeared, belongs to the first phase of the second wave of twentieth-century feminism. So too its take on Canadian nationalism. At the same time, it deals with fundamental ontological issues and numerous passages relate the specifics of the narrator's predicament to concerns that interrogate the Enlightenment privileging of the Anthropocene. The passage that opens the second of the novel's three sections goes to the heart of the Cartesian separation of mind from body and in so doing highlights and criticizes ways in which humans distinguish themselves from animals on the grounds that they have reasoning capacities:

> The trouble is all in the knob at the top of our bodies. I'm not against the body or the head either: only the neck, which creates the illusion that they are separate. The language is wrong, it shouldn't have different words for them. If the head extended directly into the shoulders, like a worm's or a frog's without that constriction, that lie, they wouldn't be able to look down at their bodies and move them around as if they were robots or puppets; they would have to realise that if the head is detached from the body both of them will die.[46]

And in this section of the novel, the narrator journeys back into the past – personal, national and prehistoric – and rediscovers a conception of self, which, as she sees it, existed before language created the illusion that body and head are separate.

Her journey is enacted on several levels. Initially it is signalled by a change in tense: up to this point she has been telling her story in the present; now the narrative moves into the past, and as she gradually uncovers buried aspects of her personal past, the novel engages in a similar process of excavation, digging into the pre-Columbian past of Canada, a past which is particularly associated with animals and Native Canadian culture. One reading of her journey has seen it as a shamanistic rite[47] and certainly she enters into a mindset which removes her from the norms of Western Anthropocene thinking.

Looking through her father's papers, she comes across some seemingly insane drawings that he has made. They include a figure that seems to combine alligator-like features with human attributes, and this therianthropic amalgam leads her to conclude that her father has become totally deranged, with the figure he has drawn possibly representing "what he thought he was turning into".[48] He has been the epitome of reason to her, even though she has discovered that the "eighteenth century rationalists"[49], personifications of the Enlightenment Anthropocene, that he admired were afflicted with a plethora of psychological problems. Consequently, she is particularly shaken by his what she views as his mad drawings. However, when she realizes that he has been pursuing an interest in Native rock-paintings, there is a sea change in her attitude. What appears crazed as the product of a supposedly rational, modern mind takes on different connotations when it is associated with an animist Indigenous view of experience. So she goes in search of her father in places where his papers suggest the rock-paintings are located and gradually her identity as a woman from contemporary consumer society is stripped away, as she travels back into a world where the norms of the Anthropocene no longer obtain.

She dives into the lake at a spot where her father has been looking for the Native paintings and *surfaces* having experienced the central epiphany of the novel. What she finds is her father's drowned body, but initially she refuses to accept this, first displacing it onto her brother, whom she has earlier said has drowned as a boy, though this turns out not to be the case. Then she further confuses the issue by conflating what she has seen with the central trauma in her past: the repressed knowledge of a child she has aborted. The passage in which she now acknowledges this has similarities with Sinha's account of Khã-in-the-Jar:

> I knew when it was, it was in a bottle curled up, staring out at me like a cat pickled; it had huge jelly eyes and fins instead of hands, fish gills. I couldn't let it out, it was dead already, it had drowned in air. It was there when I woke up, suspended in the air above me like a chalice, an evil grail and I thought, Whatever [sic] it is, part of myself or a separate creature, I killed it. It wasn't a child but it could have been one, I didn't allow it.[50]

So the shock of seeing her father dead brings her aborted parenthood to mind and she likens the foetus to an animal that may or may not be part of herself. The feminist aspects of the text make it clear that patriarchal repression has been a major factor in her alienation from self and her father's death releases her from one kind of male logic, even though he has been less rational than she has assumed. More significantly, she emerges as the victim of her married former lover, who has talked her into the abortion, telling her the child "wasn't a person, it was only an animal".[51]

She has come to regard herself as the murderer of this animal, and traumatic though the abortion has been for her, this takes on resonances that go far beyond her personal angst, since, along with wilderness space and Indigeneity, animals come to represent a prehistoric, pre-Anthropocene order of existence, which is being destroyed by contemporary 'civilization'. In the action that follows she discards the trappings of such 'civilization' and reverts to an animal-like state of being. Throughout the text animals have been associated with a *pre*human order and there are several allusions to prehistoric species – mammoths, pterodactyls and mastodons[52] among them – as well as numerous references to the contemporary fauna of the region. Animals in the narrator's imagination, as she undergoes this return to Nature, have no need of language; they represent a pre-linguistic order, in which Anthropocene binaries such as the split between mind and body do not exist.

After discovering her father's drawings, she believes that her mother must have left her a similar legacy and she finds this in a scrapbook in the form of a picture she herself has drawn as a child. This depicts a pregnant woman, whose unborn baby, her pre-natal self, is "sitting up inside her gazing out", and opposite the woman is another therianthropic being: "a man with horns on his head like cow horns and a barbed tail".[53] This is glossed as a representation of God, in which the Manichean binary that separates God and the Devil has been broken down, but it could equally well be seen as a transgression of the human-animal binary. Again, there is a striking similarity to the experience of Animal in Sinha's text, where during his time in the forest he sees two-legged figures with horns and tails.

During this phase of the action, the narrator removes herself from the norms of human behaviour, first identifying herself as an animal – discarding clothes, making herself a lair, defecating outdoors – and subsequently imagining herself going beyond this into a state of being in which she envisages herself being absorbed into a complete animist oneness with Nature:

> The animals have no need for speech, why talk when you are a word
> I lean against a tree. I am a tree leaning [...]
> I am not an animal or a tree, I am the thing in which the trees and animals move and grow, I am a place.[54]

At this point her rejection of life in the Anthropocene is total and she resolves to raise the baby she believes she may now be carrying as an animal-like being, whom she "will never teach [...] any words".[55]

Her visionary experience outside social norms has marked affinities with Animal's hallucinatory time in the forest and also promotes a view that undermines Anthropocene notions of normality predicated on reason: during this period, she says at one point, "From any rational point of view I am absurd; but there are no longer any rational points of view".[56] The novel ends with her suspended between nature and culture, being called to return to society, but not, like Sinha's Animal, actually having done so. In both cases the conclusion leaves the protagonist in an interstitial situation. Sinha's Animal appears to be choosing to continue viewing himself as an animal; Atwood's narrator knows that her extra-social experience has been an interlude, but she has learnt a non-human wisdom from it, and as yet remains poised between animal and human worlds.

In conclusion, where *Animal's People* looks towards a *post*human condition, albeit without any great optimism as to whether this can be attained, *Surfacing* posits a *pre*human state, in which animal identity is sovereign. In both cases the perspective is ultimately inextricable from the human, but the therianthropic imagination holds out the promise of a less ethically compromised way of perceiving experience and combatting the neo-colonial Anthropocene world order.

Notes

[1] Rothfels (2002) (emphasis in the text).

[2] Needless to say, as the above quote from Nigel Rothfels suggests, there are also considerable variations in human responses to particular animal species, e.g. characterizing big cats as ferocious (see my remarks on Kipling's tiger, Shere Khan, below) and sheep as meek, but I have not extended this essay into a discussion of such differences, since for the most part the two main texts I am discussing, *Animal's People* and *Surfacing*, take a broad-brush approach to animality.

[3] See Loisel (1912); and Hoage and Deiss (eds.) (1996).

[4] At the time of writing, geologists remain locked in debates about when the Age of the Anthropocene began, but as a working premise for this essay I am viewing it as starting in the late fifteenth century, when so-called Renaissance humanism was dawning, and solidifying in the eighteenth century in the so-called Age of Enlightenment.

[5] Sinha (2008).

[6] Atwood (1979 [1972])

[7] Thieme (2016:131-178).

[8] Narayan (1983 [1961]).
[9] Ihimaera (2006 [1987]).
[10] Gowdy (1999).
[11] Sinha (2008:1).
[12] *Ibid.*, *passim.*
[13] Atwood (2003); --- (2009).; --- (2013).
[14] Campbell (1949).
[15] Swift (1976 [1726]).
[16] Wells (1962 [1896]).
[17] Kipling (1973).
[18] See my discussion in *Postcolonial Geographies*, 141-142; and Nyman (2003:42).
[19] Burroughs (2008 [1912]).
[20] Conrad (1994 [1902]:71-72).
[21] Huggan and Tiffin (2010:141).
[22] Golding (1960 [1954]).
[23] For details of such readings, see Gilmour (2011:92 and 110).
[24] The Bhopal disaster occurred in December 1984 at the Union Carbide pesticide plant in the city. Estimates of the death toll vary between just under 4,000 and 16,000. More than half a million people are believed to have suffered injuries from their exposure to methyl isocyanate gas and other chemicals.
[25] Sinha (2008:15).
[26] *Ibid.*, 208.
[27] *Ibid.*, 223.
[28] *Ibid.*, 25.
[29] *Ibid.*, 284.
[30] *Ibid.*, 12.
[31] *Ibid.*, 3.
[32] *Ibid.*, 35.
[33] Soyinka's poem "Abiku" glosses its title with the words: "Wanderer child. It is the same child who dies and returns again and again to plague the mother – Yoruba belief". Soyinka (1968:28).
[34] Walcott (1970).
[35] See, e.g., Ashaolu (1977).
[36] Sinha (2008:337).
[37] *Ibid.*, 32.
[38] *Ibid.*, 328.
[39] *Ibid.*, 345.
[40] *Ibid.*, 347.
[41] *Ibid.*, 342.
[42] *Ibid.*, 352.
[43] *Ibid.*, 366.

[44] *Ibid.*
[45] Atwood (1979:123).
[46] *Ibid.*, 70.
[47] Annis Pratt (1981).
[48] Atwood (1979:95).
[49] *Ibid.*, 32.
[50] *Ibid.*, 137. This is anticipated by an earlier passage, in which, speaking of her own pre-natal experience, the narrator says "I believe that an unborn baby has its eyes open and can look out through the walls of the mother's stomach, like a frog in a jər" (*Ibid.*, 26).
[51] *Ibid.*, 138.
[52] *Ibid.*, 3, 57 and 138.
[53] *Ibid.*, 152.
[54] *Ibid.*, 175.
[55] *Ibid.*, 156.
[56] *Ibid.*, 163.

Works Cited

Ashaolu, Albert. (1977). "Allegory in Ti-Jean and His Brothers." *World Literature Written in English* 16.1, 202-211.

Atwood, Margaret (1979). *Surfacing* [1972]. London: Virago.

--- (2003). *Oryx and Crake*. London: Bloomsbury.

--- (2009). *The Year of the Flood*. London: Bloomsbury.

--- (2013). *MaddAddam*. London: Bloomsbury.

Burroughs, Edgar Rice (2008). *Tarzan of the Apes* [1912]. London: Penguin.

Campbell, Joseph (1949). *The Hero with a Thousand Faces*. Princeton, NJ: Pantheon Books.

Conrad, Joseph (1994). *Heart of Darkness* [1902]. Harmondsworth: Penguin.

Gilmour, Rachael (2011). "The Entropy of Englishness; Reading Empire's Absence in the Novels of William Golding." *End of Empire and the English Novel since 1945*. Ed. Rachael Gilmour and Bill Schwarz. Manchester: Manchester University Press, 92-113.

Golding, William (1960). *Lord of the Flies* [1954]. Harmondsworth: Penguin.

Gowdy, Barbara (1999). The White Bone. London: Flamingo.

Hoage, R. J., and William A. Deiss (eds.) (1996). *New Worlds, New Animals: From Menagerie to Zoological Park in the Nineteenth Century*. Baltimore: Johns Hopkins University Press.

Huggan, Graham, and Helen Tiffin (2010). *Postcolonial Ecocritism: Literature, Animals, Environment*. Oxford and New York: Routledge.

Ihimaera, Witi (2006 [1987]). *The Whale Rider*. Berlin: Cornelsen

Kipling, Rudyard. (1973 [1895]). *All The Mowgli Stories*. London and Basingstoke: Macmillan.

Loisel, Gustave (1912). Histoire *des ménageries de l'antiquité à nos jours*. 3 vols. Paris: Octave Doin et Fils and Henri Laurens.

Narayan, R. K. (1983). *The Man-Eater of Malgudi* [1961]. Harmondsworth: Penguin.

Nyman, Jopi (2003). *Postcolonial Animal Tale: From Kipling to Coetzee*. New Delhi: Atlantic.

Pratt, Annis (1981). "Surfacing and the Rebirth Journey." *The Art of Margaret Atwood: Essays in Criticism*. Ed. Arnold E. Davidson and Cathy N. Davidson. Toronto: Anansi, 139-157.

Ritvo, Harriet (1987). *The Animal Estate: The English and Other Creatures in the Victorian Age*. Cambridge, MA: Harvard University Press.

Rothfels, Nigel (2002). *Savages and Beasts: The Birth of the Modern Zoo*. Baltimore: Johns Hopkins University Press.

Sinha, Indra (2008 [2007]). *Animal's People*. London: Simon and Schuster.

Soyinka, Wole (1967). *Idanre and Other Poems*. New York: Hill and Wang.

Swift, Jonathan (1976 [1726]). *Gulliver's Travels and Other Writings*. London: Oxford University Press.

Thieme, John (2016). *Postcolonial Literary Geographies: Out of Place*. London: Palgrave Macmillan.

Walcott, Derek (1970). *Dream on Monkey Mountain and Other Plays*. New York: Farrar, Straus and Giroux.

Wells, H. G. (1962 [1896]). *The Island of Doctor Moreau*. Harmondsworth: Penguin.

Jonathan Skinner (Warwick)

Call the Pulsing Home: Poetry, Fascination and Resonance in Ecocritical Environments

In the following slice of thinking and sounding (with) animals, I aim at two concepts from communications theory that articulate what it might mean for communication to occur between species: fascination and resonance. I appropriate these concepts from social theorist Niklas Luhmann's notion of communication as "the differentiation of special experiential objects that are either extraordinary or fascinating".[1] While Luhmann is addressing the evolutionary sequence of language, writing, printing (which "fascinate and preocuppy the mind and thereby secure its participation" in communication)[2], I'd like to draw the notion sideways, to include the fascination of experiential objects generated by other life forms, especially the uncanny fascination of objects like bird song or whale music, which seem extraordinary to us because they sound so much like human language. We can call such vocalizations 'objects' because of the development of our recording and transmission technologies, whose evolution should not be considered separately from (though of course not conflated with) that of 'natural' sounds. The object 'whale song' is a co-evolved kind of performance, much in the way that bird song and lyric poetry, it could be argued, are now irreversibly entangled, in evolutionary terms. The postulate involved in this detournement of systems thinking is that something communicates between species – even if, or especially because, we don't know what it is. Communications do not occur in isolation or a vacuum, but resonate through matter and reverberate in spaces, as a pulse, a dawn chorus, a refrain that we might observe in terms of acoustic ecology or in terms of the special forms our fascination takes as poetic language. Participating in such language, as an ecopoetics, entails a systems-based rather than values-based understanding of environment – one that does not posit 'the environment' as background to human activity. Rather, distinctions between self and environment are internal to human, and indeed to all, forms of life. What we call 'the environment' emerges constructively, to the extent that we sound and are sounded by the pulsing of these myriad life forms. This essay is an effort to sound the animal, in resonance and dissonance, and to explore what it might mean, to borrow a phrase from poet Maggie O'Sullivan, to "call the pulsing home"[3].

Resonance takes up a special understanding of communication in systems theoretical terms, as the "constant process of reduction and opening of connective possibilities" in the contact between autopoetic systems.[4] Only resonance can mediate the irreducible distinction between message and information that is a requirement for participation in communication. We address ourselves to another, Luhmann seems to say, by making this distinction. (We might say that self and other are emergent properties of these distinctions.) How do we address ourselves to animals? Some poetic language seems comfortable with this kind of address. Humanist language, on the other hand, by definition excludes animals' access to language and narrowly limits the possibility of animal messages, consigning them to the realm of information. I am interested in the disturbance that poetry brings to such language. Resonance, as a way for communication to happen without consciousness, is a theoretical opening for communication between species, precisely in the ways the mind acts to disturb, stimulate, and irritate communication: there is no resonance without dissonance.

Such communication is of ecocritical interest insofar as it challenges epistemological and ontological frames, frames ecocriticism should query: nature, environment, animal, and the concept of species itself. This query draws me to posthumanism – not transhumanist posthumanism but the sort that, on the contrary, affirms embodiment, rejecting the use of language to draw a line between humans and animals (as if we were not animals or of the same fabric made). This strand within posthumanism asks, what is an animal? Finally, I am drawn to ecopoetics, a practice-led form of ecocriticism that challenges the extent to which criticism seems willing to exclude its own methods from the implications of its research. If texts have agency, at the very least as communicating bodies, then we can no longer unselfconsciously treat them as objects or exhibits: How do we develop relations in our reading practices?

Ecopoetics questions the panoptic competence of criticism, or adapts it, for a more constructivist practice. By "constructivist" I mean acknowledging the presence of the observer in the system that comprises text, reader and world. Ecopoetics takes the root senses of ecology (*oikos* + *logos*, or household accounting), and poetry (*poiein*, or making) at face value, to engage poetics in the unfinished work of 'household Earth'.[5] (Gary Snyder's hopeful phrase, "etiquette of the wild", judges the human species to be the adolescent at the evolutionary household table, still learning basic manners[6]). Ecopoetics also questions the primacy of (human) language and literature for ecocriticism – hence the framing of this essay in terms of communication. It is a disciplinary frame that tests the segregation of disciplines, the primacy of theoretical over generative, critical over creative modes of inquiry, and the insulation of critical inquiry from advocacy and activism. Ecopoetics, finally, questions the restriction of materiality in ecocritical discussions of poetics, which tend to subordinate excessive signifying, characteristic of texts sometimes called 'postmodern', to signified master narratives ('Anthropocene' being only the latest). Ecopoetics is post-representational, post-correlationist – challenging some of the ways in which poetics thematizes materiality by emphasizing the analogical dimensions of poems or through a topical focus on reference, narrative, or voice. Instead, poetics might seek to describe how a work is partly the experience of its own entropy, as it undergoes the disorder of embodiment. Ecopoetics furthermore embeds innovation in the ethnopoetics of cross-cultural encounter, where nature is always already human, necessitating the kinds of self-awareness (experiencing observations of one's own ethnicity) only possible through dialogical engagement and moments of translation, even and especially when encountering 'nature'. The essay centers on two moments, two encounters with animal vocalizations, which fascinate us because they seem to echo our own vocalizing habits, and which, when grasped outside the scale of human listening, might be understood as acoustic homologies: bird song and whale song.

In 1879 Helen Hunt Jackson closed a letter to her friend Emily Dickinson with the suggestion: "What should you think of trying your hand on the oriole? He will be along presently." Poet Dickinson obliged, noting in her response, "To the Oriole you suggested I add a Humming Bird and hope they are not untrue". Three years later Dickinson wrote, in a letter to her friend Mabel Loomis Todd, "I cannot make an Indian Pipe but please accept a Humming Bird"[7]. The idea of 'trying one's hand on' or 'making' a bird in poetry certainly fits 19th century conventions of collecting and depicting natural objects, and plays on various meanings of correspondence (encoded in, for instance, the "language of flowers"[8]), but Dickinson's poem, which recombines descriptions of the hummingbird from T. W. Higginson's and J. J. Audubon's natural history prose with phrases from Shakespeare's "The Tempest" is anything but conventional:

> A Route of Evanescence
> With a revolving Wheel –
> A Resonance of Emerald –
> A Rush of Cochineal –
> And every Blossom on the Bush
> Adjusts it's tumbled Head –
> The mail from Tunis, probably,
> An easy Morning's Ride –[9]

In the Western lyric tradition, most likely imported from Persia, sound patterns do not merely reinforce meaning in poetry – twelfth-century Occitan troubadours deliberately kept sound separate from meaning by rhyming only the ends of their words. French poet Jacques Roubaud speculates that the troubadours modeled rhyme, "sound full of meaning that is not a word and seeks its mate", on bird song.[10] In her blossom-heads, Dickinson invites us to imagine the words of the poem itself, "tumbled" by the hummingbird, whose distance-zapping transit through the poet's hearing organizes phonetic structures into clusters of periodic assonance and consonance, a "resonance" drawing language away from its conventional literary meanings.

Focusing on the non-semantic layers of sound in "A Route of Evanescence" allows us to consider intensifications such as: Route, rev, Res/ scence, nance/ Evan, evolv, ever/ Wheel, neal, mail/ ald, Head, Ride/ Rush, bush, Adjusts/ tum, Tun/ every, easy. These clusters revolve around a lone sound at the center of the poem, "Coch", whose semantic pun lies exposed, in which perhaps we hear the turning axle of the mailman's coach. Dickinson's "Humming Bird" operates a kind of writing machine, an imagination of relinquishment, as Prospero yields organizational agency to Ariel's phenomena, arranging human memory and association in uncanny patterns, making a mockery of human scale ("The Mail from Tunis . . . An easy Morning's Ride"). Yet, vivid though its "Emerald" and "Cochineal" be, description is bound to follow "A Route of Evanescence":

like the bush, the poem is left to "adjust" its "tumbled Head", only registering contact with another lifeform on its own, intertextual terms. A bird that does not really sing (to our ears) is made to sing in human words.

In this "adjustment", a message appears to resolve from the poem's information, illusory as the zoetrope's "revolving Wheel", as connective possibilities are only opened through the constant reduction of its meaning to words. It is our fascination with the "revolving Wheel" that allows the poem to do its work, connecting Dickinson with her correspondents, connecting readers of Dickinson and Shakespeare, connecting humans to hummingbirds. At the same time, there is really no message: as we adjust our "tumbled Heads", we cannot doubt that a poem has gone through us, but what is communicated, the new connective possibilities, by definition remain inaccessible to our consciousness. We each make our own adjustments, opening up possibilities for some other observer. What communicates is "A Resonance of Emerald".

The title of Maggie O'Sullivan's volume *In the House of the Shaman* cues us to magical expectations, as we come to the poem "Starlings". If we know some natural-cultural history, we also might expect a Shakespearean resonance, since the virtuosic starling, Mozart's darling, became a pest once introduced to America by an enthusiast who, the story goes, set out to release all of Shakespeare's birds into Central Park. Like starlings, perhaps, what we encounter challenges our attention, with a different kind of fascination, sounds invading our sense-making capacities that exceed or fall short of meaning:

Lived Daily
        or Both
    Daily
 the Living
        structuring
        Bone-Seed,
   Pelage,
        Aqueous,
                        YONDERLY —
                                lazybed of need —
  CLOUD-SANG
        Tipsy Bobbles, Dowdy
                wander.Halt upon

grinned jeers, gin's note
someone's in the leading
of small & the pitch meander ears
tune me gold
Dulthie pods,
Lipper
"Ochre harled
ELECTRIC
CONTORTIONS —[11]

As sound, starlings "pitch meander ears// tune me gold/ Dulthie pods". As sight, they are "Ochre harled". Charles Bernstein has noted how O'Sullivan's poems "lend themselves to recitation, while resisting thematization".[12] To carry out the instructions fixed on the page is a transformative way of discovering one's objective nature: as breath, tongue and lips, performing "Dulthie pod", undergo "Kinship with Animals" (the title of the section of the book from which this poem is taken). Indeed, it is impossible to recite the poem and not in some sense become its matter, to get the "Tipsy Bobbles" as one sings "gin's note", in what O'Sullivan calls "a Mattering of Materials"[13]. Part of the physical here is the page (this is the first of two-and a half pages), in its "intervals between"[14] often an active part of the composition rather than neutral support, not to speak of the changes of font. Words here seem more attracted to one another than to our will to make sense of them, like the starlings they mimic in the poem's final lines, "scrapey syncopated/ iridescent// magnets".[15]

Louis Zukofsky called poetry, "An integral / Lower limit speech / Upper limit music"[16]. For Zukofsky, the essence of poetry is more like hearing something in a language one doesn't know than like not hearing something (overhearing or interpreting it) in a language one does know. Poetic language, it could be argued, organizes acoustic signals before coding them as meaning. Theorist Reuven Tsur's "cognitive poetics" articulates a "nonspeech" mode, drawn from neuroscience and psychoacoustics, that contributes to the expressiveness (and affectivity) of poetic sound patterns: "we hear it as if we heard music sounds or natural noises. We attend away from overtone structure to tone color."[17] As poet Steve McCaffery puts it, "even a single voice resonates as a simultaneity of corporeal, acoustic events"[18].

Tropes of sound in ecopoetics mind the gap between acoustics and phonetics: in the evocation of her mother's disability in her autobiographical poem "Paean to Place", the mimesis of Lorine Niedecker's "sora/ rail's sweet / / spoon-tapped waterglass-/ descending scale-/ tear-drop-tittle", referencing a resemblance that birders instantly recognize, descends into a thicket of alliteration, ending with hyphenated and enjambed, nursery rhymed "nonsense":

> I mourn her not hearing canvasbacks
> their blast-off rise
>   from the water
>   Not hearing sora
> rails's sweet
>
> spoon-tapped waterglass-
> descending scale-
>   tear-drop-tittle
>   Did she giggle
> as a girl?[19]

On the one hand, Niedecker's sounds activate the nonspeech mode of poetry, attending to acoustic signals prior to their organization as "words". Hearing seems to offer a bridge, however enjambed, between human and nonhuman. On the other hand, the meaning of "tear-drop-tittle" remains irreducibly human, an isolated sense the deafness of Niedecker's mother might be proxy for, whose "not hearing canvasbacks/ their blast-off rise" the poet mourns. Phonetics at once imagines communication and constellates a consciousness incapable of communication, organized only in relation to itself.

Within critical attention to the sound of poetry there has been an effort to uncouple sound from poetic 'voice' (the dominant, self-present, culturally authoritative 'voice' of the 'creative writing' industry, where poets are trained to 'find their voices'). For Charles Bernstein, the aesthetic significance of the acoustic inscription of the poet's voice lies in the fact that it "returns voice from sometimes idealized projections of self in the style of a poem to its social materiality, to voicing and voices"[20]. As Steve McCaffery says, and demonstrates,

> Voice is a polis of mouth, lips, teeth, tongue, tonsils, palette, breath, rhythm, timbre, and sound. Less a component than a production of a materiopneumatic assemblage […] a simultaneity of corporeal, acoustic events.[21]

Deconstructing, or otherwise constructing, voice opens poetry up to the more-than-human soundscape. "Performance", Bernstein continues,

> always exceeds script, just as text always outperforms audibility. The relation of script to performance, or performance to script, is necessarily discrepant, hovering around an original center in a complex of versions that is inherently unstable.[22]

I am interested in finding ways to talk about the sound of poetry as a critique of humanist prosody, attentive to ways in which the sounds of poetry are both closed off and radically open, subject to the impulses and vicissitudes of the sonic environment and yet uncannily apart.

Flashback: January 1979. Or was it later? Exploring the back-issues of National Geographic Magazine? Early vinyl memories are stuck on a repeat of the afternoon I first pulled *Never Mind the Bollocks, Here's the Sex Pistols* from its pink sleeve and took advantage of my grandmother's vacuuming to play it on her old turntable console. I couldn't tell you if that was 1977 (the year of the album's release) or 1980 or later. It seems strange to me now that I can't just 'google' those autobiographical details. Somewhere in the morass of pre-digital memory (early teens for me) I certainly pulled page 24A-B from the January 1979 issue of *National Geographic Magazine*, the *Songs of the Humpback Whale* 33 1/3 Flexi-Disc ('soundsheet') produced by Eva-Tone[23], laid it on our family Thorens turntable, with perhaps a quarter set on the label to keep it in place, and put the needle in the wobbly groove: whale song.

One can, as a matter of fact, google the artifact. 10.5 million of them were printed with that issue of *National Geographic* – the largest single pressing of any record in history.[24] *Songs of the Humpback Whale* was originally released in 1970 by the Wildlife Conservation Society at the Bronx Zoo, from recordings made by Roger Payne, Frank Watlington (a Navy hydrophonics operator, who had caught the sounds almost twenty years earlier while conducting sonar surveillance in Bermuda) and others, selling 45,000 copies in less than a year, and becoming the best-selling nature recording of all time, a multiplatinum album that has sold more than thirty million copies.[25] Listening to the Flexi-Disc now, via YouTube, its vinyl surface noise mingling with the oceanic background noise of the recording itself, I am as struck by the calm and precise enunciation of the narrator, whale biologist and activist Roger Payne, as I am by the blowing of these Ornette Coleman humpback whales:

> The recording you will now hear was carried onboard a Voyager spacecraft into outer space. The reason for including such a strange message, one of many greetings from earth, is that there is a remote chance sometime within the next 1.2 billion years, the expected lifetime of the spacecraft, that some other spacefaring civilization may find this bottle tossed into the cosmic ocean, and decode its message from Earth. That idea stops my heart. The songs of whales, so long confined within the vaults of the sea, have in span of just twenty years, burst through its surface, flowed over the land, conquered the hearts of their age-old enemy, man, and are now bound on a 1.2 billion-year journey that will spread them throughout the galaxy.[26]

Embedded in this statement, besides many other odd notions, such as the longshot hope that an alien civilization might be able to "decode" what we earth dwellers could not, is a belief in the transubstantiation of sound recording: as itself embodying the "songs of whales", which have been somehow decanted from the seas, and bottled in this high tech vessel to be "tossed into the cosmic ocean". The phrase "strange message" contains the contradiction of 'animal communication': vocalizations (and other information) whose meaning remains a mystery to us yet nevertheless is perceived to carry a 'message'. The agency of these nonhumans also remains ambiguous, as active verbs like "burst", "flowed", "conquered" are neutralized by the substance, the Golden Record (or vinyl phonosheet) into which they are pressed, "bound" on a galactic journey. Finally, the time scale of 1.2 billion years – a period of time within which chances are high that life on Earth as we know it will have vanished – seems out of scale with the presumed "message" of this phonosheet, which is, in popular terms, to 'save the whales'.

It would be hard to deny that *Songs of the Humpback Whale* did as much to put 'ambient music' on the commercial map as did Wendy Carlos, Brian Eno, Miles Davis, Pink Floyd, Jean Michel Jarre, Tangerine Dream, etc. It certainly impacted the map of my own listening development as much as the work of those other artists. (R. Murray Schafer notes how "the exaggerated echo and feedback effects of modern electronic and popular music re-create for us the echoing vaults, the dark depths of ocean"[27]). It would also be hard to deny that Payne's whale song album, which was just one part of a campaign Payne and his allies waged to get the International Whaling Commission to place a moratorium on commercial whaling in 1982, contributed more than any other intellectual or aesthetic production to the protection of the whales.

Yet according to the ecocritique of Timothy Morton and associated 'posthumanist' thinkers, whale music, and ambient art in general, render a fantasy of immersion in and interconnection with "the one thing that maintains an aesthetic distance between us and them, us and it, us and 'over there'".[28] In the case of ecology, this thing is "Nature", which any "dark ecology" – cleaving to "the dark, depressive quality of life in the shadow of ecological catastrophe" – must let go of, especially if human and nonhuman actors are to advance together in sounding future possibilities of coexistence.[29] Ambience does not just feed the phantasmagoria of 'nature', it also lures listeners into an ethical breach: if we do not want to resonate with ethically objectionable power structures, if we want to extend social relations to whales (for instance), then we might want to resist the special objects that fascinate and preoccupy our minds in order to secure our participation.

> In its refusal to produce an idea of nature as a way of being [à la Adorno's 'halting the mastery over nature through which nature continues its mastery'], dark ecology is one of the aspects of this 'halting', generating not the relaxing ambient sounds of ecomimesis, but the screeching of the emergency brake.[30]

To consume the renderings of ambient whale music, according to Morton's critique, is to linger in the tabernacle of the beautiful soul, ignoring the killing and machinery of the extraction industry. In his anatomy of the processing of a sperm whale on a midcentury American whaler, in the novel *Moby Dick*, Herman Melville dramatizes the rendering process (of whale blubber into oil) in the "try-works" of the whaling vessel and marvels at the conversion from the industrial gore of extraction, where "the entire ship seems great Leviathan himself", to the slick cleanliness of commerce, where "you would all but swear you trod some silent merchant vessel".[31] We are to be troubled by the double sense of "rendering" – an extraction of immediacy from the media of ambient poetics but also of a resource from living creatures. "Instead of whistling in the dark, pretending that we're part of Gaia", Morton asks, "why not stay with the darkness?"[32].

I would like to stay with the darkness *and* with the whistling (and groaning) of these whale songs, especially with the groans that are so far down, in a zone where only the lowest and slowest sounds travel, that our unaided human ears can't even hear them. Real deep darkness. My teenage self listening to the vinyl phonosheet of *Songs of the Humpback Whale* could hardly have imagined nearly fourty years later clicking a button on a screen in Europe to link to live streaming audio of a humpback whale singing into a robotic "wave glider" hydrophone in the Pacific Ocean.[33] As I listen to this transmission, I cannot avoid the fantasy that the whale 'knows' it is singing at a microphone, to humans listening around the planet. I post the link on Facebook and other humans tune in, each adjusting our own consciousness to this new fascination, as the communication spreads. Alvin Lucier seemed to ask, in his piece "Quasimodo, The Great Lover", what the body of such communication might be.[34] I can hear the reverberation of the spaces into which the whale is singing, but does that sound die in my space? How do I pay it (play it) forward? If I irritate and disturb the channels of communication with my fascination, it may resonate more than when I transmit whatever I perceive to be the "message" of the whale. Such disturbance could take the form of activism to protect whales, to draw attention to the threatened state of our oceans. There is resonance when the singing whale benefits from our fascination. We have been drawn into an alliance, whether we like it or not, that demands some very close listening. Not just to whales, of course, but to all manner of species, to buildings and stones and rivers, even, perhaps, to clouds of data. Of course I'd also like to leave some room for science fiction narratives about whales who use humans to broadcast their SOS into deep space.

In Ronald Johnson's *ARK*, a long poem that Johnson claimed would need "no reference except itself" and "be read by spaceships on the way to Alpha Centauri"[35], Johnson notes it is "by ear" that we stand up: "*Here, also, is couched our sense of the vertical*". We gain our direction in a labyrinth of sound: in "Beam 20, Labyrinthus", "It rises and falls through the repercussions of songs of birds".[36] "The mind begins early to select from the buzz and humdrum", Johnson writes in "Beam 7", "till most men end hearing nothing, when the earth speaks, but their own voices".[37] Johnson's field guide poetry[38], as in "ARK 37, Spire called Prospero's Songs to Ariel (constructed in the form of a quilt from Roger Tory Peterson's *A Field Guide to Western Birds*)", extends objectivist 'homophonic' explorations from a mimetic fascination with sound to a reverberational and repercussive engagement, admitting into the soundscape the maker's role as an emitter and reflector of sound:

hear hear hear hear
see-see-see
"upcurled" uttered like a mallet driving a stake
a tick of white, pale buff
constantly changing speed and direction
immutabilis
with an air-splitting stitch at the "focus"
"dead-leaf " pattern
in falling diminuendo blending into a broad terminal band of
"code" [39]

Johnson has written about this poem and its companion piece ("ARK 38"):

> I guess I wanted one coast to reverberate the other coast. I took the *Peterson's Field Guide to Eastern Birds* and just snipped it up and made a quilt out of it. Not all bird song, but bird songs are in it. And then I did a real piece of music where I took a record of the Western birds—the first one was called "Prospero's Songs to Ariel" . . . and this one was called "Ariel's Songs to Prospero", as if going from the east coast to the west coast. I used records and stitched together a music with a sound technician.[40]

A useful context for "ARK 38" might be musique concrète – the "concrete experiment in music", which, as its inventor Pierre Schaeffer defined it, "consists of building sonorous objects, not with the play of numbers and seconds of the metronome, but with pieces of time torn from the cosmos"[41]. Such "sonorous objects" might include the metallic whirr of the wood thrush as much as the fluting melody of the hermit thrush, or the cacophonic range of a Harry Partch composition – to whom one of the sections of "ARK 38" makes homage. This pairing of invisible Spire ("ARK 38") and silent Spire ("ARK 37") – "hear hear hear hear / see-see-see" – inviting their mutual reverberation and intertwining, their dissonance and resonance, emphasizes ARK's place in the world, somewhere between sound and vision, as material, embodied architecture.

Composer Pauline Oliveiros notes how "[t]he natural and urban environments are full of pulses and patterns. Try to record", she suggests, "the most interesting pulses or patterns that you can find in your daily environment"[42]. I am not merely a passive receiver of sounds, nor am I the only listener: my participation in the soundscape, even the mere fact of my 'listening', is bound to impact other listeners, and to affect their sounding, i.e. what I hear. We might call this feedback of organic transducers within a sonic environment resonance, and the parallel feedback loop of vocalizations reverberation. Except that would be too neat, as well as ignore the vast dimension of non-vocalized sounds. But the play of resonance and reverberation – or, in Johnson's terms, repercussion – might be an adequate way to conceptualize the relationship of poetry to soundscape.

If language is "no longer seen (as it is in philosophical humanism) as a well-nigh magical property that ontologically separates *Homo sapiens* from every other living creature", states philosopher Cary Wolfe, then we are bound to pay attention to "larger processes of social interaction and communication among animals including but not limited to *Homo sapiens*"[43]. Wolfe's key move here, taking his cue from the natural sciences and social sciences, is the separating out of language from communication: just because animals don't speak and write doesn't mean they don't communicate, and just because humans have language, doesn't mean 'we', the subjects in language, communicate – we are precisely not where our communications are. Biologists Humberto Maturana and Francisco Varela, and the later work of sociologist Niklas Luhmann, conceptualize such processes around the notion of autopoesis and

> the seemingly paradoxical fact that systems are both open *and* closed; to exist and reproduce themselves, they must maintain their boundaries and integrity through a process of self-referential closure; and it is only on the

basis of this closure that they can then engage in 'structural coupling' with their environment.[44]

An example of operational closure/ structural openness might be the homology between whale and bird song, which can be seen and heard to follow similar reiterative patterns ('rhythm and rhyme') when speeded up and/or slowed down. Despite the radically different operation and scale of their organisms, structural coupling seems to occur around patterns of sound. (A track on David Rothenberg's *Whale Music* CD includes a catbird song slowed down to sound like a humpback whale[45]; Payne's *Songs of the Humpback Whale* flexidisc includes a segment of humpback whale song speeded up to sound like a catbird[46].) Or it may be that a song system – Australian aboriginals might say a 'songline', Deleuze and Guattari a "refrain"[47] – transects these organic autopoetic systems. The prosthetic (or "schizophonic", to borrow a term from R. Murray Schafer[48]) binding, manipulation, and even graphing of acoustic time, afforded by our listening technics, by which we register signals and events beyond the scope of the human ear, both reinforces the incongruent boundedness of our hearing, the hearing of catbirds, and the hearing of whales, *and* makes us aware of the noise of our self-production. A (second-order) systems approach to communication deconstructs the signal/ noise binary, allowing us to 'read' noise as communication, including (importantly) the noise of interdisciplinary communication. It becomes more critical than ever to 'listen' to noise, from a standpoint where disruptive, counter-hegemonic, compositional practices of "disquiet" (à la Jacques Attali[49] or poet Lisa Robertson[50], as she has it in a recent essay by that title) are not at odds with the conservationist and preservationist care of a biopolitics and its focus on the integrity of signaling systems.

The case against nature poetry is compelling: the "relaxing ambient sounds of ecomimesis" might reasonably be indicted – not only for silencing "the screeching of the emergency brake" we so need to hear but for actively participating in the rendering process itself.[51] (Timothy Morton's critique of ecomimesis asks us to consider whether the consumption of "whale music" perpetuates the very rendering process its production is meant to decry.) Ecopoetics today, such critique runs, might better turn aside from the prosody of nature, and, as in Ariana Reines's *The Cow*, "get to the other side of the animal"[52], scanning language from

Carcass Disposal: A Comprehensive Review for valences that distort the language of interpersonal (and by extension, human-animal) relations.

> **STICK LIQUID OR STICK WATER:** THE VISCOUS LIQUID LEFT IN THE RENDERING TANK AFTER COOKING PROCESS

> Because remembering could be loose like interpersonal relations, I am only a citizen. Nothing is required of me. Certain things. Maybe speaking. This doesn't have to be speaking. Under speaking. Low. Down. Under speaking. [53]

If ecopoetics listens to animal sounds, this poetry seems to say, it is for the noise of human relations, not for signals from another world. And yet the poet invokes the "under speaking" of a communication that is not language. John Clare's verse may begin with the song of the nightingale, but it ends in the madhouse. If the delight of Les Murray's "Lyre Bird" lies in its vertiginous mimicry of the "Tailed mimic aeon-sent to intrigue the next recorder", its instruction remains, how "I alter nothing. Real to real only I sing":

> Liar made of leaf-litter . . .
> Tailed mimic aeon-sent to intrigue the next recorder,
> I mew catbird, I saw crosscut, I howl she-dingo, I kink
> forest hush distinct with bellbirds, warble magpie garble, link
> cattlebell with kettle-boil; I rank ducks' cranky presidium
> or simulate a triller like a rill mirrored lyrical to a rim.
> I ring dim. I alter nothing. Real to real only I sing [...][54]

Luhmann's shorthand for the paradoxical structure of consciousness is that "humans can't communicate"[55], which seems to assume that consciousness is a human attribute. If we remove this premise (and simply affirm that consciousness doesn't communicate) or if we expand our definition of "human" (as in animist cultures, where to be human is to have a point of view, regardless of physical attributes[56]) the structure of the observation holds. Lyrebird is catbird, saw, dingo, forest hush, bellbird, magpie, cattlebell, kettle-boil, duck, triller; we can participate in lyrebird's fascination with these sounds, to the point where lyrebird tells more than our carefully constructed 'nature' narratives about the forest –

as in David Attenborough's famous lyrebird episode, where the lyrebird brings camera shutter and chainsaw sounds back into the frame.[57] Nevertheless, the information does not resolve a message. Consciousness can't communicate, only adjust itself, but it is through that very adjustment and increasing points of contact in the environment that communication happens, as a kind of *resonance* – one that it takes a posthumanist ear to detect.[58] "To know the humpback song", writes David Rothenberg, "is to feel its resonance and its power, and to fathom a reason for its shape and its form"[59]. Jane Bennett, in her pursuit of a theory of vital materiality uses "resonance" to describe how various actants assemble: "In nonlinear assemblages, 'effects' resonate with and against their 'causes,' such that the impact of any added element [...] cannot be grasped at a glance".[60]

The posthumanist ear, I argue, takes in *both* the Sex Pistols and Brian Eno, both the screeching of the emergency brake and *The Song of the Humpback Whale*, both Ariana Reines's conceptual unmasking of the gendered landscape of slaughterhouses *and* Les Murray's expressive mimicry of the mimic "Lyre Bird". The posthumanist ear turns to poetry for its sonic techniques, for how its prosody amplifies the ways in which human language renders the nonhuman world. Poets emphasize our uncanny relationship to language, as always at least partially exterior to consciousness and culture, a prosthetic by which ideas and affect get around. Poetry, despite its role in anchoring a humanist narrative about culture, is well positioned to sound the "ahuman" qualities of this language.[61] What communicates through language, but not only through language, in an ecological sense can only be, as Luhmann suggests, a communication of ignorance.[62] Of course the relationships that subtend these communications are unequal (between disciplines, groups of humans, humans and other animals), and traversed by power structures that both channel and limit resonance. Any significant change in these relationships threatens the communication – or, conversely, something more violent than resonance may be necessary to effect change. It may be that invoking 'resonance' or 'ignorance' (like the supposedly self-regulating homeostases of 'Gaia') is just another appeal to magic; even worse, such an appeal may 'greenwash' our ears, encouraging acquiescence with the business as usual models of 'sustainable development'. We also need the howls of refusal that eco-consciousness brings to these communications, the disturbances that shake apart entrenched habits of sounding: we need both 'fracktivism' and activism.

When we withdraw (from) our fascination with the vibrant matter of a more than human world, however, when we bind our ears to the enchantment of sound, bird, insect or whale song, when we turn away from the brightly patterned worlds of sexual selection, because we fear our fascination can make us communicating vessels for compromising power structures, we limit possibility. The withdrawal of media from communication, and reduction of information to message or critique, also leaves entrenched power structures in place. Life continues, fending for itself. Here I have focused largely on how sound, and especially the acousmatic object of recorded sound, what Hildegard Westerkamp calls the "naked" ear of the microphone[63], connects us to, at the same time that it disconnects us from the environment, offering a texture for what poet Nathaniel Mackey calls forms of "discrepant engagement".[64] In the "sand-anointed wind [that] spoke of / survival", a landscape of "blown/ rush, thrown voice, legbone/ flute", Nathaniel Mackey's poem "Sound and Semblance" sounds "a new mood suddenly, blue/ but uptempo,/ parsed, bitten into".[65] This "new mood" invokes the dissonances and gapped rhythms of free jazz, accenting "fissure, fracture, incongruity, the rickety, imperfect fit between word and world". Mackey's poetry amplifies this "creaking of the word . . . the noise upon which the word is based". In its power to disturb, stimulate, and irritate, noise sounds the gap between message and information, consciousness and communication, provoking adjustments in the contact between systems, coaxing new orders of "identity and signification"[66].

With Bruno Latour's critique of "Nature" and his call for a multi-disciplinary sounding of the "tangled objects"[67] of (small s) science, as with Cary's Wolfe's emphases on "the estranging prostheticity and exteriority of communication" in the context of disciplinary specificity[68], I hear a case for listening to animal vocalizations as poetry (or 'songs') and for listening to poetry as acoustic ecology, for poetics as a site for interdisciplinary if not cross-species resonance. I would sound the acousmatic object, modeled so concisely by the sound recordist's microphone, for a prosody emerging from the necessity of the other.[69] Listening can be understood as a stance of participatory receptiveness, as much as an aural faculty (we can 'listen' with our eyes or 'sound' with science). Listening also means not subordinating poetry as a mode of thought – signaled through creative-critical formulations explored here, such as Mackey's "discrepant engagement", Dickinson's "resonance", Johnson's "repercussion", O'Sullivan's "mattering of matter" – to a 'prior' critical formulation.

Jacques Derrida urges us to deconstruct the singular "animal" – that criminal "confounding of all non-human beings under the common and general category of the animal"[70]. As a protest, Derrida's *Ecce animot* lodges the humanist's cogito acoustically, between animals ("animaux") and word ("mot").[71] Or, as Giorgio Agamben writes,

> if the caesura between the human and the animal passes first of all within man, then it is the very question of man—and of 'humanism'—that must be posed in a new way. . . . What is man, if he is always the place—and, at the same time, the result—of ceaseless divisions and caesurae?[72]

These are the divisions, the discrepant engagements, the segments and caesurae that poetry animals, in different ways, ceaselessly scan. "Loue is blynd alday and may nat see", wrote Chaucer[73]; how easily fascination turns to love, singers croon. Indeed, in the very blindness (and deafness) of our fascination with the material events of life, we multiply points of contact. It is in our disconnections that we connect – to participate in a dawn chorus or refrain, to resonate with other disciplines, to amplify noise in the system, as we face the challenge human success presents all life on earth – to act in critically and materially meaningful ways for other life forms, to finally "call the pulsing home":

when your animal is brought back
you
too
water & ice & leaves & snow become
you
too
Day Door Sky & Sing
you
too
scald & crow down ink
you
too

stiffen swoop on ridge
you
too
topple turn hills many more turns
you
too
the Beasts to the rain not the Birds do another
you
too
call the Pulsing home. [74]

Notes

[1] Luhmann (1994:375).
[2] *Ibid.*, 376.
[3] O'Sullivan (1993:17)
[4] Luhmann (1994:375)
[5] *Earth House Hold* is the title of Gary Snyder's 1969 collection of "Technical Notes & Queries" (New York: New Directions).
[6] Snyder (1990:22).
[7] Dickinson (1955:1011-1012).
[8] Farr (2005:39-70).
[9] Dickinson (1955:1010).
[10] Roubaud (1994) [1986]:274). The translation is my own.
[11] O'Sullivan (1993:41).
[12] Bernstein (2011).
[13] O'Sullivan (2003:65).
[14] *Ibid.*, 64.
[15] O'Sullivan (1993:43).
[16] Zukofsky (1978:138).
[17] Tsur (1992:18).
[18] McCaffery (1998:160).
[19] Niedecker (2002:263).
[20] Bernstein (2009:144).
[21] McCaffery (1998:160). See also McCaffery's performance of "Carnival" at the Instal 09 festival in Glasgow:

<https://youtu.be/Z5sB_YvvSS4?list=PL711942F2263A094D> (Accessed 24 May 2017.)
[22] Bernstein (2009:148).
[23] Payne (1979).
[24] Rothenberg (2008:9).
[25] *Ibid.*,17-23. Payne. *Songs of the Humpback Whale*. Album. CRM Records, 1970.
[26] <http://www.youtube.com/watch?v=0WOjJIynHgM> (Accessed 24 May 2017.)
[27] Murray Schafer (1977:118).
[28] Morton (2007:204).
[29] *Ibid.*, 187.
[30] *Ibid.*, 196.
[31] Melville (1930 [1851]:615).
[32] Morton (2007:187).
[33] See Jupiter Research Foundation's Wave Glider-Hydrophone Project. Web. 24 May 2017 <http://jupiterfoundation.org/projects.shtml>.
[34] Lucier (1970). "Quasimodo, The Great Lover." With Matt Rogalsky, Laura Cameron et al. Transnational Ecologies 1: Sounds Travel Project. Institute of Geography, University of Edinburgh, 10 May 2007. <https://mattrogalsky.bandcamp.com/track/quasimodo-the-great-lover-alvin-lucier> (Accessed 24 May 2017.) See also Kahn (2013:167-169).
[35] Johnson (1985-1986:2).
[36] Johnson (2013 [1996]:51).
[37] *Ibid.*, 23.
[38] Skinner (2008:397-420).
[39] *Ibid.*, 106-107.
[40] O'Leary (1996:50).
[41] Herbert (1972:85).
[42] Oliveiros (2005:27).
[43] Wolfe (2010:120).
[44] *Ibid.*, 111.
[45] Rothenberg (2008:248-249). Rothenberg (2008) "The Far Field." *Whale Music*.
[46] Payne (1979).
[47] Deleuze and Guattari (1987 [1980]:310-350).
[48] Schafer (1977: 90-91).
[49] Attali (1985).
[50] Robertson (2012:55-70)
[51] Morton (2007:196).
[52] Reines (2006:63).
[53] *Ibid.*, 71.
[54] Les Murray (1993:21).

[55] Luhmann (1994:371).
[56] Viveiros de Castro (1998:447).
[57] Attenborough (2007). "Bird Sounds From The Lyre Bird." *BBC Wildlife*. <https://www.youtube.com/watch?v=VjE0Kdfos4Y> Accessed 24 May 2017.
[58] Luhmann (1995) [1984]:37).
[59] Rothenberg (2008:132).
[60] Bennet (2010:42).
[61] Wolfe (2010:119).
[62] Luhmann (1998 [1992]).
[63] Westerkamp (2001:148).
[64] Mackey (1993:19-21).
[65] Mackey (2006:55-56).
[66] Mackey (1993:19).
[67] Latour (2004:22).
[68] Wolfe (2010:119).
[69] *Ibid.*, 46.
[70] Derrida (2008:48).
[71] *Ibid.*, 41.
[72] Agamben (2004:16).
[73] Chaucer. "The Merchant's Tale." line 385.
[74] O'Sullivan (1993:17).

Works Cited

Agamben, Giorgio (2004). *The Open, Man and Animal.* Stanford, CA: Stanford University Press.

Attali, Jacques (1985). *Noise: The Political Economy of Music.* Minneapolis: University of Minnesota Press.

Bennett, Jane (2010). *Vibrant Matter: A Political Ecology of Things*. Durham, NC: Duke University Press.

Bernstein, Charles (2009). "Hearing Voices." *The Sound of Poetry, the Poetry of Sound*. Eds. Marjorie Perloff and Craig Dworkin. Chicago: The University of Chicago Press

--- (2011) "Colliderings: O'Sullivan's Medleyed Verse." *The Salt Companion to Maggie O'Sullivan*. Ed. Ken Edwards. Cambridge: Salt Publishing

Buell, Lawrence (1995). *The Environmental Imagination: Thoreau, Nature Writing, and the Formation of American Culture.* Cambridge, Mass.: Belknap Press of Harvard University Press.

Castro, Eduardo Viveiros de (1998). "Cosmological Deixis and Amerindian Perspectivism." The Journal of the Royal Anthropological Institute. 4.3, 469-488.

Deleuze, Gilles, and Felix Guattari (1987) [1980]. *A Thousand Plateaus: Capitalism and Schizophrenia.* Trans. Brian Massumi. Minneapolis: University of Minneapolis Press.

Derrida, Jacques (2008). *The Animal That Therefore I Am.* Trans. David Wills. New York : Fordham University Press.

Descola, Philippe (2005). *Par-delà nature et culture.* Paris: Ed. Gallimard.

Dickinson, Emily (1955). *The Poems of Emily Dickinson.* Ed. Thomas H. Johnson. Cambridge: Belknap Press of Harvard University Press.

Farr, Judith (2005). *The Gardens of Emily Dickinson.* Cambridge: Harvard University Press.

Feld, Steven (1982). *Sound and Sentiment: Birds, Weeping, Poetics, and Song in Kaluli Expression.* Philadelphia: University of Pennsylvania Press.

Johnson, Ronald (1985-86). "The Planting of the Rod of Aaron." *Northern Lights Studies in Creativity* 2, 2.

--- (2013) [1996]. *ARK.* Chicago, Flood Editions.

Kahn, Douglas (2013). *Earth Sound Earth Signal: Energies and Earth Magnitude in the Arts.* Berkeley: University of California Press.

Latour, Bruno (2004). *Politics of Nature: How to Bring the Sciences into Democracy.* Trans. Catherine Porter. Cambridge: Harvard University Press.

Luhmann, Niklas (1994). "How Can the Mind Participate in Communication?" *Materialities of Communication.* Ed. Hans Ulrich Gumbrecht and K. Ludwig Pfeiffer. Stanford, CA: Stanford University Press.

--- (1995 [1984]). *Social Systems.* Trans. John Bednarz, Jr. Stanford, CA: Stanford University Press.

--- (1998 [1992]) *Observations on Modernity.* Trans. William Whobrey. Stanford, CA: Stanford University Press.

Mackey, Nathaniel (1993). *Discrepant Engagement: Dissonance, Cross-Culturality, and Experimental Writing.* Cambridge: Cambridge University Press.

--- (2006) *Splay Anthem.* NY: New Directions.

McCaffery, Steve (1998). "Voice in Extremis." *Close Listening: Poetry and the Performed Word.* Ed. Charles Bernstein. Oxford: Oxford University Press.

Melville, Herman (1930). *Moby Dick.* New York: Modern Library.

Morton, Timothy (2007). *Ecology Without Nature: Rethinking Environmental Aesthetics.* Cambridge: Harvard University Press.

Murray, Les (1993). *Translations from the Natural World.* Manchester, UK: Carcanet.

Niedecker, Lorine (2002). *Lorine Niedecker: Collected Works*, ed. Jenny Penberthy. Berkeley: University of California Press.

O'Leary, Peter (1996). "An Interview with Ronald Johnson." *Chicago Review* 42.2, 32-53.

Oliveiros, Pauline (2005). *Deep Listening: A Composer's Sound Practice.* New York: iUniverse, Inc.

O'Sullivan, Maggie (1993). *In the House of the Shaman.* London: Reality Street Editions.

--- (2003) *Palace of Reptiles*. Willowdale, ON: The Gig.

Payne, Roger. (1979). "Humpbacks: Their Mysterious Songs." *National Geographic* 155.1 Jan., 18-25.

Perloff , Marjorie, and Craig Dworkin (2009). *The Sound of Poetry, the Poetry of Sound.* Chicago: The University of Chicago Press.

Reines, Ariana (2006). *The Cow.* Albany, NY: Fence Books.

Robertson, Lisa (2012). *Nilling.* Toronto: BookThug.

Rothenberg, David (1997) "Music from Nature: The *Terra Nova* CD." *Terra Nova* 2.3, 121-137.

--- (2008). *Thousand Mile Song: Whale Music in a Sea of Sound.* New York: Basic Books.

Roubaud, Jacques (1994 [1986]). *La Fleur Inverse: L'Art des Troubadours*. Paris: p

Russcol, Herbert (1972). *The Liberation of Sound: An Introduction to Electronic Music.* Englewood Cliffs: Prentice Hall.

Schafer, R. Murray (1977). *The Soundscape: Our Sonic Environment and the Tuning of the World.* Rochester, VT: Destiny Books.

Skinner, Jonathan (2008). "Upper Limit Tu-Whit: Ronald Johnson's Field Guide Poetries." *Ronald Johnson: Life and Works*. Ed. Joel Bettridge and Eric Murphy Selinger. Orono, ME: The National Poetry Foundation.

Snyder, Gary (1969). *Earth House Hold.* New York: New Directions.

--- (1990). *The Practice of the Wild.* New York: North Point Press.

Tsur, Reuven (1992). *What Makes Sound Patterns Expressive?: The Poetic Mode of Speech Perception.* Durham, NC: Duke University Press.

Viveiros de Castro, Eduardo (1998). "Cosmological Deixis and Amerindian Perspectivism." *The Journal of the Royal Anthropological Institute*. 4.3, 469-488.

Westerkamp, Hildegard (2001). "Speaking from Inside the Soundscape." *The Book of Music and Nature*. Ed. David Rothenberg and Marta Ulvaeus.

Wolfe, Cary (2010). *What is Posthumanism?* Minneapolis: University of Minnesota Press.

Zukofsky, Louis (1978). "A." Berkeley: University of California Press.

Ioannis Tsitsovits and Pieter Vermeulen (Leuven)

The Anthropocene Scriptorium: Writing and Agency in Ben Lerner's *10:04* and Tom McCarthy's *Satin Island*

1. Introduction: Big Data, Geological Agency, and the Literary

U., the narrator of Tom McCarthy's 2015 novel *Satin Island*, works as a corporate anthropologist charged with writing the "Great Report" – an all-encompassing, comprehensive account of contemporary life.[1] Given this daunting task, it is unsurprising that he hits a wall: "I'd begun to suspect", he notes, "that this Great Report was un-plottable, un-frameable, un-realizable: in short, [...] *un-writable*"[2]. U. gains an insight into his impasse when he begins to understand that, in a data-saturated world, in which movements, consumer transactions, keystrokes, and click-throughs are relentlessly recorded, tabulated, and cross-indexed, the Great Report is not so much "*un-writable*" as being written in real time:

> The truly terrifying thought wasn't that the Great Report might be un-writable, but – quite the opposite – that it had *already been written*. Not by a person, nor even by some nefarious cabal, but simply by a neutral and indifferent binary system that had given rise to itself, moved by itself and would perpetuate itself: some auto-alphaing and auto-omegating script – that that's what it *was*. And that we, far from being its authors [...] were no more than actions and commands within its key-chains.[3]

Writing, in *Satin Island*, morphs from being an exclusively human act into a nonhuman action, and this occasions a crisis of agency: human life is not only writing, but is constantly being written by algorithms. And this undermining of human autonomy and human action's participation in assemblages of other non-autonomous agents is not only a problem of agency: it is also a peculiarly *literary* problem, as the continuous recording, tagging, and tabulating of human life comes to usurp some of the traditional tasks of literature. These days, McCarthy writes in an essay, it is software that "maps our tribe's kinship structures, our systems of exchange, the webs of value and belief that bind us all together"; algorithms transcribe human life into a "regime of signals" that is "omnipresent and insistent" and elides the role of a creative human author.[4] As the distinction between human and nonhuman agency threatens to collapse, so does that between literary and nonliterary writing.

Satin Island not only links this altered understanding of human and literary activity to the ascendency of what is often called Big Data – a term that captures the increasingly intensified capture, analysis, curation, and monetization of behavioral data – but also to the Anthropocene. As is familiar by now, this term reflects the insight that human life has become a geological agent affecting the chemical and climatological make-up of the planet. These two developments complement one another: just as the rise of Big Data entangles human agency with nonhuman and technological actions, the Anthropocene underlines the reciprocal implication of human and natural life. U. is obsessed with a widely mediatized oil spill – a process he describes as "Earth open[ing] its archives"[5], as "Earth well[ing] back up and reveal[ing] itself; nature's hidden nature gush[ing] forth"[6]. Yet the oil spill is also a writing event: watching "the streaks and clusters taking shape as oil spread slowly inland", U. imagines "ink polluting paper, words marring the whiteness of a page".[7] As this vision comes to U. when he is fruitlessly trying to write the Great Report, it illustrates the shift from human creativity to geological agency. In *Satin Island*, not only algorithms, but also the environment is constantly writing – that is, leaving traces of its actions; and as human life, in the Anthropocene, is a geological force in its own right, it is co-writing the geological record it inhabits, just as it is co-writing the databases that, in their turn, increasingly shape the lives we are living (and writing into archives again).

Satin Island's relevance for contemporary nature writing not only has to do with its thematic occupation with environmental issues, but also with its sustained focus on the contemporary vagaries of writing. It positions the notion of writing at the heart of the feedback loops through which algorithms and geological agency give rise to a proliferation of data that in their turn shape the assemblages of human and nonhuman forces that we inhabit. This reciprocally reinforcing entanglement of living and writing characterizes what Mark Seltzer has called the "official world" – his term for modernity, which he sees as a world consisting "both of itself and its self-description, denotation, or registration".[8] In the modern age, our lives are marked by a comprehensive process of self-writing (the "auto-alphaing and auto-omegating script" McCarthy refers to)[9] and this writing becomes coterminous with human action: "It is not merely that there is nothing in the world that is not in the files", Seltzer writes; "the correlate is that there is then nothing in the files that is not in the world".[10] What Kate Marshall has called "the Anthropocene's reflexive phase"[11] does not mark a real departure from the modern, official world; it is an intensified recognition that the reciprocal imbrication of human and geological life operates through processes of notation, of "observation and depiction".[12] The Anthropocene, then, is also a matter of writing; and as *Satin Island* suggests through its organizing preoccupation with ethnography, which McCarthy sees as a form of writing that is more literary than most literature[13], it is also essentially a *literary* concern.

Ecocriticism traditionally – that is, in its first and second waves[14] – valorized literature's mimetic and expressive qualities, and was justly suspicious of the human- and language-centeredness of critical theory, which often ascribed an agency to writing that seemed unhelpfully divorced from the material processes that, on a traditional understanding, make up nature. Recently, the promiscuous proliferation of the geological and algorithmic writing that *Satin Island* plugs into gives some seemingly obtuse critical elevations of writing an unexpected relevance. Jacques Derrida's easily ridiculed "Il n'y a pas de hors-texte"[15] seems hardly extravagant when there is no part of nature that is *not* co-created by human action, and when the power of the Google search engine is such that what it cannot find might as well not exist.[16] (In *Satin Island*, the announcement of U.'s friend Petr's death is sent via Petr's mobile phone, with Petr's name showing up as the message's sender, making U. consider that "[t]o almost all intents and purposes", Petr is still alive.)[17] Or take Maurice Blanchot's hyperbolic assertion that, because the act of writing both creates a new reality and in the process affirms the writer as a historical agent, "a writer's activity must be recognized as the highest form of work"[18]. This does not sound nearly so inflated when work, writing, and living have become overlapping practices, and when so much remunerated as well as invisible labor consists of writing data into databases.

McCarthy himself points to Michel de Certeau's imagining of social life as a vast "scriptural enterprise" – a massive process of notation that comes to shape and control human life. The result is life's "incarceration within the operations of a writing that constantly makes a machine of itself and never encounters anything but itself".[19] For de Certeau, the only ways out of this self-perpetuating scriptural machine were "fictions, painted windows, mirror-panes"[20] – illusory constructs that allow readers a measure of freedom. Readers, de Certeau writes, produce "gardens that miniaturize and collate a world"; they are "travellers" that "deterritorialize" themselves and cannot be captured by the scriptural apparatus.[21] In the age of the Anthropocene and Big Data, de Certeau's 1980 exaltation of the reader (which echoes the work of Roland Barthes) sounds decidedly dated; even if pattern recognition and data processing is more important than ever, it is hard to see such activities as alternatives (rather than prized contributions) to the contemporary "scriptural enterprise". As more and more reading takes place on computer screens and online, acts of reading are tracked, stored, tagged, and monetized – they are, in other words, forms of inscription, recording, and writing. As Wendy Chun notes, Big Data has "turned once silent and private acts – such as reading a book – into noiselessly noisy ones, eroding the difference between reading, writing, and being written"[22]. Critical theory's engagement with writing becomes surprisingly relevant for understanding changes to human agency in the Anthropocene, even if its elevation of reading and writing as affirmations of freedom stands in need of a sobering update.

Recent ecocritical accounts of literature's recalibrated relation to the environment and to nonhuman agency tend to either heighten or slight human responsibility. Adam Trexler's book *Anthropocene Fictions*, for instance, upholds the resilience and elasticity of narrative, as literary fiction manages to "give room to nonhuman things to shape narrative"[23]; in this way, Anthropocene fiction testifies to the need for "a tremendous, common response from humanity", or, failing that, to the possibilities of "mass adaptation".[24] In contrast to this emphasis on narrative and human exceptionalism, more avant-garde experiments and theories celebrate art's capacity to display the mismatch between the human and the natural agencies afflicting it; it prefers works that emphasize "disjunctiveness, a being-overwhelmed by contexts in which the human perceiver is deeply implicated but cannot hope to command or sometimes even to comprehend"[25]. As Timothy Clark has remarked, such edgier accounts typically have little patience for literature, which through its partiality to narrative, perspective, and pattern seems fatally anthropocentric.[26]

This essay complements such extant approaches – which either perpetuate an only slightly altered liberal notion of human agency or flatten the distinction between human and nonhuman agency – by situating the contemporary environmental relevance of literature less in its evocative and affective capacities than in its concern with writing. 'Writing' now also names human life's geological agency[27] *and* its participation in processes of data storage and transmission; in a time "when our most pervasive surrounding environment is technological"[28], self-conscious literary engagements with writing offer an occasion to tease out the implications of the entanglement between living and writing, between the human and the nonhuman. These engagements are not merely thematic, but concern the very possibility of literature as a distinct activity. In *Satin Island*, U.'s account of his life writing a "Great Report on our data-saturated present becomes *part* of that Great Report"; in Ben Lerner's *10:04*, which we will discuss later in this essay, the narrator's account of his attempt to try to write a commissioned novel comes to *replace* that novel as if to underscore that life, in the novel's hypermediated and climate-changed world, is *already* a form of writing.

These novels underline that registration technologies and human geological impact are two sides of the same coin. As Nicholas Mirzoeff has remarked, climate change and global geological change can only be observed through "computational models supported by a knowledge infrastructure" such as "weather observations, satellite data, radar readings, and so on".[29] At the same time, digital technologies leave a considerable environmental footprint through their vast expenditure of (often unclean) energy as well as through the use of rare minerals and the proliferation of e-waste; as Jussi Parikka has shown, "the purified industries of computing [are] secretly just as dirty as the industrial ancestors", as media technologies "retain their toxic materiality".[30] If human life now participates in "terraforming assemblages"[31], it does so in part through the inevitably material processes of data processing that make its geological agency visible in the first place. *Satin Island* and *10:04* underline that this multiply overdetermined context is the environment in which contemporary literary writing participates, even if these novels are less certain how literature can still make a difference to it. One challenge, as we will see, is that algorithmic and geological writing display some of the very features – notably performativity[32] and reflexivity[33] – that have traditionally marked out literary writing.

2. Self-Writing and the Literary Environment: Reflexivity, Performativity, and Human Difference

Geological writing, like algorithmic writing, is never just mere notation, but also always constitutes action. Writing on the power of science to read the human impact on the Earth, Tobias Boes notes that "our very planet has become a medium for the storage and recursive transmission of human-generated messages"[34]. Clouds, rocks, and water are now "repositories of readable data", and become essential parts of semiotic and hermeneutical operations (which is not to say, of course, that they can ever be fully decoded or understood).[35] What is remarkable about the assumed consequences of human geological agency – rising temperatures, sinking pH levels, species extinction, deforestation – is that they are "not merely legible signs of our impending catastrophe, they *are* the catastrophe itself"[36]. What we find, in other words, is a "conflation of message and medium", in which "textuality is inseparable from materiality".[37] The Anthropocene, then, "is not simply something that is written *about*; it is also something that is actively shaped and created through acts of human inscription".[38] Geological agency manifests itself as a "peculiarly embodied form of writing"[39], in which reading, writing, and living operate on the same plane – as so many actions that generate effects that require (even if they continue to complicate) reading. Human life, in the Anthropocene, does not express itself "in denotative speech acts but rather in performative interventions in which humankind functions as both subject and object"[40] – interventions that redefine even as they perform human action.

Human action, in the Anthropocene, is constitutively self-reflexive, autopoietic, and performative. So how can literature mark its difference from this dynamic? The opening of Ben Lerner's 2014 novel *10:04* finds its semi-autobiographical narrator and his literary agent celebrating the contract and the sizeable advance he was offered on the basis of "an earnest if indefinite proposal"; all he had to do was "promise to turn [a story he had published] into a novel".[41] Together with its thematic occupation with energy depletion, climate change, and superstorms, it is

10:04's sustained semi-autobiographical mode that signals its ambition to tap into the Anthropocene ecology of writing: in this ecology, all writing is also self-writing (as human action comes to *define* what it means to be human in the Anthropocene), and no form of writing is fully autobiographic (as there is no human agency that is not entangled with nonhuman others). In both *Satin Island* and *10:04*, the continuity between living and writing and between fiction and nonfiction is underlined by including essayistic writings by these novels' authors into their narrators' streams of consciousness. In this new ecology, a life led in preparation of the writing of a novel is *already* writing, and *10:04*'s narrator gradually comes to realize that his meticulous, nervous, and hyper-self-conscious notation of everyday life is *already* a novel, and will come to be published (as *10:04*) instead of the novel he had promised to write. *10:04*'s central movement, then, precisely echoes U.'s discovery in *Satin Island* that the Great Report, far from being unwritable, is already being written, and even being co-written by U. himself. Living, writing, and reading all operate on a continuous plane, and there are no clear-cut distinctions between the production of signs, the materiality of the signs, and the act of reading them – all count as inscriptions in this Anthropocene ecology.

10:04 collapses the distinction between writer, reader, and text through several strategies. There are the intermittent second-person addresses to the reader, which position the reader as a fellow New Yorker, rather than a disembodied abstraction ("You might have seen me sitting there on the bench that midnight."[42]). The narrator underlines his ambition to "insert some physical particulars" into the letters he writes – an ambition he links to John Keats "always describing his bodily position at the time of writing, the conditions of his room".[43] The narrator's ambition to include the media of inscription into his text is compared to "the red-eye effect in the photographs of my youth, the camera recording the light of its own flash, the camera inscribing itself in the image it captured"[44]. The most extensive invitation to "coeval readership"[45] comes when the narrator describes a trip to Marfa and cancels the distance between remembrance, writing, and reading: "I remember the address (you can drag the 'pegman' icon onto the Google map and walk around the neighborhood on Street View, floating above yourself like a ghost; I'm doing that in a separate window now)."[46] Moments such as these synchronize the occasion, the production, and the consumption of writing; they shift readers from the external position of interpreters to that of agents in a textual process in which they, in Bruno Latour's words, "share agency with other subjects that have also lost their autonomy"[47] – with the author, the character, the computer screen, the interface.

10:04 emphasizes that experiences of shared agency are always mediated; in the above example, the computer interface is a crucial agent in the assemblage the reader participates in. When in the face of an approaching superstorm New York City is described as congealing into "one organism [...] an aerial sea monster" (a recurring image in the novel, often in the guise of an octopus), the novel underlines how this image "constitut[es] itself in relation to a threat viewable from space" (and thus depends on the mediation of satellites), and is produced by "a million media, most of them handheld".[48] The autopoietic logic of Anthropocene writing interacts with that of contemporary digital media, which also operate according to a comprehensive self-writing dynamic. In the Big Data ecology, human behavior is recorded, stored, and algorithmically processed in order to affect future behavior, which will then itself be processed in turn, etc. The upshot is that the distinction between life and its algorithmic processing has disappeared: the Internet has turned into "the greatest laboratory ever for consumer research and lead generation"[49], in which behavior provides feedback that will enable algorithms to further map and shape lives – what *Satin Island* calls "real-world R&D".[50]

In this logic, software has a performative dimension, as the real world becomes an encompassing and continuous beta test that writes, reads, and implements its own test results in real time. Orit Halpern has noted that in a condition of "ubiquitous computing", "bandwidth and life [are] inextricably correlated for both profit and survival".[51] Wendy Chun has shown how algorithms both capture and inculcate habits – they naturalize particular preferences while circumventing moments of individual deliberation: "Habits are trained algorithms, stored in involuntary memory."[52] Software is a performative process that "does what it *says*"[53]: "Software is word become action: a replacement of process with inscription that makes writing a live power by conflating force and law."[54] Because of their performative and autopoeietic operations, Big Data environments, like the Anthropocene environments from which they are inseparable, are essentially *literary* environments that perform and recursively actualize themselves in a way traditionally ascribed to literary texts.

So where does this leave human freedom? One feature of the data-saturated present is that information no longer simply translates into liberty. As Frank Pasquale writes, "[d]ata is becoming staggering in its breadth and depth, yet often the information most important to us is out of reach"[55]. Contemporary data processing has actualized and updated the aim of what Fredric Jameson influentially called "cognitive mapping" – the challenge to locate individual action within the bewildering reality of global capitalism:[56] while data processing has managed to establish ever "larger connections", these cognitive achievements have not "enabled individual subjects to understand and change the system".[57] For Wendy Chun, far from empowering individuals, "[c]onstant participation grounds surveillance. The erasure of the separation between reading and writing – reading as a writerly process – has not liberated, but rather domesticated"[58]. As Bernard Harcourt argues, there is now "[n]o need to distinguish ordinary life from the supervised correctional condition, since we will be watched, tracked, analyzed, and known at every moment of the day", as "the formerly coercive surveillance technology is now woven into the very fabric of our pleasure and fantasies".[59]

Human life is never simply the author or the reader in processes of data transmission, but is instead distributed across these processes. Orit Halpern has mapped a shift toward "an attentive and affective global information-consumer space" that requires users (who write even as they read) rather than observing subjects.[60] Users, in this constellation, are no longer discrete bodies but "composed of agglomerations of nervous stimulation; compartmentalized units of an individual's attentive, even nervous, energy and credit"; at the same time, they are *being used* by networks composed of human, nonhuman, and technological actors.[61] Big Data, then, are a crucial component in what the introduction to this volume calls "new materialist conceptualisations of shared materiality" – what it calls a materiality that "circumvent[s] the dualisms between matter and meaning or nature and culture", and instead emerges in the "dynamic interactions between physical characteristics and signifying strategies" (the introduction borrows this last phrase from Katherine Hayles).

10:04 and *Satin Island* are attentive to the challenges to both human and literary distinctiveness in these novel environments – new realities that, as these novels show, also furnish a new habitat for the novel form. Crucially, neither of these novels identifies the human, or indeed the individual subject, with the literary; for both, finding a new footing for literature instead signals an openness to a shared life that is distributed among human and nonhuman agents. While thoroughly immersed in the Anthropocene and Big Data ecologies they aim, in Wendy Chun's words, to establish a position "away from preemption and predictable yet rampant consumption toward political contestation and sustainable habituation"[62]. These novels' engagement with the present modalities of writing, we argue, constitute their ethical and political dimensions – an ethics and politics that, as the introduction to this volume has it, are situated less in texts' "referential, mimetic or didactic dimensions" than in "the transformative agency of aesthetics itself". *10:04*'s term for literature's aesthetic agency is "a proprioceptive flicker"[63] – a glitch that creates a moment of opportunity and openness from *within* the environments the literary work inhabits yet momentarily suspends. The rest of this essay shows that both novels elaborate such a minor yet ineluctable role for literature – a role that emerges through their engagement with (rather than their withdrawal from) their novel environments.

3. Parachute Writing: *Satin Island*

Satin Island is obsessed with images of hyperconnectedness and encompassing infrastructures; its first chapter finds U. at the Torino-Caselle airport – which, significantly, is a "hub-airport"[64] – bombarded by screens, vibrating phones, Skype calls, assorted noises, and involuntary memories. *Satin Island*'s world is a world where it is impossible to escape and go off the grid. As McCarthy underlines in an essay, "[t]here is no space outside this matrix, no virgin territory of pure 'aesthetics' or neutral 'reflection' on which it hasn't impacted"[65]. For U., this means that he must firmly locate himself "*inside* events and situations *as they unfolded*" – a "participation-from-within" he calls "Present-Tense Anthropology™".[66] The trademark is significant, and it signals that, in this dispensation, even "vanguard theory" is being fed "back into the corporate machine".[67]

This encompassing machine figures in the novel as the so-called "Koob-Sassen Project". Inscrutable, boring, and sprawling, the project serves as the invisible infrastructure on which contemporary life operates:[68] "Koob-Sassen involved many hook-ups, interfaces, transpositions – corporate to civic, supranational to local, analogue to digital and open to restricted and hard to soft and who knows what else."[69]

If this description of Koob-Sassen echoes the rhetoric of immateriality and cloudy weightlessness through which digital capitalism officially promotes itself, *Satin Island* consistently insists on the Project's ineluctable materiality – its status as, precisely, an infrastructure project to be compared to "poldering and draining landmasses of thousands of square miles, or cabling and connecting an entire empire"[70]. The Project, in other words, is not only an autopoietic process of self-writing and data processing, it is also a form of geological inscription: "The Project was supra-governmental, supra-national, supra-everything – and infra-too."[71] As we will see, *Satin Island* refuses to collapse the tension between the two sides of the Anthropocene scriptorium, and it locates the residual force of literature in such a refusal.

Readers of McCarthy's breakthrough novel *Remainder* will recognize this concern with the unavoidable material dimensions of human designs. In *Remainder*, "surplus matter, mess or clutter" continuously disrupts all human schemes, and attempts at transcending matter irrevocably fail.[72] While *Remainder* emphasized the inevitable victory of matter over design, *Satin Island* is a sustained effort to inhabit an Anthropocene ecology in which the mobilization of matter to some extent *works* – but not as smoothly and seamlessly as many cheerleaders of digital capitalism assume. The cover of the American edition of *Satin Island* displays struck-through genre categories: "a ~~treatise~~", "an ~~essay~~", "a ~~report~~", "a ~~confession~~", "a ~~manifesto~~"; the only label that remains is "a novel". The distinctiveness of the novel, in *Satin Island*, is not a matter of a distinctively literary format: the book is made up of numbered sections, as if it were an anthropological report, and more than one critic has remarked on its formlessness.[73] Instead, it distinguishes itself as an environment in which the imperfect articulation of data and materiality is inhabited only to be momentarily suspended. In contrast to *Remainder*, *Satin Island* is not a representative for triumphant, but inarticulate, matter[74] – a job description that hints at Latour's notion of a "Parliament of Things", in which human representatives take up the case of mute objects.[75]

In *Satin Island*, matter is not inarticulate – instead, it *writes*, and it feeds (only to resist) the fantasy that it can seamlessly be enlisted for data-processing. In an imaginary lecture, U. enthuses that the oil from the oil spill should not be brushed away, but that instead, we should be

> lowering a needle to its furrows and replaying it all, and amplifying it all the while to boot: up and up, exponentially, until from littoral to plain to mountain, land to sky and back to sea again, the destiny of every trilobite resounds.[76]

U. also hallucinates the Koob-Sassen Project as a picture of wholeness – as "hordes of people" coalescing "into one larger, more coherent pattern" that moves "towards its glorious realization, at which point *all* would become clear".[77] The novel shows that data, like the oil spill, foster the "almost sublimely reassuring" image of a "bottomless and inexhaustible torrent of giving": "*Datum est*: it is given."[78] At the same time, it underlines that this vision of infinite fungibility is an unsustainable illusion. This illusion emerges precisely when there is a glitch in the system – when U.'s computer is "afflicted by frequent bouts of buffering", which inspire visions of "hordes of bits and bytes and megabytes", of "a giant *über*-server".[79] *Satin Island* juxtaposes this fantasy of "unconditional and grace-conferring act[s] of generosity" with the sobering awareness that the buffering sign may be only that – "just a circle, spinning on […] screen, and nothing else".[80]

The novel personifies the dream to articulate matter with design through the character of Peyman, who runs the Company. Peyman, we read, connects all "scattered, half-formed notions and intuitions" to "a world of action and event, a world in which stuff might actually *happen*; connected us, that is, to our own age […]. He connected the age to itself".[81] If this illustrates the performative dimension of data processing, the error the novel diagnoses is to see this as a form of *human* agency (through its personification as Peyman), rather than as the onset of a radical recalibration of the very distinction between human and nonhuman agency. The articulation of data and geology never obeys merely manmade designs, and interferes in human life as delays, errors, and glitches: the novel is filled with delayed flights, missed meetings, cancers – "all the extraneous clutter, all the world-debris" that refuses to stop interfering.[82] Importantly, U.'s writing itself is imagined as "the damp, pulpy mass" of paper that separates "evidence-based research" on the one side from "epic art" on the other.[83] *Satin Island* suspends the opposition between the two, yet articulates them as a thoroughly material medium – as a book, as data, or as another form of geological inscription.

Satin Island reflects on this position of a fully material suspension through U.'s obsessive engagement with the widely mediated case of a parachute murder. Like the buffering sign and the oil spill, the image of the parachute combines fantasies of plenitude (flying) with intimations of radical finitude (falling). In the case of the sabotaged parachute, the crime itself cannot be accurately pinpointed (is it the moment of sabotage? Is it when the victim discovers he gets no purchase on the air around him? Or when he notices his reserve chute is not working either? Or when he hits the ground?) but is in fact distributed across Earth and sky – all places on which the crime "left [its] imprint".[84] The parachute murder, then, redefines the atmosphere and the Earth as crime scenes[85] – as media in which different agents leave their imprint. The victim's experiences of falling are, U. reasons, "mere side effects of a technical delay, a pause, an interval"; like the buffering sign or the delays besetting Skype conversations, they are merely "the hiatus created by the passage of a command down a chain".[86] *Unlike* staring at buffering signs or oil spills, skydiving consciously *inhabits* a situation of distributed agency, a vast scriptural environment that human agents co-write. If *Remainder* is more interested in the confrontation between design and matter (a confrontation the oil spill and the buffer signal emblematize), *Satin Island*'s mode of writing, like the parachute, aims to remain "*in transit*": the Project U. co-writes "has to be conceived of as in a perpetual state of passage, not arrival – not *at*, not *between*".[87] In the world of *Satin Island*, there is no nature that remains exterior to human and nonhuman agency: that outside, in the parachute image, is the "ground-target" where "the parachute stops playing its role"[88] – and where the skydiver dies. Life and writing, again, are co-extensive, and halting the process of writing – that is, living – means death.

Satin Island, for all its lack of plot and suspense, seems to move toward an illusory outside in its last chapters – only to abandon the reader with a failed epiphany, which underscores the reader's, the text's, and the author's implication in the encompassing scriptorium it taps into. U. finds himself traveling to Staten Island in New York – "the forgotten borough, the great dump"[89] collecting the continent's waste, which "seemed to resist all incorporation into any useful or productive screed".[90] Staten Island – which is mixed up in U.'s thoughts with the mysterious signifier "Satin Island" – "radiat[es] with a prospect, with an overwhelming promise, of significance" precisely because it seems a residue that has escaped the autopoietic system that has spawned it.[91] Yet the meaning of the term 'Satin Island' turns out to be prosaic at best (which allegorizes *Satin Island*'s own decidedly non-epiphanic and non-heroic operation),[92] and U. fails to take the ferry to Staten Island. The novel (almost) ends with a description of a homeless guy at the ferry terminal, who is holding the receiver of a payphone "making no attempt to listen or to talk into it"[93]. U. wonders whether the payphone even works. Meeting the eyes of the homeless guy, U. disconnects from him only to plug "back into the city"[94] and return to the scriptorium he has been co-writing.

Near the end of the novel, U. entertains different strategies for undermining the system from within – by providing faulty data, or by conceiving of "Present-Tense Anthropology™" as "an armed resistance movement".[95] U.'s girlfriend reminds him that such a conception of agency is fatally anthropocentric, reflecting an all too masculine desire "to be the hero in the film who runs away in slo-mo from the villain's factory that he's just mined"[96]. In the Anthropocene scriptorium, there are no human heroes, and no one is running away, least of all from the factory – the scriptorium where we labor, live, write. Still, there is slo-mo: U.'s girlfriend notes there is no need for mining the factory, as "the explosion's taking place already [...] it's always been taking place. You just didn't notice"[97]. What makes *Satin Island* a novel rather than a manifesto, an essay, or a report, is its effort to make visible the entangled agencies that slowly exhaust even as they encompass the planet. While it does not simply reject or deflate fantasies of immateriality and delusions of human exceptionalism (as *Remainder* does), it shows how these illusions are caught up in crisscrossing and recursive dynamics that render them as groundless as they are material.

4. Proprioceptive Flickers: *10:04*

If *Satin Island* signals the friction between data and matter through buffering, glitches, and delays, *10:04* registers discontinuities in the Anthropocene scriptorium through occasional flickers. Flickering invariably indicates moments of transition – between absence and presence[98], between life and death[99], "between temporalities"[100], between fiction and nonfiction[101], or "across genres"[102]. As in *Satin Island*, indeterminate moments of transition generate new intensities and potentialities – when, for instance, the powers of Big Data fall short and "[a]nother historic storm […] failed to arrive, as though we lived outside of history or were falling out of time"[103]. The failure of a preprogrammed future to materialize shifts attention to the attempt to find "a way to inhabit the present"[104], and to test "what possibilities of feeling [are] opened up in the present tense of reading"[105]. Crucially, *10:04* sees works of art and literature, and therefore also itself, as sites where such frictions and flickers are generated. They are sites, moreover, that are written on and across the borders between fiction and autobiography, in a domain where "the distinction between fiction and nonfiction [does]n't obtain"[106]. In this domain, writing is "neither fiction nor nonfiction"[107], as *10:04* operates "on the very edge of fiction"[108], and thus in a place where flickers can occur.

10:04 situates itself in a world saturated by media and is obsessed with its geological agency, which appears in the novel through two major black-outs, the prospect of New York's future "underwater"[109], a fascination with dinosaurs, and evocations of "both galactic space and geological time"[110]. Like *Satin Island*, then, it has no illusions about the possibility of a critical position *outside* of the Anthropocene scriptorium; instead, it generates what it calls "proprioceptive flicker[s]" from *within* the scriptorium. *10:04* repeatedly imagines its own position in that scriptorium as a technology for registering and storing data – as a registration machine that, unlike traditional novels, does not immediately convert data into literary significance. The novel's careful, hyper-self-conscious, and almost pedantic notation of events, thoughts, and stimuli is part of an effort to "detect local texture variations", without "integrat[ing] that information into a larger picture".[111] This mode of notation is a strategy to "resist the will to integration"[112] and to decline "*pareidolia*" – the process "when the brain arranges random stimuli into a significant image or sound".[113] *10:04*'s storage work suspends such meaningful articulation, and instead insists on the continuities between writing, reading, and living as so many forms of inscription.

As in *Satin Island*, the ethics and politics of *10:04*'s archival work emerge in encounters with assemblages that are neither fully human nor resolutely natural, but rather partly manmade environments. On one of his walks through New York, the narrator becomes intensely aware of the infrastructure surrounding him, "of the delicacy of the bridges and tunnels spanning it"; this intensity is like "a cortical reorganization", and it generates "a proprioceptive flicker in advance of the communal body".[114]

This last phrase recurs later in the novel through another confrontation with built space: the city afflicts the narrator as "[b]undled debt, trace amounts of antidepressants in the municipal water, the vast arterial network of traffic, changing weather patterns of increasing severity". This is an assemblage of human and nonhuman, technological and computational agents that together serve as "the material signature" of "a collective person who didn't yet exist, a still-uninhabited second person plural" to whom *10:04* is addressed.[115]

10:04's emphasis on images of infrastructure shows that the communal body that its archival work intimates will not be a merely human one.[116] So how is this imagined collectivity different from the data amassed by algorithmic processes – the archival work with which the novel competes? The novel's motto gives a clue to this difference. It presents a passage from the work of Walter Benjamin, which offers a particular understanding of messianism. According to this understanding, the messiah will not alter the world, but merely leave it as he finds it: "everything there will be just as it is here [...]. Everything will be as it is now, just a little different"[117]. The novel links this minor, imperceptible difference – in which everything is "a little changed, a little charged"[118] – to the full availability of the past, and thus to the archiving work in which the novel engages. In another (unacknowledged) borrowing from Benjamin, *10:04* images a future "where everything is the same but a little different because the past will be citable in all of its moments"[119]. The difference between literary data storage and Big Data, then, is that this future database will also contain potentialities and virtualities that were never actualized; it will include "those [moments] that from our present present happened but never occurred"[120]. Literature, on this account, is a technology that confronts algorithmic writing with its exclusive focus on actualities and on actual inscriptions; it borrows Big Data's ambition to store and collect everything, but it does so by *also* including potentialities that were never actualized. It is the friction between digital archives and *10:04*'s archiving of virtualities that digital archives cannot contain: that generate the flickers that in turn intimate a coming "communal body", a "still-uninhabited second person plural".[121]

So, what does this archiving of potentiality have to do with a future second person plural, with a 'you'? How, in fact, do databases or their literary alternatives even address a 'you'? Here, the insight that writing, in the Anthropocene scriptorium, is a performative act becomes helpful.

Wendy Chun has shown that, unlike mass media that carved out a 'we' and a 'they', social media – in many ways the interface of Big Data – always produce a 'you'; in a situation in which "[t]he media have imploded in the social", 'you' always remains distinguishable, trackable, captured, and updated.[122] Big Data and social media are relentlessly individualizing as well as consistently tracking individual's connections to groups, patterns, habits.[123] In this dominant logic, the second person is "never singular, but singular-plural"[124]. *10:04*'s address to a second person plural engages this dominant logic, while bending it to a less constraining "communal body"; its second person plural is "still-uninhabited" – it is the effect of a literary and archival logic that refuses to exhaust the future 'you'.[125] By enlisting reader, text, media, environment, and writer in collaborative processes of inscription, *10:04* addresses a virtual community; in Chun's words, it "inhabit[s] [...] the singular plural that is the you" in order to "produce a 'we' that does not flatten or align identity, but rather [...] exposes that singularity is fundamentally plural".[126] This demonstrates the particular agency of literature in Anthropocene and Big Data ecologies; it invites us to think of literature as a nonhuman agent that mediates and generates new modes of association between other agents – human as well as nonhuman, organic as well as technological.

When *10:04* ends with the words "I am looking back at the totaled city in the second person plural"[127], it underlines that the urban assemblage it has generated is a co-creation of different agents. Chun emphasizes that effective strategies for affirming community in Big Data environments do not (impossibly) withdraw into an illusory privacy, but rather aim for "community through exposure"[128] – the exposure, for instance, of an awkwardly oversharing narrator who is (almost) the novel's author, but also that of a reader who participates in the novel's operation. Rachel Sagner Buurma and Laura Heffernan have noted how "novels of commission" (their term for novels that are organized around commissioned but unwritten works of literature) like Lerner's shift from product (the commissioned novel that never gets unwritten) to procedure, and also from claims of representativeness to enactments of relation.[129] In this way, *10:04* bends Big Data's logic of prediction and surveillance to the intimation of "a second person plural on the perennial verge of existence"[130]. It "embrace[s] the fundamentally nonpersonal nature of our networked communications"[131] in order to reimagine it as a conduit for community – the community it enacts in the present of writing, living, and reading.

In an environment in which human action has become a form of writing, and in which writing has also become a feature of nonhuman agents, the positions of both human life and literature need to be reimagined. It may seem, as Christina Lupton has remarked, that machines and nature are now able "to 'speak' to themselves and to each other through networks and systems that bypass human cognition" – a condition of "high technology" in which, in words she quotes from Friedrich Kittler, "literature has nothing more to say", but just becomes an effect of media.[132] *10:04* and *Satin Island* both imagine literary activity as thoroughly immersed in the networks and systems through which geological agency and data operations are articulated in the Anthropocene; they both see literature as a place where the glitches, delays, and frictions in these networks and systems – hiccups that dominant discourses tend to neglect – can be registered. For both these novels, literature is decidedly *not* a placeholder for human distinctiveness, but instead an intimation of an assemblage in which agency is distributed across human and nonhuman agents. If it alters the ways different agents relate to one another through a recalibration of writing, it also calls on readers to develop new ways to understand the relation between writing and reading.

Notes

[1] McCarthy (2015a:63).
[2] *Ibid.*, 126.
[3] *Ibid.*, 133-134.
[4] McCarthy (2015b).
[5] McCarthy (2015a:118).
[6] *Ibid.*, 116.
[7] *Ibid.*, 98.
[8] Seltzer (2016:6).
[9] McCarthy (2015a:134).
[10] Seltzer (2016:143).

[11] Marshall (2015:25).
[12] Seltzer (2016:5).
[13] Cf. McCarthy (2015b:n.pag).
[14] Cf. Buell (2005).
[15] Derrida (1976:158).
[16] Peters (2015:26-27); Pasquale (2015:69).
[17] McCarthy (2015a:149).
[18] Blanchot (1995:313).
[19] de Certeau (1984:150).
[20] *Ibid.*
[21] *Ibid.*, 173-174.
[22] Chun (2016a:94).
[23] Trexler (2015:26).
[24] *Ibid.*, 236.
[25] Clark (2015:183-184).
[26] *Ibid.*, 187.
[27] Cf. Chakrabarty (2012:2); Steffen, et al. (2011:843).
[28] Peters (2015:2).
[29] Mirzoeff (2015:219); cf. Edwards (2010).
[30] Parikka (2015:111-113).
[31] Woods (2014:134).
[32] Culler (2000); Miller (2002); Bennett (2009:262-269).
[33] Alter (1975); Hutcheon (1980).
[34] Boes (2016:97).
[35] Peters (2015:4).
[36] Boes (2016:107).
[37] *Ibid.*, 107, 98.
[38] Boes and Marshall (2014:64).
[39] Boes (2016:107).
[40] Boes and Marshall (2014:64).
[41] Lerner (2014).
[42] *Ibid.*, 109.
[43] *Ibid.*, 212.
[44] *Ibid.*, 166.
[45] *Ibid.*, 93.
[46] *Ibid.*, 163.
[47] Latour (2014:5); italics in original removed.
[48] Lerner (2014:17).
[49] O'Neil (2016:75).
[50] McCarthy (2015a:52).
[51] Halpern (2015:4).
[52] Chun (2016a:81).

[53] *Ibid.*, 82.
[54] *Ibid.*
[55] Pasquale (2015:191).
[56] Jameson (1990:51-54).
[57] Chun (2016a:40).
[58] Chun (2016b:367).
[59] Harcourt (2015:21).
[60] Halpern (2015:239).
[61] *Ibid.*, 249.
[62] Chun (2016b:363).
[63] Lerner (2014:28).
[64] McCarthy (2015a:4).
[65] McCarthy (2015b:n. pag).
[66] McCarthy (2015a:78).
[67] *Ibid.*, 33.
[68] Hageman (2016). "Infrastructure and the Anthropocene in Tom McCarthy's *Satin Island*." *Alluvium* 30 Oct. 2016: n. pag. Web. 7 December 2016.
[69] McCarthy (2015a:13-14).
[70] *Ibid.*, 29.
[71] *Ibid.*, 135.
[72] McCarthy (2006:159).
[73] Ammah-Tagoe (2016). "Letters from 'The Contemporary': Letter 3." *Post45* 4 Nov. 2016: n. pag. Web. 7 December 2016; Miller, Christopher Patrick (2016). "Letters from 'The Contemporary': Letter 1." *Post45* 1 Nov. 2016: n.pag. Web. 7 December 2016.
[74] Cf. Vermeulen (2012).
[75] Latour (1993:142-145).
[76] McCarthy (2015a), 118. Given repeated references to the work of Rainer Maria Rilke in McCarthy's interviews, this image likely riffs on Rilke's well-known thought experiment with the "primal sound" generated by lowering a needle to a human skull: "What if one changed the needle and directed it on its return journey along a tracing which was not derived from the graphic translation of sound but existed of itself naturally – well, to put it plainly, along the coronal suture, for example A sound would necessarily result, a series of sounds, music…". Rilke, Rainer Maria (2001). "Primal Sound." *The Book of Music and Nature: An Anthology of Sounds, Words, Thoughts*. Ed. David Rothenberg and Marta Ulvaeus. Middletown: Wesleyan University Press, 22. This fantasy also recalls archaeoacoustic attempts to recreate ancient sounds from marks and grooves inscribed in archeological finds – a process in which rocks and other materials are treated as data repositories (although, given these endeavours' lack of success, such repositories, in an archaeoacoustic sense, remain unreadable).
[77] McCarthy (2015a:69).

[78] *Ibid.*, 73.
[79] *Ibid.*
[80] *Ibid.*, 73-74.
[81] *Ibid.*, 44-45.
[82] *Ibid.*, 97.
[83] *Ibid.*, 125.
[84] *Ibid.*, 40.
[85] *Ibid.*, 41.
[86] *Ibid.*, 60.
[87] *Ibid.*, 87.
[88] *Ibid.*
[89] *Ibid.*, 144.
[90] *Ibid.*, 146.
[91] *Ibid.*, 178.
[92] *Ibid.*, 180.
[93] *Ibid.*, 189.
[94] *Ibid.*
[95] *Ibid.*, 137.
[96] *Ibid.*, 140.
[97] *Ibid.*, 140.
[98] Lerner (2014:15,136,201).
[99] *Ibid.*, 238.
[100] *Ibid.*, 21, 67.
[101] *Ibid.*, 194.
[102] *Ibid.*, 239.
[103] *Ibid.*, 230.
[104] *Ibid.*, 137.
[105] *Ibid.*, 171.
[106] *Ibid.*
[107] *Ibid.*, 194.
[108] *Ibid.*, 237.
[109] *Ibid.*, 40.
[110] *Ibid.*, 11.
[111] *Ibid.*, 6-7.
[112] *Ibid.*, 53.
[113] *Ibid.*, 69; italics in original.
[114] *Ibid.*, 28.
[115] *Ibid.*, 108.
[116] Elsewhere, one of us has shown that *10:04* neutralizes a humanist poetics of the person in order to open up a "transpersonal" dimension of connectedness. Cf. Vermeulen, Pieter (2016). "How Should a Person Be (Transpersonal)? Lerner,

Ben, Roberto Esposito, and the Biopolitics of the Future." *Political Theory* 7 Sept. 2016: n. pag. Online first. Web. 7 December 2016.
[117] Lerner (2014: epigraph).
[118] *Ibid.*, 18.
[119] *Ibid.*, 109.
[120] *Ibid.*
[121] *Ibid.*, 28 and 108.
[122] Chun (2016a:22-23).
[123] *Ibid.*, 120.
[124] Chun (2016b:363).
[125] Lerner (2014:28 and 108).
[126] Chun (2016b:379).
[127] Lerner (2014:240).
[128] Chun (2016b:379).
[129] Buurma and Heffernan. (2014:89)
[130] Lerner (2014:157).
[131] Chun (2016a:13).
[132] Lupton (2016:504).

Works Cited

Alter, Robert (1975). *Partial Magic: The Novel as a Self-Conscious Genre*. Berkeley: University of California Press.

Ammah-Tagoe, Aku (2016). "Letters from 'The Contemporary': Letter 3." *Post45* 4 Nov. 2016. Web. 7 December 2016.

Bennett, Andrew, and Nicholas Royle (2009). *An Introduction to Literature, Criticism and Theory*. 4th ed. London: Routledge.

Blanchot, Maurice (1995). *The Work of Fire*. Stanford: Stanford University Press.

Boes, Tobias (2016). "Reading the Book of the World: Epic Representation in the Age of Our Geophysical Agency." *Novel* 49.1, 95-114.

Boes, Tobias, and Kate Marshall (2014). "Writing the Anthropocene." *Minnesota Review* 83, 60-72.

Buell, Lawrence (2005). *The Future of Environmental Criticism: Environmental Crisis and Literary Imagination*. Malden: Blackwell.

Buurma, Rachel Sagner, and Laura Heffernan (2014). "Notation after 'The Reality Effect': Remaking Reference with Roland Barthes and Sheila Heti." *Representations* 152, 80-102.

Chakrabarty, Dipesh (2012). "Postcolonial Studies and the Challenge of Climate Change." *New Literary History* 43.1, 1-18.

Chun, Wendy Hui Kyong (2016a). *Updating to Remain the Same: Habitual New Media*. Cambridge, MA: MIT Press.

--- (2016b). "Big Data as Drama." *ELH* 83.2, 363-382.

Clark, Timothy (2015). *Ecocriticism on the Edge: The Anthropocene as a Threshold Concept*. London: Bloomsbury.

Culler, Jonathan (2000). "Philosophy and Literature: The Fortunes of the Performative." *Poetics Today* 21.3, 503-519.

de Certeau, Michel (1984). *The Practice of Everyday Life*. Berkeley: University of California Press.

Derrida, Jacques (1976). *Of Grammatology*. Baltimore: Johns Hopkins University Press.

Edwards, Paul (2010). *A Vast Machine: Computer Models, Climate Data, and the Politics of Global Warming*. Cambridge, MA: MIT Press.

Hageman, Andy (2016). "Infrastructure and the Anthropocene in Tom McCarthy's *Satin Island*." *Alluvium* 30 Oct. 2016. Web. 7 December 2016.

Halpern, Orit (2015). *Beautiful Data: A History of Vision and Reason since 1945*. Durham: Duke University Press.

Harcourt, Bernard (2015). *Exposed: Desire and Disobedience in the Digital Age*. Cambridge, MA: Harvard University Press.

Hutcheon, Linda (1980). *Narcissistic Narrative: The Metafictional Paradox*. New York: Methuen.

Jameson, Fredric (1990). *Postmodernism, or, The Cultural Logic of Late Capitalism*. Durham: Duke University Press.

Latour, Bruno (1993). *We Have Never Been Modern*. Cambridge, MA: Harvard University Press.

--- (2014). "Agency at the Time of the Anthropocene." *New Literary History* 45.1, 1-18.

Lerner, Ben (2014). *10:04*. London: Granta.

Lupton, Christina (2016). "The Novel as The Book's Future Anterior: Tom McCarthy's *Remainder* and Ali Smith's *The Accidental*." *Novel* 49.3, 504-518.

Marshall, Kate (2015). "What Are the Novels of the Anthropocene? American Fiction in Geological Time." *American Literary History* 27.3, 523-538.

McCarthy, Tom (2006). *Remainder*. London: Alma Books.

--- (2015a). *Satin Island*. New York: Knopf.

--- (2015b). "The Death of Writing: If James Joyce Were Alive Today He'd Be Working for Google." *The Guardian* 7 Mar. 2015, Web. 7 December 2016.

Miller, Christopher Patrick (2016). "Letters from 'The Contemporary': Letter 1." *Post45* 1 Nov. 2016. Web. 7 December 2016.

Miller, Joseph Hillis (2002). *Speech Acts in Literature*. Stanford: Stanford University Press.

Mirzoeff, Nicholas (2015). *How to See the World*. London: Pelican Books.
O'Neil, Cathy (2016). *Weapons of Math Destruction: How Big Data Increases Inequality and Threatens Democracy*. New York: Crown.
Parikka, Jussi (2015). *A Geology of Media*. Minneapolis: University of Minnesota Press.
Pasquale, Frank (2015). *The Black Box Society: The Secret Algorithms That Control Money and Information*. Cambridge, MA: Harvard University Press.
Peters, John Durham (2015). *The Marvelous Clouds: Toward a Philosophy of Elemental Media*. Chicago: University of Chicago Press.
Rilke, Rainer Maria (2001). "Primal Sound." *The Book of Music and Nature: An Anthology of Sounds, Words, Thoughts*. Ed. David Rothenberg and Marta Ulvaeus. Middletown: Wesleyan University Press, 21-24.
Seltzer, Mark (2016). *The Official World*. Durham: Duke University Press.
Steffen W., et al. (2011). "The Anthropocene: Conceptual and Historical Perspectives." *Philosophical Transactions of the Royal Society A* 369, 842-867.
Trexler, Adam (2015). *Anthropocene Fictions: The Novel in a Time of Climate Change*. Charlottesville: University of Virginia Press.
Vermeulen, Pieter (2012). "The Critique of Trauma and the Afterlife of the Novel in Tom McCarthy's *Remainder*." *Modern Fiction Studies* 58.3, 549-568.
--- (2016). "How Should a Person Be (Transpersonal)? Ben Lerner, Roberto Esposito, and the Biopolitics of the Future." *Political Theory* 7 September 2016. Web. 7 December 2016.
Woods, Derek (2014). "Scale Critique for the Anthropocene." *Minnesota Review* 83, 133-142.

Rainer Emig (Mainz)

"Because I am a man, and I have acid hands": Environment, Ethics and Masculinity in Contemporary Welsh Poetry in English

1. Introduction: The Feminisation of Nature and Its Blind Spots

Environmental approaches in literature and the arts often associate nature and femininity. Masculinity is relegated to the realm of civilization and particularly to technology – and therefore often placed in opposition to nature and the environment. This is, of course, a short-sighted view and, more problematically, one that reproduces established clichés, both of gender and nature. The traditional patriarchal model associates femininity with nurturing and protecting, while masculinity is generally seen as active and outgoing – and therefore often as aggressive and even destructive. While traditional feminism, such as that of Mary Wollstonecraft's famous *Vindication of the Rights of Woman* (1792), was still happy to embrace such a view of the world, modern feminism has been critical of it.[1] Gender Studies have gone further and propose to see femininity and masculinity as mutually dependent constructions, while its offshoot, Queer Theory, challenges all normative views of reality and tries to undermine them with subversive gestures and projects that expose what is viewed as essential and unchanging as historical and biased.

In this respect, it is noteworthy that ecocriticism, itself a fairly recent theoretical development in Literary and Cultural Studies, has, in many of its ideas, gone back behind the claims of modern feminism and Gender Studies. Its understandable aim to re-evaluate nature and, consequently, to problematize the achievements of civilization and technology, lead to several impasses, two of which are connected to what new approaches to ecocriticism describe as entanglements and older ones viewed as problematic binaries: feminine against masculine and nature against civilization. Cheryll Glotfelty acknowledges this unwittingly in the

"Introduction" to the immensely influential *Ecocriticism Reader* that she co-edited with Harold Fromm. In it, she proposes to view the development of ecocriticism analogously to that of modern feminism as outlined by Elaine Showalter:

> The first stage in feminist criticism, the 'images of women' stage, is concerned with representations, concentrating on how women are portrayed in canonical literature. These studies contribute to the vital process of consciousness raising by exposing sexist stereotypes – witches, bitches, broads, and spinsters – and by locating absences, questioning the purported universality and even the aesthetic value of literature that distorts or ignores altogether the experience of half of the human race. Analogous efforts in ecocriticism study how nature is represented in literature. Again, consciousness raising results when stereotypes are identified – Eden, Arcadia, virgin land, miasmal swamp, savage wilderness – and when absences are noticed: where is the natural world in this text? But nature per se is not the only focus of ecocritical studies of representation. Other topics include the frontier, animals, cities, specific geographical regions, rivers, mountains, deserts, Indians, technology, garbage, and the body.
>
> Showalter's second stage in feminist criticism, the women's literary tradition stage, likewise serves the important function of consciousness raising as it rediscovers, reissues, and reconsiders literature by women. In ecocriticism, similar efforts are being made to recuperate the hitherto neglected genre of nature writing […] [2]

By trying to get feminism (and by extension ecocriticism) to redress a critical position "that distorts or ignores altogether the experience of half of the human race", they themselves are in danger of doing exactly that – by not leaving space for the critical discussion of masculinity. It might feature implicitly (in "frontier", "cities", "technology", perhaps also "garbage"), but is not addressed explicitly. In fact, in Glotfelty's summary at the end of the above quotation, nature writing has become the equivalent of feminist criticism – and thus narrowed down to one side of the traditional gender binary.

When Glotfelty discusses a third phase in feminism (and thus ecocriticism), masculinity features briefly:

> The third stage that Showalter identifies in feminist criticism is the theoretical phase, which is far reaching and complex, drawing on a wide range of theories to raise fundamental questions about the symbolic construction of gender and sexuality within literary discourse. Analogous work in ecocriticism includes examining the symbolic construction of species. How has literary discourse defined the human? Such a critique questions the dualisms prevalent in Western thought, dualisms that separate meaning from matter, sever mind from body, divide men from women, and wrench humanity from nature.[3]

But just as one welcomes a broader perspective, the door closes again in the very next sentence: "A related endeavor is being carried out under the hybrid label 'ecofeminism,' a theoretical discourse whose theme is the link between the oppression of women and the domination of nature." Glotfelty and Fromm's *Ecocriticism Reader* features examples of ecofeminism in Annette Kolodny's essay "Unearthing Herstory: An Introduction" and Vera L. Norwood's "Heroines of Nature: Four Women Respond to the American Landscape".[4] Later examples of ecofeminism often combine their approach with a postcolonial one. A typical example is Swarnalatha Rangarajan, "Women Writing Nature in the Global South: New Forest Texts from Fractured Indian Forests".[5] Investigations that focus on masculinity as part of ecocriticism or cultural economy, however, have been noticeably rare.

The present essay does not wish to set an 'ecomasculinism' against ecofeminism.[6] Rather it wishes to acknowledge that masculinity – as much as femininity – is a construction, and one that is in itself as insubstantial and without essence as its binary opposite. This, however, does not mean that it is powerless. On the contrary, as Stuart Hall reminds us,

> cultural meanings are not only 'in the head'. They organize and regulate social practices, influence our conduct and consequently have real, practical effects. The emphasis on cultural practices is important. It is participants in a culture who give meaning to people, objects and events.[7]

The participants in the culture to be examined in the present chapter are men and women. It will assess the mutual construction of their roles, but also their entanglement, an entanglement that is, of course, as metaphoric as many of the images of the analysed poetic texts. The analysis will also examine the entanglement of the participants and protagonists and their roles with 'nature'. The inverted commas imply that nature, too, cannot simply be taken to be a given, an already existing undisputable fact. As the alternative use of 'environment' in ecocriticism signals, concepts as 'nature' and 'environment' are created by human beings, and these human beings remain the origin and also the orientation of the concepts they design. This problem of ecocriticism is called 'anthropocentrism', the fact that in human thinking the human being remains firmly in the centre. This is true even when humans attempt to overcome this centrality, when they want 'nature to speak for itself'. Which nature is meant to speak here, and in whose language? A nature following human definitions, is the answer, and in signs that humans can understand. Moreover, nature and environment are complex and partly contradictory terms, one only has to think of 'human nature' (is it inside or outside all other 'nature'?) or 'urban environment' ('natural' or not?).

This complexity does not make ecocriticism obsolete. Yet it adds to the already complicated investigation a further difficulty. If, in keeping with the theme of the present collection of essays, ethics are meant to be in the focus of the debate, these ethics as patterns or systems of right and wrong need to be erected between humans, between human cultures' models of gender, and between human ideas about themselves and human ideas about a supposed Other: nature. Once again, a paradox raises its head here: of course, nature is and is not Other to humans. It may be the opposite of human civilization and technology (although many features of the two are borrowed from what we call nature), yet few humans would regard themselves as entirely 'unnatural'. Our bodies and their functions, desires, ultimately also their material fragility and transience are reminders of the artificiality of the human-versus-nature divide. Its simplistic overcoming in the idea of 'human nature', however, is no less problematic. The term is either tautological (if humans are natural anyway) or oxymoronic (if humanity and nature are opposed). Yet it is tellingly employed exactly when we wish to have our cake (the essential 'naturalness' of some ideas or supposed 'facts') and eat it too – in the shape of appropriating these supposed facts for historically very specific reasons – as the empowerment of some factions of our culture.

Recent attempts at a so-called posthumanist ecocriticism have argued for a radical re-imagination of this conundrum. Thus, Iovino claims that

> these boundaries, especially those between human and nonhuman, are not only shifting but also porous; based on the – biological, cultural, structural – combinations of agencies flowing from, through, and alongside the human, the posthuman discloses a dimension in which 'we' and 'they' are caught together in an anthropological dance whose choreography follows patterns of irredeemable hybridization and stubborn entanglement.[8]

Serpil Oppermann appears to comment on Iovino's definition when she writes,

> In this ecocritical perspective, whether elemental, biological, geological, climatic, or technological, the world's manifold agencies are always deeply interlaced with human mindscapes, reflexivity, and imagination.[9]

In doing so, she also pinpoints some of the conceptual weaknesses of this new posthumanist ecocritical approach: despites its professed interest in materiality and its appropriation of both biology and technology, it relies largely on metaphoricity for its claims. When flows become "an anthropological dance", it is already squeezed into patterns that are also anthropocentric, as the term further choreography emphasises. Oppermann is very clear on this when she ultimately performs a linking back of theoretisation to the Romantic imagination. Jane Bennett, whose treatise *Vibrant Matter: A Political Ecology of Things* is an important source for this posthumanist ecocriticism, also identifies the problem in terms that were addressed above:

> What method could possibly be appropriate for the task of speaking a word for vibrant matter? How to describe without thereby erasing the independence of things? How to acknowledge the obscure but ubiquitous intensity of impersonal affect?[10]

The present essay intends to put some flesh on the bones of the issues outlined in such abstract shape above. It will look at a specific form of interaction between humans and between humans and the non-human, here nature, namely the latter's poetic representation. After what has just been stated about recent posthumanist trends in ecocriticism, this might not appear entirely off-target. If gender relations are a construction, in the broadest sense an ideology, and if our understanding of nature and the ethics of dealing with this nature are also concepts that form part of entangled ideologies, it makes sense to look at imaginary models inside which these relationships are enacted. Psychoanalysis would claim that similar things are observable in dreams, where the censorship of our culturally shaped super-ego is temporarily suspended. Freud eventually links creative activity and day-dreaming.[11] Louis Althusser, the great Marxist theorizer of ideology, ultimately claims with regard to ideology that

> it is not their real conditions of existence, their real world, that 'men' 'represent to themselves' in ideology, but above all it is their relation to those conditions of existence which is represented to them there. It is this relation which is at the centre of every ideological, i.e. imaginary, representation of the real world. It is this 'cause' which has to explain the imaginary distortion of the ideological representation of the real world.[12]

The distorted world of the poem is thus a playing field in which imaginary representations of the real world, but also imaginary constructions of possible alternative worlds are attempted. Poetic representations hint at how human beings in their unpoetic reality conceive their reality to be – and how they not only make sense of it, but also fashion, change, and sometimes destroy it (in imaginary and non-imaginary ways) – with effects both on other humans and that which they call nature.

2. The Celtic Fringe as a Popular Field of Projections

Choosing texts by two poets from Wales, Owen Sheers and Meirion Jordan, for the inquiry of the present chapter serves a double purpose. On the one hand, as was stated at the opening of the argument, it is meant to counteract the frequent impression that 'nature' and environmental themes in art and literature 'naturally' belong to women.[13] A brief look at the origins of ecocriticism in Romanticism will redress this mistake, for although the English Romantics were strongly influenced by successful women writers of their time, such as Charlotte Smith for poetry, Joanna Baillie for drama, and Ann Radcliffe for prose, it was male figures such as the first-generation Romantics William Wordsworth and Samuel Taylor Coleridge who set the tone for the Romantic interplay of nature

and human subjectivity and whose 'Romantic ideology' (to borrow the words of the critic Jerome McGann) has continued to shape us.[14] Ecocriticism also owes much of its early structures to American Romantics, especially Henry David Thoreau, whose *Walden; or, Life in the Woods* of 1854 has remained a foundational text for those seeking to rediscover 'nature' as a remedy against the ills of civilization.[15] Thus, masculinity in literature is, from the start, entangled with ecocriticism.
The so-called Celtic Fringe, which, with reference to the British Isles means Ireland, Scotland and Wales, also owes its popularity to the Romantics. While England was becoming increasingly industrialized by the end of the eighteenth and the beginning of the nineteenth century, Ireland, Scotland and Wales largely remained a backwater (with the exception of the iron and coal mines of South Wales). It was not merely this 'unfallen' state that attracted artists and writers looking for an unspoiled counterpart to modern life, but also the fictions and myths surrounding them. It is exactly the imagined separateness, and more than that, the not so imaginary historical role as victims of English oppression, that makes the Celtic fringe interesting for the analysis of the present chapter. Victimhood is again commonly a state associated both with femininity and, in the view of many ecocritics, with nature. Once again, this harks back to highly problematic ideological images, such as that of the Scottish *bean nighe* and the Irish *bean sídhe* (Anglicised as 'banshee'), supernatural women dressed in green who wash the blood of the fallen or those about to die in battle in streams. Femininity is coupled with nature (in the colour green and the location at streams) to produce a strong national symbol construed in terms of possession, mastery and control, whose origins are certainly historical – in the many occasions for such activities in Scottish or Irish history.

In terms of poetic fashions, Scotland produced its national poet Robert Burns, whose *Poems Chiefly in the Scottish Dialect* (1786) helped as much to popularise rural Scotland in the public's imagination as did Thomas Moore's *Irish Melodies* (1808-1834) for Ireland.[16] Wales had to wait a little longer for the English Victorian gentleman-rambler George Borrow to publish *Wild Wales: Its People, Language and Scenery* in 1862.[17] It was partly this belatedness, this always coming last – not only in the imagination of the English, but also in the context of Britain's Celtic fringe nations – that prompted the present chapter to look at Welsh rather than Scottish or Irish poetry. Another reason is that many female poets in

Wales, Gillian Clarke being the foremost example, have already achieved international reputations – as well as also being strongly associated with nature writing.[18]

In choosing two very different male poets from Wales who both make nature their theme, the present essay intends to correct this imbalance. It also aims at tackling in one assessment three different ethical issues: the relation of masculinity and femininity, or men and women as depicted in the fictional universes of the respective poems; the relation of human beings and nature in the texts; and the implicit issue of marginality – of location as well as gender and its perspectives.

3. Two Male Welsh Poets Writing (about) Nature

Owen Sheers is an unusual poet who does not conform to the cliché of withdrawn recluse occasionally issuing a new volume of poems. Sheers is very much a media person. He is the author of novels, plays and a film script as well as several volumes of poetry, many of which won awards, but he has also worked as a television presenter. Born in 1974 in the Fiji Islands, he grew up in Abergavenny in South East Wales, and, after a stint in London, has now relocated there again. Much of his work is influenced by rural Wales, although his themes also embrace war and industrialisation. In 2011 Owen Sheers, himself a keen rugby player, became the first Artist in Residence for the Welsh Rugby Union.[19]

But it is not merely the tantalising biographical mixture that makes Sheers a good candidate for an ecocritical and gendered analysis of ethics in Welsh writing, but his writing itself. In the volume *Skirrid Hill* of 2005 (named after a mountain near his home), there are several poems depicting a particularly gendered interaction with nature. "The Farrier", although opening realistically with a depiction of the blacksmith of the title ("Blessing himself with his apron, / the leather black and tan of a rain-beaten bay"), soon drifts into more complicated territory.[20] Already the unspectacular opening contains complex symbolisms and a shift between nature and civilization. The blessing of the poem's opening is of course a religious gesture, only here tied to a sign of the smith's craft – and thus to work rather than faith. Celtic mythology attaches great importance to smiths. The very town of Abergavenny, where Sheers grew up, is supposedly named after the Old Welsh *Gobannia*, which translates as "river of the blacksmiths".

Another loaded symbolism rests in the black and tan colouring of the leather, "Black and Tans" being the nickname of Irish paramilitaries, the Royal Irish Constabulary Special Reserve, whose official function was to fight the IRA, but who ended up terrorising parts of the Irish population. Into the seemingly idyllic image of a rural scene enters the threat of violence. It does so also through the apron, for the leather is that of a rain-beaten bay, a chestnut coloured horse. One horse has already been sacrificed before the action of the poem even begins, before another one ("the mare") is "led from the field to the yard" in the second stanza:

> For the mare to be led from the field to the yard,
> the smoke slow-turning from his mouth,
> and the wind twisting his sideburns in its fingers.
>
> She smells him as he passes, woodbine, metal and hoof,
> careful not to look her in the eye as he runs his hand
> the length of her neck, checking for dust on a lintel.[21]

The poem's most significant shift occurs in the third stanza, when the perspective so suddenly shifts to the female horse that an initial reading might suspect the beginning of a love poem: "She smells him as he passes, woodbine, metal and hoof". Horses, like most other animals, identify other creatures by their smell, but here the smell is culturally encoded. The woodbine is hardly the fragrant flower, but much rather the cheap cigarette. And how would a horse know the smell of hot metal and burned hoof – unless of course it was part of the horse's existence on a farm?

The poem, it quickly turns out, is not about a human taking possession of a natural being, a horse, but about a careful, almost tender, interaction between two beings, an interaction that has to be careful because it could easily turn into violence – a violence that can be exerted by the human as well as the heavy horse. Here, one can find what ecocriticism is concerned with; the transformation of hierarchical relations between human beings and the nonhuman into more equal ones. Thus the unnamed protagonist is "careful not to look her in the eye", folds "her leg with one arm, he leans into her flank / like a man putting his shoulder to a knackered car".[22] Lest the romanticism (here in lower-case, since it merely plays with conventions of love) become too dominant, a machine image, the car, is introduced. And yet the potential eroticism does not disappear, perhaps also because many men treat cars like love objects. Indeed, the description of checking the hoof before reshodding it is that of "a romantic lead dropping to the lips of his lover".[23] Like the black and tan colour, it contains a spike, however, for who is the leading part in the interaction, and who is being led? An unsentimental view would regard the animal as the object and the smith as the subject inflicting a civilizing modification onto nature. Horses only need horseshoes when they have to function for humans in a human environment.

And yet the poem does not work that way, despite all evocations of "branding on a shoe // in an apparition of smoke, / three nails gritted between his teeth".[24] For the protagonist is then immediately imagined as "a seamstress pinning the dress of the bride", and as if this image was not strange enough, it is followed in the subsequent stanza by "Placing his tools in their beds".[25] What could have been a rustic poem describing replacing a lost or worn horse shoe mutates into an awkward epithalamion, a bridal poem, only that its awkward love-making is between a blacksmith and a horse. The horse ultimately leaves the scene after the smith "gives her a slap", although it is still "awkward in her new shoes, walking on strange ground".[26] The isolated final line of the poem continues this subtle defamiliarization: "The sound of his steel, biting at her heels".[27] Yet the world has not only become unfamiliar to the horse – whose new horse shoes still have to be worn in. It has also become at least temporarily unfamiliar for the smith, whose role is described as hovering between that of a masculine car mechanic (even implicitly a terrorist) and a feminine film star coyly waiting for her lover's kiss or an equally feminine seamstress busily preparing a wedding dress.

It proves futile to search for unambiguous signs of domination in this poem, although it ends with the horse being affected by what has happened. The attentive reader, however, will be just as affected as the mare, and will carry the bite of the poem with her or him for a while. This bite also rests on blurring not merely the distinctions between masculine and feminine, but also nature and civilization ("from the field to the yard"), since the two are entangled here. The horse is not wild – and probably would not exist were it not for the presence of a farm. The threat of its replacement by a machine is implied in the poem, but also the reason for its continued presence, a Romantic (and now the capital letter can be justified) relation between human actors and animals in which the identities of both undergo a tantalizing metamorphosis that is as defamiliarizing as it is enriching.

The poem "Winter Swans" in the same collection continues this Romantic trajectory in the direction of the interaction of human and nonhuman as a mutually modifying continuum – at least in the imagination of the human protagonist and witness. Swan poems have a long tradition, and the self-declared "last Romantic", William Butler Yeats, also produced poems such as "The Wild Swans at Coole" at a time, 1917, when others were already writing more obviously experimental modernist verse.[28]

Sheers winter swans take three stanzas to appear, stanzas in which other elements of nature dominate, clouds and rain, "the waterlogged earth" and "the lake, silent and apart".[29] Here we have a speaker simultaneously observing nature and, while doing so, feeling separated from it, at least initially. It is united rather with a second person, which explains the "we" and "our" – and perhaps also the detached perspective.

This changes when the swans appear – in a typically sublime Romantic moment that makes the human beings realise their limited importance and therefore exactly their humanity when faced with the larger creation:

> until the swans came and stopped us
> with a show of tipping in unison.
> As if rolling weights down their bodies to their heads
>
> they halved themselves in the dark water,
> icebergs of white feathers, paused before returning again
> like boats righting in rough weather.[30]

The swans stop the onlookers as much as they take over the two central stanzas of the poem. That they are sublime is attested in images like "icebergs" or "boats" who are given the unusual participle "righting" that forms an alliteration with the "rough" of the weather. Yet, as in "The Farrier", the action is not one-sided (which would here mean: nature at least momentarily takes over and takes control of humans). The speaker calls the swans' actions "a show". It knows how to compare their movements to acrobatics. It can quantify them ("halved"), structure them ("paused before returning again") and ultimately compares them to the very civilized "righting" that is not done by a boat itself, but by its experienced human crew. Once again, the interaction between humans and nature is a give and take, here a challenge and response. This, however, does not mean that the roles in this exchange are clearly demarcated. Stability as well as instability are addressed in the poem in the swans' mating for life and the rough weather. The imaginary transformation of the swans into boats in the simile can be viewed as an intrusion, even as a violation. But it might also be a gesture of imaginary support. Once again, new entangled relations are envisaged that might hint at different non-hierarchical ethics, as they already did in the poem "The Farrier".

This becomes obvious when categories of gender enter the poem. The hitherto unidentified second person suddenly makes herself heard in the fifth stanza with the unprepared statement "'They mate for life'". Its accompanying phrase "you said as they left, / porcelain over the stilling water" is as important as the subsequent statement "I didn't reply". Only what follows then permits the interpretation of this second person as female and, in a heteronormative view that is still the dominant one in literature, the poem as a love poem. What made the speaker think of acrobatics and mastering a boat would then, in a clichéd manner, make the female think of relationships. Her interjection is almost experienced as a violation in the near-perfect aesthetics of the scenario of porcelain and stilling water. At the same time, the initially denied male response is exactly that, aesthetic and even aestheticist – in the sense of cherishing the moment for its own sake.

But life, movement and relationships continue, as the pragmatic female statement implies. As it turns out in the poem's conclusion, both the sublime experience of the ascending swans and the intervention of his partner have altered the speaker's perspective: "I noticed our hands". These "had, somehow, / swum the distance between us // and folded, one over the other, / like a pair of wings settling after flight".[31] The defamiliarising description of human hands as nonhuman wings is here subtler than in the temporary sex change of "The Farrier". Nonetheless, something has happened that leaves the lyrical I changed. His hands are now part of "our hands", and how this came about can only be explained unconvincingly ("somehow") in an analogy to the natural beasts, the swans. What remains as an explanation is a poetic image: they have "swum the distance between us", only to then become folded on top of each other like swans' wings.

In terms of movement and repetition (something that the poem itself uses as an explanation for a natural phenomenon), it has itself repeated the swans' movements in an act of human beings imitating the agency of nature – or finding in nature patterns that help explain human emotions and behaviour. That this explanation is a scaffold rather than a certainty is made obvious in the suspicious term "somehow", but also in the clearly inappropriate statement "'They mate for life'", which neither matches the unidentified number of swans described nor makes sense in the swans' universe, which lacks awareness of the duration humans call a 'life'.

Owen Sheers has thereby created a perfect contemporary variant of the prototypical Romantic moment that Wordsworth famously describes in the Preface to the second edition of *Lyrical Ballads*:

> [...] poetry is the spontaneous overflow of powerful feelings: it takes its origin from emotion recollected in tranquillity: the emotion is contemplated till, by a species of reaction, the tranquillity gradually disappears, and an emotion, kindred to that which was before the subject of contemplation, is gradually produced, and does itself actually exist in the mind.[32]

In terms of ethics, however, the potential conflicts of this poem, though subtle, remain unresolved. This, and its entangled relation in terms of gender roles as well as its hierarchies of human and nonhuman, helps it go beyond the modern epistemological norms that are inscribed both in the Romantic and also much post-Romantic imagination, norms that grant the human ultimate control – over himself (the gendered pronoun is apt here) and about his environment. Who or what triumphs at the end of Sheers' poem "Winter Swans", though? Does anybody or anything in it (literally) gain the upper hand – the feminine perspective or the masculine one, nature or humans, human nature even?

Some of Sheers' earlier poems use less subtlety in the confrontation of humans and animals. In *The Blue Book* (2000), there are poems such as "Hedge Foal" or "Lambing" that present images connected to the birth of a foal or lamb to describe human astonishment when faced with nature.[33] "Old Horse, New Tricks" uses the well-known saying of its title as a cruel introduction to a scene in which a horse is shot by a vet. There are gendered elements in all three poems, and there are indications of ethical questions, especially in the last poem, which makes the horse a "she" who obliges and succumbs, but also performs her part in a comedy for the unmoved onlookers ("We watched, an audience expecting tricks").[34] Only in the final stanza, which describes the dead horse's mouth touching the ground, does a strongly loaded image appear: "like a child, stealing a taste of the cake / before it is served". Unemotional, even cruel detachment is replaced by its opposite, for children generally elicit a strong response in the audience. Now the sick horse is an innocent creature, and more than that, a subversive one that aims to have a final taste of what is served – here clearly to others.

That "the earth below" is now a cake is an ethical challenge. It implies added value, symbolic and real, but also turns the earth into a commodity. It clearly does not belong to all creatures that inhabit it, at least not in equal measure. Once again, domestication and appropriation, possession and consumption are invoked – in the entangled poetic form of simile and metaphor. The poem affects its readers more strongly because it does not formulate this as an accusation or question, but leaves them with the ambiguous formula "before it is served".

A culmination of the combined issues of gender and ethics can be found in an at first glance innocuous little poem in Sheers' oeuvre, also in *The Blue Book*. "Harvest" describes a speaker and his partner or lover gathering conkers, horse chestnuts. Yet, as in "Farriers" and all the other poems analysed above, the seemingly familiar scenario is quickly subverted. The first instance of this subversion still seems humorous, when the falling chestnuts are compared to "Miniature mines".[35] Yet the theme of destruction (and its counterpart preservation) are then quickly established when the second person begins to "gather them in". In fact, the action is a two-fold one: "those you picked you kept, / holding them tight to your stomach". In line with several other poems by Sheers that discuss motherhood, this can be interpreted as a feminine gesture. That it is not an entirely selfless one is already implied in the line that disturbingly intervenes between gathering and keeping, a line that speaks about "squeezing out their secrets". Masculinity is traditionally associated with keeping one's counsel and preserving one's secrets. Already the Old English poem "The Wanderer" declares,

> [...] and I know it for a truth
> That in a man it is a noble virtue
> To hide away his thoughts, lock up
> His private feelings – however he may feel.[36]

In the gendered scenario of Sheers' poem, the forcible extraction of secrets (here from chestnuts – a pretty dry affair) is also a form of attack – like that of the miniature mines above.

The poem then quickly retaliates – by making the image shade over into one of injury: "as if you had been stabbed, and were / bleeding conkers from the wound". The surreal image of the stabbed partner then becomes even further defamiliarised, as if the scene were now a Freudian dream-scenario. "When they [the chestnuts] became too many, / you trusted me with some, which I held". Freud interprets the child's triumph in controlling its bowel movements and the resulting possibility to please its parents by equating excrement and gift.[37] Here, the imagined blood-clots/chestnuts become a strange gift for the speaker. That he is "trusted" with them also aligns them with a possible birth. Yet no matter how one reads the strange scene, the destructive masculinity of the speaker (which is still evident when he holds them like "a bunch of knuckles in my fist") is confronted with a feminine gesture of trust. Are we back in the traditional gender binary, the one that was criticised above as at work in much ecocriticism, of men as destroyer and woman as giver and preserver of life?

Yes and no is the answer, for the speaker does indeed protect the chestnuts and even returns them. But nonetheless, something has altered, and it is the second person who comments on this change: "my sweat dulled their sheen". "[Y]ou said it would always be this way; / because I am a man, and I have acid hands." The poem seemingly ends in what one can only call essentialism ("always be this way"). Masculinity means destruction (or at least deformation) of nature, as the provocative final image of the "acid hands" implies.

But is the poem's conclusion so simple? What is the "it" that "would always be this way"? Destruction as the consequence of trust between the sexes – or a continuing ritual of acting out gender in an expected way, a choreography of perception and imagination that rests as much on dream-like or traumatic scenarios as it shapes the experience even of everyday moments like that of gathering chestnuts? What goes on in the poem, we should never forget, largely does so in the views of the two speakers represented in it in poetic fashion. Poetic here does not necessarily mean pleasing, for while the male speaker envisages his female counterpart as possessive, then injured and finally judgmental, his imagined female Other (and it is important that it is the speaker who represents this counterpart to the reader) is the more active, more successful one (in squeezing out secrets) and ultimately the one who has the final word – which contains a verdict on masculinity. The encounter with the materiality of the nonhuman, here embodied in the innocuous image of the chestnut affirms the dominance of what is human and what is masculine – and shows the limitations of both in the subtle and very symbolic deterioration of what is most beautiful and cherished in it. Once again, the hierarchies are challenged, and a very real material entanglement triggers a reflection about the power of epistemological power. Who has knowledge of what in the poem? The female of the male, humans of the nonhuman – or vice versa, if this was possible and would make sense (which would be a radically alternative one)?

If Owen Sheers is the rugby-playing Wordsworthian, Meirion Jordan is perhaps best described as a more introvert follower of the great modern Welsh poet Dylan Thomas. Born in 1985 in Cwmllynfell, a village north of Wales's second city Swansea, he studied Mathematics at Oxford before switching to Creative Writing. His poems won him the Newdigate Prize in 2007.[38] While Sheers writes about nature, but also war, Jordan is fascinated by Welsh mythology (an entire volume entitled *Regeneration: White Book – Red Book* of 2012 retells Welsh myths in poetic form),[39] but, like Sheers, also by metamorphoses and dream-like scenarios. "Poppy Field" is a short poem from the collection *Moonrise* (2008) that equates a field with a body, yet a body that appears to resist human interference cunningly: "October, you slaked the dry furrows with grain / and June the fields came blistering with poppies, / winking their black eyes in the breeze".[40] The poem is unusual in that it sports a lyrical "you", an unidentified addressee that could be anyone. It is also characterised by odd juxtapositions (instead of the expected crops, poppies have grown) and the repeated use of "as though" to indicate an imaginative interpretation in the form of an unusual simile.

In all its images, nature functions like a body, and human attempts to discipline this body are counteracted and ridiculed ("winking") by this very body's unruly and uncanny agency. Poppies, though pretty, are weeds, and farmers dislike them. They are of course also flowers associated with death, with the loss of blood, as is attested by their use as commemorative symbols on Armistice Day, 11 November, to remember the end of the First World War. That the poppies have black eyes is a further hint at violence, a repeated hint, since the poem also ends with the phrase "grasping black eyes".

The poem works with slightly mismatched terms, such as the "slaked" in its opening line or the "grasping" in its final ones. Why would one quench a furrow – unless, as in Greek mythology, the earth demands a sacrifice? How can eyes grasp? Jordan's world is mythological and it is also thoroughly animated. As in many poems by his predecessor Dylan Thomas, seemingly inanimate things become active and can even be potentially hostile. In "Poppy Field", "the hedge extends / a rain of hands snatching the light",[41] a comment on the fact that hedges are human constructions that violate the growth patterns of the plants used for them. In later lines, there is mention of "the bruise of foxgloves, a septicaemia of primrose, an unintended gift". Now weeds are simultaneously interesting names, beautiful flowers, but also injuries and illnesses. The perspective has shifted to that of human anthropocentrism again, but with a twist. What violates human order is actually a gift, unintended, because not part of rational planning, but in its aesthetic beauty something that adds to civilization. Wordsworth never worried if his daffodils were weeds and in the way of sensible farming. Jordan does. His nature, however, is not half as docile as are Wordsworth's gently swaying daffodils. In "Poppy Field" "from the hill's scalp / down to where the river rattles in the limestone throat / the slope gushes with fists, blood red".[42]

Jordan's nature is an alternative body, one that challenges the human onlooker through its potential power and destructiveness, an onlooker who is only seemingly in control and sensibly active. Once again, the agency of nature challenges the power hierarchy between the human and the nonhuman through its disruptive materiality. That the competition also involves gender can be seen in the clash of traditionally feminine images, such as those of flowers (whom already Edmund Burke relegated to the realm of the beautiful rather than the sublime[43]) with violent 'masculine' ones, such as that of scalp, throat, fists and blood. Yet they all belong to the same paradigm 'nature', while the human "you" of the poem remains strangely faceless.

This potential struggle between human and nature is brought to a traumatic climax in the poem "The Wasp Queen", also from *Moonrise*. It initially seems to depict the cruel experiment of a lyrical I involving a trapped wasp: "she will not sleep. / her wings trouble the glass".[44] It soon becomes apparent, though, that this is more than a casual act of torturing an insect. Why is the wasp female, even a "Wasp Queen"? And why does the poem continue by referring to the wasp "seeking the heat, / my breath. Her lips are moist"? The line "my breath. Her lips are moist" is repeated in the second stanza, where the invoked lips even end up parting "like mine". What is described here is a strangely erotic confrontation of a lyrical I – not so much with a real wasp (do wasps have lips?), but with a combined phantasm of nature and femininity. That this femininity is not necessarily inferior or weaker than the implied masculinity of the speaker becomes obvious in another repetition in the subsequent lines of the poem, that of "the whiteness of my skin". The inevitable happens, "her sting", but then also the incredible, traumatic and dream-like: "she crawls in / seeking the heat".

Ted Hughes used the image of a fox on snow to express his shamanistic idea of poetic creativity in his famous poem "The Thought-Fox" (1957).[45] Jordan is more radical, since his white page is formed by the body of his speaker, and the inspiration does not rest safely outside the window as in Hughes' poem, but crawls under the skin of the speaker, one can only assume on its way to the source of heat and inspiration, the heart. Nature becomes internalised here, but in a much less comfortable way than in traditional Romanticism, where it functions as an emotional trigger, and it is the emotion that is then safely recollected and reworked into art later. This is what happens in Sheers' poems, too, despite the fact that they leave their speakers and readers shaken. In Jordan, the confrontation of self and nature happens on a level playing field, that of the body, and both bodies involved risk dramatic consequences in the encounter.

In "The Owls", also in *Moonrise*, this consequence is an Ovidian metamorphosis: "In February Mark began to grow a beak". What can at first be read as a lyrical I observing fledgling birds growing up and getting ready to leave the nest ("He was the first to go. Then Aled, […] / Two weeks later I found Sam and Marie / preening each other in my hay-loft") soon turns out to be a surreal scenario: "I knew it. My neighbours were turning into owls."[46] Owls are mythological animals. In Greek mythology, they are the birds of the goddess of wisdom, Athena. Welsh mythology contains the story of the unfaithful flower-woman Blodeuwedd, who is turned into an owl as a punishment, since the owl is hated by all other birds. But owls also feature prominently in a famous modern Welsh poem, Dylan Thomas' "Fern Hill", where the speaker reports, "As I rode to sleep the owls were bearing the farm away"[47]. In Thomas' poem, this functions as a childhood description of dreaming.

In Jordan's poem, the speaker remains remarkably detached vis-à-vis what is happening in his environment: "At first I thought nothing of it", "I grew used to the ghosts of wings crossing my windows." His (unrealistic) response is ambivalent – and epistemologically self-destructive: it combines the supposed control of routine with the Gothic image of ghostly wings crossing the windows. The nonhuman once again challenges epistemological categories as well as the power hierarchies of human and nature. It is therefore almost like an attempt at human re-empowerment when the speaker's observations become coldly empirical again: "my barns / stank of the cold sweat of mice each morning". That the street he lives in slowly turns into "a gust of boarded doorways" of "windowless" houses can be read as a poetic consequence and as a very real acknowledgment of the many abandoned communities in the poorer parts of Wales. The poem's 'nature' images are therefore also cultural ones, here of politics and the economy, in the same way as they are magical and mythological. In terms of gender, the detachment of the observer and his evident lack of concern or fear firmly relegate him to the masculine position – as does his seeming inability to immerse himself imaginatively into what is happening. That this position is only assumed during daytime, however, is betrayed in the poem's final four lines:

> And each night I sit under the last lamp in the house
> hearing the clink and rasp of their claws at the slate,
> each night I dream of snow under the huge moon,
> my shadow broad and beating it like down.[48]

The scenario resembles a Gothic or adventure tale in which the lonely observer can only wait until his last source of light goes out, before he becomes exposed to the forces of darkness. We also know the employment of birds as agents of fear from films such as Alfred Hitchcock's *The Birds* (1963). Yet, as in Thomas' "Fern Hill" and Jordan's own "The Wasp Queen", there is also a desire for this to happen, "each night I dream", a desire for the speaker to become an owl himself.

One can read this, as was done with "The Wasp Queen", as a precarious meditation on creativity and the imagination. One can even read "The Owls" as a study of mental instability – with everything that goes on in the poem as happening inside a deranged mind. Nonetheless, in terms of gender, the environment and ethics it poses interesting questions, especially if one sees them framed – much more strongly than in Owen Sheers' poem – by the position of contemporary Wales between deindustrialisation, the dwindling of rural communities and the effects these factors have on traditional gender roles (with masculinity relegated to that of the reasonable and detached observer or active breadwinner). Then, what is represented in a nightmarish scenario would be a renegotiation of knowledge, of epistemology, that is, and power. Who or what is in control – and who or what loses it? Is this loss of control merely negative – as a loss of identity – or does it not also hold potential, perhaps that of reconceptualising of the human and its borderlines?

Nature can be seen to make a return in "The Owls", but just as in "Poppy Field" and "The Wasp Queen", this return is neither peaceful nor harmonious, but brings conflict and strife into the lives (and minds) of humans. In Jordan, nature is not in itself good. It is not even always good for you, the "you" being the unnamed humans that act as stand-ins for everyone and for the poetic imagination.

4. Conclusion: Conflicting Ethics and Attempts at Dialogue

The two contemporary Welsh poets presented in the above readings, Owen Sheers and Meirion Jordan, have much in common. They both use nature and its images as sources of inspiration in the tradition of the Romantic poets, but also their modern successor Dylan Thomas. Yet in neither of their works is nature unproblematic or even clearly locatable. Instead, it is shown to possess an active, unruly agency that challenges human dominance and epistemological certainties. In Sheers, nature prompts strong emotional responses, as it did for Wordsworth, but it can also intervene in gender relations and even put the shortcomings and isolation of masculinity on the spot. In Jordan, the masculine desire for possessing and controlling nature meets an almost vicious response by natural phenomena that (often quite literally) undermine supposed masculine identity and dominance. The body, traditionally associated with the feminine, is at least partly relocated to the masculine sphere by both authors. Materiality thus features on both sides of the human-nonhuman divide and contributes to their complex entanglements.

Much of this is connected to the authors' special relation to nature, having grown up in an environment where nature is both visible in its still relatively unspoilt rural variety, but also in its 'damaged' shape after becoming the object of centuries of industrialisation and its aftermath. Gender positions, especially those of masculinity, are inseparable from those of political and economic marginalisation. The Welsh are for many English still the butt of jokes, and while a Welsh accent is seen as friendly and trustworthy, it also often implies simplicity of mind, something that clashes drastically with contemporary expectations of men.[49] Poetry as a decidedly 'unmanly' genre (at least since the end of the nineteenth century) might have an easier time, or at least a freer interaction, with the combined challenges of the ecology and of masculinity.[50] Coming from a rural background, the two authors use their experiences to confront their readers with images of a nature that does not conform to idyllic clichés. Yet they remain aware that their versions of interaction between human and nature are therefore neither more realistic nor objective. Both of them see their view of nature as shaped by previous ideas, literature in the case of Sheers and mythology in that of Jordan, as ideological that is. The bias in viewing nature is the equivalent of the bias in viewing gender, as was shown in Sheers' poem "Harvest" that presented a male speaker imagining (or remembering) the views of a female Other or in Jordan's poem "The Wasp Queen" that depicted seemingly detached observation sliding into uncomfortable eroticism.

All this means that their poems refuse to provide easy answers concerning the relationship of humans and nature or of the sexes. This seeming shortcoming, however, is exactly the start of ethics as a system of demarcations and borderlines that are not (any longer) prescribed by a vengeful or charitable God or by a nature whose will and direction is clearly identifiable. Bruno Latour indeed sees the start of a real ethics in the recognition that it also necessarily manifests itself beyond the human:

> Just as a geologist can hear the clicks of radioactivity, but only if he is equipped with a Geiger counter, we can register the presence of morality in the world provided that we concentrate on that particular emission. And

> just as no one, once the instrument has been calibrated, would think of asking the geologist if radioactivity is 'all in his head,' 'in his heart,' or 'in the rocks,' no one will doubt any longer that the world emits morality toward anyone who possesses an instrument sensitive enough to register it.[51]

Ethics require ongoing dialogues, and they require imagination, also the imagination to see beyond self and Other, yet without merely turning the Other (be it the supposedly opposite gender or the nonhuman) into a conveniently malleable object. The beginning of a gendered environmental ethics, the poems of both authors imply, is the understanding that taking possession of an Other also means that this Other gains possession of us.

Notes

[1] Wollstonecraft (1792).
[2] Glotfelty (1996:xxii-xxiii).
[3] *Ibid.*, xxiv.
[4] Kolodny (1996). Norwood (1996).
[5] Rangarajan (2016).
[6] This is done by Allister (ed.) (2004). *Eco-Man: New Perspectives on Masculinity and Nature*. Charlottesville, VA: University Press of Virginia. What remains troubling in this collection of essays, though, is its neo-liberal attitude of 'making ecology work' for 'modern man'.
[7] Hall (1997:3).
[8] Iovino (2016:11).
[9] Oppermann (2016:30).
[10] Bennett (2010:xiii).
[11] Freud (1953-1974:24-28).
[12] Althusser (1971:164).
[13] See, for instance, Anderson (ed.) (2003). See also "Five Women Poets on Nature [Special Section]." *Callaloo: A Journal of African Diaspora Arts and Letters*. 34.3, 759-793.
[14] McGann (1983).
[15] Thoreau (1854).
[16] Burns (1786).
[17] Borrow (1862).

[18] See (2015).
[19] Sheers. "Biography." Web. 31 December 2016 <http://www.owensheers.co.uk/about-owen/biography/>.
[20] Sheers (2005:2).
[21] *Ibid.*
[22] *Ibid.*
[23] *Ibid.*
[24] *Ibid.*
[25] *Ibid.*
[26] *Ibid.*
[27] *Ibid.*
[28] Yeats (1917:9).
[29] Sheers (2005:7).
[30] *Ibid.*, 7.
[31] *Ibid.*
[32] Wordsworth (1800: xxxiii-xxxiv). On the connection between Romanticism and ecocriticism, see also Coupe (ed.) (2000); Rigby (2014:60-79) and Buell (1995). *The Environmental Imagination: Thoreau, Nature Writing, and the Formation of American Culture*. Cambridge, MA and London: The Belknap Press of Harvard University Press.
[33] Sheers (2000:16).
[34] *Ibid.*, 13.
[35] *Ibid.*, 17.
[36] Anonymous (2015:176).
[37] Freud (1908).
[38] "Meirion Jordan." *Versopolis: European Review of Poetry, Books and Culture*. Web. 31 December 2016 <http://www.versopolis.com/poet/8/meirion-jordan>.
[39] Jordan (2012).
[40] Jordan (2008:8).
[41] *Ibid.*, 8.
[42] *Ibid.*, 8.
[43] Burke (1757).
[44] Jordan (2008:17).
[45] Hughes (1957:14).
[46] Jordan (2008:48).
[47] Thomas (1945:21).
[48] Jordan (2008:48).
[49] Already George Borrow wrote about "the noble simple-minded, genuine Welsh" in *Wild Wales*, 64.
[50] Compare Sinfield (1992:274).
[51] Latour (2013:456).

Works Cited

Allister, Mark (ed.) (2004). *Eco-Man: New Perspectives on Masculinity and Nature*. Charlottesville, VA: University Press of Virginia.

Althusser, Louis (1971). "Ideology and Ideological State Apparatuses (Notes towards an Investigation)." *Lenin and Philosophy and Other Essays*. Trans. Ben Brewster. New York: Monthly Review Press, 127-186.

Anderson, Lorraine (ed.) (2003). *Sisters of the Earth: Women's Poetry and Prose about Nature*. London: Vintage.

Anonymous (2015). "The Wanderer." *A Choice of Anglo-Saxon Verse*. Ed. Richard Hamer. Revised ed. London and Boston: Faber & Faber, 176-185.

Bennett, Jane (2010). *Vibrant Matter: A Political Ecology of Things*. Durham; NC and London: Duke University Press

Borrow, George (1862). *Wild Wales: Its People, Language and Scenery*. London: John Murray.

Buell, Lawrence (1995). *The Environmental Imagination: Thoreau, Nature Writing, and the Formation of American Culture*. Cambridge, MA and London: The Belknap Press of Harvard University Press.

Burke, Edmund (1757). *A Philosophical Enquiry into the Origin of Our Ideas of the Sublime and Beautiful*. London: R. & J. Dodsley.

Burns, Robert (1786). *Poems Chiefly in the Scottish Dialect*. Kilmarnock: John Wilson.

Coupe, Laurence (ed.) (2000). *The Green Studies Reader: From Romanticism to Ecocriticism*. New York: Routledge.

Emig, Rainer (2015). "Towards a Biodegradable Subjectivity: Two Women Poets from the Celtic Fringe." *Weeds and Viruses: Ecopolitics and the Demands of Theory*. Ed. Cordula Lemke and Jennifer Wawrzinek. Trier. WVT, 49-65.

"Five Women Poets on Nature [Special Section]." *Callaloo: A Journal of African Diaspora Arts and Letters*. 34.3, 759-793.

Freud, Sigmund (1908). "Character and Anal Erotism." *The Standard Edition of the Complete Psychological Works of Sigmund Freud*. Vol 9. Ed. James Strachey. London: Hogarth Press, 167-176.

Freud, Sigmund (1953-1974). "Creative Writers and Daydreaming." *The Standard Edition of the Complete Psychological Works of Sigmund Freud*. Vol. 4. Ed. James Strachey. London: Hogarth Press, 24-28.

Glotfelty, Cheryll (1996). "Introduction: Literary Studies in an Age of Environmental Crisis." *The Ecocriticism Reader: Landmarks in Literary*

Ecology. Ed. Cheryll Glotfelty and Harold Fromm. Athens, GA, and London: University of Georgia Press, xv-xxxvii.

Hall, Stuart (1997). *Representation: Cultural Representations and Signifying Practices*. London et al. Sage.

Hughes, Ted (1957). *The Hawk in the Rain*. London: Faber & Faber.

Iovino, Serenella (2016). "Introduction: Posthumanism in Literature and Ecocriticism." *Relations: Beyond Anthropocentrism*. 4.1, 11-20.

Jordan, Meirion (2008). *Moonrise*. Bridgend: Seren.

Jordan, Meirion (2012). *Regeneration: White Book – Red Book*. Bridgend: Seren.

Annette Kolodny (1996). "Unearthing Herstory: An Introduction." *The Ecocriticism Reader: Landmarks in Literary Ecology*. Ed. Cheryll Glotfelty and Harold Fromm. Athens, GA and London: University of Georgia Press, 179-181.

Latour, Bruno (2013). *An Inquiry into Modes of Existence: An Anthropology of the Moderns*. Trans. Catherine Porter. Cambridge, MA: Harvard University Press.

McGann, Jerome J. (1983). *The Romantic Ideology: A Critical Investigation*. Chicago and London: University of Chicago Press.

"Meirion Jordan." *Versopolis: European Review of Poetry, Books and Culture*. Web. 31 December 2016 <http://www.versopolis.com/poet/8/ meirion-jordan>.

Moore, Thomas (1808-1834). *A Selection of Irish Melodies*. 10 Vols. Dublin: William and James Power.

Oppermann, Serpil (2016). "From Posthumanism to Posthuman Ecocriticism." *Relations: Beyond Anthropocentrism*. 4.1, 23-37

Norwood, Vera L. (1996). "Heroines of Nature: Four Women Respond to the American Landscape." *The Ecocriticism Reader: Landmarks in Literary Ecology*. Ed. Cheryll Glotfelty and Harold Fromm. Athens, GA and London: University of Georgia Press, 323-350.

Rangarajan, Swarnalatha (2016). "Women Writing Nature in the Global South: New Forest Texts from Fractured Indian Forests." *Handbook of Ecocriticism and Cultural Ecology*. Ed. Hubert Zapf. Berlin and Boston: de Gruyter, 438-458.

Rigby, Kate (2014). "Romanticism and Ecocriticism." *The Oxford Handbook of Ecocriticism*. Ed. Greg Garrard. Oxford et al.: Oxford University Press, 60-79.

Sheers, Owen (2000). *The Blue Book*. Bridgend: Seren.

--- (2005). *Skirrid Hill*. Bridgend: Seren.

Sheers, Owen. "Biography." Web. 31 December 2016 <http://www.owensheers.co.uk/about-owen/biography/>.

Sinfield, Alan (1992). "Cultural Imperialism and the Primal Scene of U.S. Man." *Faultlines: Cultural Materialism and the Politics of Dissident Reading*. Berkeley, CA et al: University of California Press, 254-302.

Thomas, Dylan (1945). "Fern Hill." *Horizon* October, 21-22.

Thoreau, Henry David (1854). *Walden; or, Life in the Woods*. Boston, MA: Ticknor and Fields.

Wollstonecraft, Mary (1792). *A Vindication of the Rights of Woman: With Strictures on Political and Moral Subjects*. London: J. Johnson.

Wordsworth, William (1800). *Lyrical Ballads: With Other Poems*. 2nd ed. London: Longman & Rees.

Yeats, William Butler (1917). "The Wild Swans at Coole." *The Little Review* 4.2, 9.

Alexa Weik von Mossner (Klagenfurt)

When Everything Is Up for Grabs: Environmental Narcissism in Percival Everett's *Grand Canyon, Inc.*

1. Introduction

Percival Everett's novella *Grand Canyon, Inc.* (2001) is an odd little book, disturbing in its casual rendering of human and nonhuman suffering, annoying in its refusal to provide readers with likeable characters or a coherent plot. It also is a grimly amusing book, ruthless and indeed merciless in its portrayal of a narcissistic sociopath who puts his own needs and desires above everything else in the world. The protagonist of the novella is Winchell Nathaniel Tanner, nicknamed Rhino, who receives a BB gun from his father when he turns eight and spends the rest of his life shooting at everything that moves. He is a boy who happily cries "I hit something!" whenever his bullet strikes a target, regardless of whether that "something" is a bird or his best friend.[1] He becomes a man whose hunting habits lead to the extinction of several species of large mammals and who does not shy away from incorporating the ecosystem of the Grand Canyon in order to turn it into a giant amusement park.

Needless to say, the tone of Everett's novella is profoundly satirical and its plot turns are often absurd. Sylvie Bauer notes that *Grand Canyon, Inc.* "enacts a simple farce of madness, in which the main character maims the landscape of the Grand Canyon, destroying what is essential in order to achieve a form of power"[2]. Tanner is a "sociopath to boot"[3] and thus devoid of empathy and related moral emotions, among them compassion, pity, remorse, shame and guilt. Even the vast natural expanse of the Grand Canyon is little more to him than a narcissistic extension of his self, its willful destruction a minor plot turn in the grandiose story he tells himself about embodying "the *real* American dream"[4]. As in all satire, however, there is political purpose behind the madness. As Bauer points out, Everett uses the narrative distortion of the real, the pathological confusion of reality with its representation, for a relentless critique of the moral heritage of America. I will argue that the novella's narrative distortion of environmental affect is just as important for this critique – a critique that is more relevant than ever in the era of Donald J. Trump. After all, it is not only the protagonist Tanner who is disturbing in his solipsistic lack of concern for sentient others and the world as a whole. The narrator, too, relates his tale with a callousness that almost forces readers to become indignant on their part and to cry out on behalf of those who are maimed and mutilated without second thought. It is this affective and ethical dimension of *Grand Canyon, Inc.* that calls for ecocritical investigation.

In what follows, I will use the analytical tools of econarratology for a closer analysis of the novella's narrative structure and rhetorical strategies. Econarratology, as Erin James defines and develops it in *The Storyworld Accord* (2015), is an analytical mode that pairs "ecocriticism's interest in the relationship between literature and the physical environment with narratology's focus on the literary structures and devices by which writers compose narratives"[5]. As such, it strikes me as particularly pertinent for the analysis of a postmodern environmental satire that thrives on irony, fragmentation, and unreliable narration. I will pay particular attention to these postmodern elements in *Grand Canyon, Inc.* because ecocritics have often privileged realist storytelling, arguing that a dedication to authentic detail and life-like characters are best suited to instill in readers awareness and affective attachment to the depicted environment.[6] There is very little realism in Everett's novella, and yet it cues strong emotional responses in readers that may easily lead to moral outrage at attitudes and practices in the extra-textual world. Ecocritic Nicole Seymour has suggested that irony "can address the problems posed by serious affective modes – and foster a self-critical attitude that does not hinder but in fact enables environmentalist work"[7]. I will show how such fostering takes places in *Grand Canyon, Inc.* and suggest that Everett's brisk satire amounts to a scathing critique of environmental narcissism.

2. Character Empathy and our Affective Relationships to Narrative Environments

People matter. This is true not only in our daily life, but also when we sit down to read a novel. Our empathetic engagement with characters – the fact that we can feel along with imaginary people, share their joys and sorrows – is one of the main reasons why we read literature. The cognitive literary scholar Blakey Vermeule goes even further, claiming that "the reasons why we care about literary characters are finally not much different from the question of why we care about other people, especially people we have never met or are ever likely to meet"[8]. While this is correct, there are nevertheless some crucial differences between literary characters and "other people" beyond our simple awareness that the former are not real in any material sense. Most importantly, literary characters are created by authors for the purpose of telling a story, which means that the authors have control over how much they reveal about their characters, from which angle, and when. All of this will influence not only how much readers *know* about individual characters but also how they *feel* about them. As Vermeule points out, "[f]iction writers have devised powerful tools for sharpening and focusing our interest and for holding it intensely for a time"[9]. One of those powerful tools is character empathy.

As readers, we have a tendency to feel along with a character whose perspective we share. Film scholar Murray Smith has explained this phenomenon in terms of 'alignment'. Alignment, he explains, is a result of "our access to the actions, thought, and feelings of a character"[10]. If we see the events from a certain character's perspective, we are aligned with that character in the sense that the character acts as focalizer of the narration.[11] Such narrative alignment makes it easy for us to imaginatively "slip into the character's shoes" and empathize with him on both the cognitive and affective level Cognitive empathy, also referred to by psychologists as Theory of Mind (ToM) refers to the cognitive effort to put oneself "into the shoes" of another person in order to understand what they think and feel and why they do the things they do. Affective empathy tends to be less controlled by cognitive processes and relies on often involuntary mirroring responses such as affective mimicry and emotional contagion. In combination, the two modes are fundamental for our understanding of the emotions, actions and intentions of both actual people and fictional characters.[12] In fiction, alignment greatly facilitates both modes of empathy by giving us information about characters' inner lives. Moreover, Smith suggests that alignment not only facilitates our cognitive and affective understanding of a character but often also leads to moral 'allegiance', a term that refers to the way in which a narrative "elicits responses of sympathy" toward that character. Such sympathetic responses to a character, Smith suggests are "triggered—if not wholly determined—by the moral structure" of the narrative.[13]

Important in my context here, narrative alignment must not *always* lead to responses of sympathy and moral allegiance. The moral structure of the narrative might be completely at odds with that of its reader, leading to 'imaginary resistance' and thus to an unwillingness to feel sympathy for a character (or any interest in reading further).[14] Just imagine the protagonist of a novel being an avid hunter and the reader a vegan animal rights activist. No matter how much the narrator lauds the joy of hunting and no matter how much the protagonist enjoys it, this particular reader will have a hard time getting sympathetic. She might even feel a deep sense of satisfaction if the protagonist gets mauled by one of the animals he pursues. Whereas a moment of tragedy might have been intended by the author, the reader will likely read it as poetic justice if she should ever make it that far into the novel. This is arguably a case of what the cognitive literary scholar Suzanne Keen has called "empathetic inaccuracy"[15], since the reader does not respond in the way intended by the author, feeling *empathy with* and *sympathy for* not the protagonist but the animal(s) he is chasing. Her moral allegiance is with the animals rather than with the protagonist, regardless of what the narrative suggests.

However, there is also a different and somewhat more complicated case of compromised moral allegiance, and that is when there is reason to suspect that the author (though not necessarily the narrator) *wants* readers to partially or fully withdraw their allegiance from the protagonist. In such cases, we cannot speak of empathetic inaccuracy since the author consciously *uses* alignment and resulting character empathy in order to make readers feel uncomfortable with the protagonist. A prime example is Richard Wright's *Native Son* (1940), which for much of the narrative aligns readers with a multiple murderer, forcing them to share his perspective and mode of thinking. For many readers – whether they were Wright's contemporaries or are reading the novel today – this makes for a disturbing read, potentially leading to the self-reflection and recognition that Wright was hoping for.[16] I will suggest that Everett is trying to do something similar in *Grand Canyon, Inc.* even though he uses very different stylistic means. Whereas *Native Son* is a naturalist novel that has been criticized for its didacticism and lengthy philosophical detours, Everett's novella is short and terse. Instead of heaps of naturalistic detail it uses hyperbole and satire to make its point.

Putting an immoral and unsympathetic character at the center of a story is a risky choice for any author since there is a good chance it will alienate readers. One way to lessen that risk is to offer some kind of compensation, something that will make readers curious enough to read on. This something might be a particularly fascinating, multi-facetted protagonist who appeals to readers' sympathy and understanding, as we find it in Vladimir Nabokov's *Lolita* (1955) and in Bonnie Nadzam's much more recent novel *Lamb* (2011).[17] It can also be morally redeeming factors as is the case in the American TV-show *Dexter*, which centers on a psychopathic killer who only kills other psychopathic killers, thus making the world a safer place. Another way of keeping readers' attention is creating a story so absurd that they want to find out just how far the madness will go and where it will lead. This is the road taken by Everett in *Grand Canyon, Inc.,* which opens with the following words:

> Winchell Nathaniel Tanner claimed at various times to be a Navy Seal, a former Army Ranger, a member of Delta Force, an on-call DEA agent, a special agent for the President of the United States and the best rifle shot on the planet. He claimed to have dispatched three Viet Cong generals from over 1500 yards away with a .50 caliber rifle.... Of all the things he claimed, only the part about being a good rifle shot was true at all, though he never fired a single shot in Vietnam or in any other war. Tanner worked hard at being a remarkably good shot, but he was not the best shot in the world, though he was however willing to shoot at anything that lived.[18]

Rhino Tanner – as he will later be called – is introduced here as someone who brags, lies, and deceives, and who has very low inhibitions when it comes to killing others. For the first-time reader, this is an intriguing, if somewhat puzzling introduction of the protagonist. It is not one that cues sympathy or admiration, but it serves to make readers curious.

Tanner, they will soon learn, is determined and unafraid of a challenge, but he only acts when it serves his own needs and desires. Standing next to his father on the rim trail of the Grand Canyon one sunny summer day, he wants to know whether they can buy this place. After his father tells him that national parks are not for sale and that it would be too expensive anyway, Tanner responds: "Everything is for sale".[19] He is ten years old then. Twenty years later he will stand at the same place again and tell BB Trane to note down that they must "[a]quire the Canyon".[20] At this point in the story Tanner has already shot BB Trane in the head with the BB rifle he received from his father as a birthday gift. BB Trane just barely survived with the ordeal of the bullet permanently lodged in his brain, but because he is "more simple" even than Tanner he has become the latter's "sidekick.... playing a fat Tonto to Tanner's maniacal Lone Ranger"[21].

It is not immediately apparent to the reader why BB Trane would stay by the side of the man who deliberately shot him, but the central function of his character in the first half of the narrative is to show that Tanner shows no empathy for anything that is alive, whether it is human or nonhuman. For a long time the boy is not able to hit anything with his rifle, and when he finally manages to fatally injure a sparrow he does not "terminate its suffering, but instead simply watche[s] it suffer" before he proceeds to shoot another bullet "into its BB-sized brain".[22] When, a few years later, he shoots BB Trane, he enthusiastically "danc[es] around" his friend, who is lying in his blood on the sidewalk, "shouting 'I hit him! I hit him!'"[23] Later the two men go to Africa, where Tanner will "kill a score of zebra in a single afternoon for no reason"[24]. The novella is full of moments like this, all of them acknowledging in a laconic, indifferent voice that Tanner kills animals irrationally and manically to the point that he is personally responsible for the extinction of several species. For readers who care about animals this is hard to take, despite the obvious hyperbole and general lack of detail regarding the individual animal's suffering. The quantity of the killing itself is disturbing, as is the fact that it is so terribly successful. Tanner makes his considerable fortune by guiding those who can afford it on illegal "killing spree[s]" in the African savanna.[25] Among his clientele is the Sultan of Brunei, with whom he kills "two elephants, three rhinoceroses, [and] sixteen gnus"[26]. As if that would not be enough of mindless cruelty, he next bets the Sultan one million dollars against ten that BB Trane can push a three inch needle into the dent on his forehead that is still left from the gunshot wound. It is a trick they do regularly (since no one believes that it is humanly possible), and so the Sultan loses when BB pushes the needle into his brain as told, providing Tanner with the eleven million dollars that he will later use to buy the Grand Canyon from the American government.

None of this is likely to make Tanner particularly endearing to readers, regardless of whether they consider themselves to be animal-lovers or not. Unless they happen to share his deep-seated hatred (or harbor an indifference) toward all living creatures, Tanner's behavior is going to strike readers as immoral. And unlike the immoral characters I have previously mentioned, Tanner possesses almost no redeeming qualities. His fervor, cleverness, and constant strife for success are all self-centered and egoistical, and he is neither attractive nor charming. We are also given very little information about the potential *causes* of his psychological pathology. The text's fragmented and unchronological plotline leaves readers for a long time without any explanation for Tanner's lust to kill other than that his childhood was determined by a brutish father who bragged that he shot down six Japanese planes during WWII and who "was never *right* even before he went off to the war".[27] Only much later will they learn about the violent and tragic death of Tanner's mother, who is first trampled down by horses, then ripped apart by an exploding rack of firework rockets, before she finally drowns in a nearby pond. The narrator casually remarks that this horrific accident "shaped [Tanner's] being, but he hardly ever thought back on it in any significant way"[28]. This might be taken as signs of an emotional trauma that helps explain Tanner's extreme hatred of horses and, by extension, other animals. But his immediate response to his mother's death puts a question mark even behind this psychological explanation as it attests to the boy's complete lack of empathy: "That was really something", he tells BB Trane. "That was the first time I was ever proud of anyone in my family. What a way to die. All lit up like that with everybody watching."[29] Instead of grieving for his mother, young Tanner is fascinated by the spectacle of her death and by the attention it has garnered. While it thus suggested that his upbringing is in part responsible for Tanner's malice, it is not depicted in a way that would help readers develop compassion for him. Instead, the narrative voice cues them to withdraw their allegiance from the protagonist and feel moral disgust toward his actions.

That Tanner is such a profoundly unsympathetic protagonist is therefore at least in part the "fault" of the narrator and, ultimately, the author, who chooses one kind of narrator over another. Everett has a predilection for unreliable narrators that reveal some important piece of information about their characters – or themselves – only relatively late in the story, thus forcing readers to reevaluate and adjust their previous interpretation of the narrated events.[30] *Grand Canyon, Inc.* is a typical example in that it initially seems to be narrated by an authorial narrator who freely moves in and out of characters' minds, revealing selected details of their thoughts and feelings, knowing their past and future, jumping forward and backward in time, and commenting on the unfolding events with a detached voice that oscillates between the ironic and the sardonic. It is only in the second half of the story that we learn that this seemingly detached and external narrator is in fact a character in the story. Worse, it is BB Trane and thus a man who at the time of writing still carries a bullet in his brain. The fact that he suffers from brain damage makes him not only the poster boy of unreliable narration but also challenges readers' understanding of everything they have learned so far. Even more important in my context here is the fact that BB shows as little concern for the lives of animals or the protection of ecosystems as Tanner does. While this is disconcerting in an omniscient narrator, it becomes even more so once we learn that the narrating voice belongs to one of Tanner's many *victims*. Why, one might ask, does BB Trane not rebel, sue, or at least walk away from his tormenter? The answer to this question, it turns out, is of central importance for the novella's stance on environmental narcissism and its enablers.

3. Irony, Environmental Ethics and Postmodern Storytelling

That BB Trane is the narrator of the story likely comes as a surprise to most readers after having previously been told – by that very same narrator – that BB Trane is fat, ugly, and even "more simple" than Tanner is.[31] But simplicity comes in many shades in *Grand Canyon, Inc.*, and BB Trane turns out to be a highly self-conscious narrator who does not shy away from metafictional deliberations. This is how he opens chapter 13 of the novella:

> I, your narrator, am in fact BB Trane and not some disembodied entity, but instead rather heavily bodied and pigeon-toed. I was or remained throughout his life the closest thing to friend or family Rhino Tanner would ever know. […] I would have run off […] long ago, but I'm profoundly weak of character and pathologically insecure. I reveal to you

> now however that I am perhaps not as stupid as previously advertised. So, still you ask why did I remain and have every right to. My answer is, because it was a good show. It's as simple as that. A damn good show. Disgusting in many respects, certainly. Degrading, yes, but only if one gives a damn about anything at all and I have not an ounce of pride. If I flatter myself, I can claim to be simply the most cynical person in the world, oddly without a sense of self, impressively anaesthetized to the external world. [32]

Not only does the narrator here openly admit his unreliability, he also is self-ironic about his character defects. He claims to be weak, insecure and extremely cynical. Even more remarkable, he claims to be both without self and without feeling toward the world around him. And it turns out that to a mind such as his there *is* in fact a redeeming quality about Tanner: his ability to put on a damn good show, something that might be degrading and disgusting if one has a sound moral compass, but that is highly entertaining if one has not.

This leaves us at a point where we need to inquire into the exact nature of both characters' pathologies. Tanner is characterized by a stunning lack of empathy in combination with ruthless egotism, self-aggrandizement, and a pervasive sense of entitlement. According to the Mayo Clinic Website, these are typical features of the Narcissistic Personality Disorder, which goes along with BB's claim that his boss is "a sociopath to boot"[33]. BB, on his part, shares some traits with Tanner – for example the near-complete lack of empathy – but he does not seem to have the latter's unquenchable bloodthirst, nor does he need to be at the center of attention all the time. The world around him, he explains, "goes into" the hole in his head left by Tanner's bullet "and nothing comes out. Until now. You're reading it"[34]. BB has a story to share and he insists that both he and his tale are much more complex than it seems at first. "[N]o thing or person is so simple", he tells the reader. "What I did get to do while Rhino Tanner killed everything in sight was read, read, and watch, read, watch and wonder."[35] BB is therefore not only a victim; he is also a witness to Tanner's actions and an enabler. Most importantly, he is the one who has control over Tanner's story. And so it is from BB's rather peculiar perspective that we are learning about Tanner's acquisition of the Grand Canyon and the miss-matched group of activists that tries to put an end to the environmental devastation.

We also learn ahead of time what it will all lead to. "What happens at the end of this story", announces BB Trane at two-thirds into the book,

> is more than poetic justice. It's real justice. There is little of that in the world, but there is some. What happens is, in a fashion, horrible, the way all just and right things are horrible in some way, and it's both surprising and not surprising. The nature of just things is that they are exercises in irony.[36]

And indeed, ironies abound in the last third of the novella, in which we learn that Tanner is able to buy the Grand Canyon from an American government that prioritizes military expenses and tax cuts, which is why it can "no longer afford to keep pristine the nation's and the world's greatest topographical treasure"[37]. This is the point where the story takes its most obvious stab at the extratextual world, a stab that is even more painful for today's reader in the face of Donald Trump's announcements about the planned opening up of protected federal lands for oil and gas exploration.[38] Tanner's insanity and ignorance – forcefully expressed in his perverse plan to turn one of the most famous national parks of the United States into an amusement park – is matched in Everett's novel by the American government's negligence. Neither of them is able to see the actual value of the enormous ecosystem or why it should be protected from capitalist exploitation. As Bauer observes, this mutual blindness and indifference is expressed in the repeated name change "from 'Grand Canyon' (the original), to 'the Canyon' (its transcription in [BB Trane's] notebook), and then to 'Grand Canyon Inc.' (its mutilation to become an amusement park)" until it "finds its ultimate transformation when it becomes 'the Grand Tanner Canyon.'"[39] In this progression, the ecosystem is first stripped of its grandeur and then objectified and incorporated. In its final incarnation, the adjective "grand" no longer qualifies the ecosystem but the narcissist Tanner.

The only person in the novella who understands the true value of the Grand Canyon is Tanner's son Niko, who is the product of a one-night stand with a Finnish-named Japanese woman in a US witness protection program who later becomes his wife and since has divorced him. When Tanner first shows him his new acquisition, Niko is stunned by the sight. Upon hearing his father's plan to turn the national park into an amusement park, however, his sense of awe changes to disbelief:

> "You're going to build here?"
> "Yes."
> "Why?"
> "Because the government is letting me."
> "Why?"
> "Because they need me. I'm going to save this place."[40]

It remains unclear whether Tanner's answer is meant to be ironic. Given his previous reasoning, it seems more likely that it straightforwardly expresses his lack of appreciation for nature and limitless belief in his own abilities. This does not change, however, that in the context of the larger narrative this exchange is deeply ironic because Tanner will, quite literally, cover the place in human excrements before dying a violent death in it.

Irony, suggests literary theorist Linda Hutcheon, "is a 'weighted' mode of discourse in the sense that it is asymmetrical, unbalanced in favor of the silent and unsaid"[41]. There is a tremendous amount of things that remain unsaid in BB Trane's narration, and this is where we can locate its complexity. Although BB professes not to care, he portrays events in a way that cues anger and moral indignation in readers. It also cues compassion, but not for the protagonist. Typical examples include the moment when the best shot in the world (who is not Tanner) cannot shoot a "pachyderm" because "[i]t's got such a sweet face" and asks Tanner do it for him.[42] There is also the incident when Tanner shoots a "peacefully browsing bull elephant" in the presence of his deeply uncomfortable son.[43] In both cases it is Tanner who kills casually and mindlessly whereas other characters feel bad when confronted with the unsuspecting animals (though they do not stop Tanner from killing them). "Does the killing bother you?" Tanner asks Niko as they both stare at the dead elephant. Before his son can answer, he already promises him that he will come to like it over time just as he does. But Niko proves him wrong. He never comes to like killing animals for no reason and this is one of the characteristics that will likely make him sympathetic to most readers because – all distancing irony notwithstanding – his dislike is in accordance with the moral structure of the story. As Kimberley Ruffin notes, "the word choice of 'killing' rather than 'hunting' gives no justification of Tanner's activities, and the government's ideological preference for bombs and tax cuts over well maintained national parks appears absurd"[44]. The tone here and elsewhere in the novella is not only ironic, but also decidedly satirical, developing the fractured plotlines to their absurdist extreme in order to make a moral and political point.

"In satire", writes Stephen Butterfield, "laughter is always with a tight mouth, and humor shifts quickly to furious anger"[45]. *Grand Canyon, Inc.* invites readers to develop *empathic* anger at the protagonists because they are so blatantly careless and cynical in their interactions with the natural world. According to psychologist Martin Hoffman, empathic anger is different from direct anger in that is a response to the suffering of another, not the self. It can consist either of a mirroring of the feeling of someone who has been slighted or express itself in a feeling of indignation and irritation *on behalf* of that person.[46] Although he is a minor character with whom readers are rarely aligned throughout the narrative, Niko invites both kinds of empathic anger to some degree. On the one hand readers might feel irritated on his behalf when he is being mistreated by his father (which happens repeatedly); on the other hand they might *share* his own growing anger, which in itself is mostly empathic in nature and directed at Tanner on behalf of everyone else he exploits and abuses. Niko eventually grows to hate his father after the latter builds the Tannerland Resort in the Grand Tanner Canyon, complete with monorail, rollercoaster, and Ferris wheel, and with sewage pipes that simply pump their content into a nearby ravine to avoid the cost for septic tanks. He befriends a group of American Indians and builds an eco-terrorist group that plans to attack and destroy the Tannerland Resort. He also plans to kill his father, whom he considers the "death of this planet"[47]. He will fail tremendously at both of these projects and yet, ironically, accomplish them both at the end of the story.

Niko is by far the most sympathetic character in the story, simply because he and his activist friends are the only ones who actively *resist* Tanner's environmental narcissism on the basis of moral principles. And yet we don't ever get close to him as readers because BB Trane does not offer enough information to make Niko fully identifiable and just cannot hide his pity and condescension for the young man: "The terrorist campaign waged by Niko and his comrades", we learn, "was little more than bad weather in the way of a herd of bison. They did not know how to stop the herd. Tanner would have known. Buffalo Bill would have known. But Niko and the others did not.". In BB's view, Niko is no match for his father, and since he admires the father's ability to put on a damn good show, he narrates the son's demise with indifference and even amusement.

On the day of the planned terrorist attack Niko is so sick and feeble from a fever that he has to be carried along on a stretcher. But there is a much more serious snag in the execution of their plan. One of the Indians has built an explosive device, but on his way to the target his "van hit a pothole, bounced and exploded, sending bits of the van and John Russel's nephew raining down all over the landscape. He was nowhere near his destination."[48] In such moments, the narrative voice of *Grand Canyon, Inc.* has a taste of Vonnegut, reporting horrific events as if they were mundane while never ceasing to point out the ironies of life in general and combat in particular:

> Though no one felt the blast, it must have sent one tiny tremor through the ground, deep into the face of the planet, not a big tremor, but the right tremor and the vibration found the wall of Glen Canyon Dam. A small crack formed at the base of the thick concrete, then the weight of all that water, all that time, all those years pressed against the monstrous construction.
>
> A wren heard a tiny noise and flew away.
>
> All the animals began to crawl, slither and fly to higher ground.
>
> The dam cracked, opened, gave up.[49]

This is the poetic justice that BB Trane rejected earlier, insisting that the dam failure was in fact *real* justice and that the "nature of just things is that they are exercises in irony"[50]. Ironies abound when, refusing to believe his eyes, Tanner fires his pistol at "the wall of water" that is suddenly mounting up behind his Ferris wheel. This time, however, his target is much mightier than he is and so "[i]t was Tanner's last stand. Everything he had built was completely defeated, washed away forever, no pieces ever to be found. The canyon became what it once was. There was no dam, no lake, only river, the mighty Colorado."[51] Evoking General Custard's notorious "last stand" during the American Indian wars, these final words of the novella are rife with tragic irony. As BB also suggests, real justice is often painful and in this case involves the erasure not only of Tanner's constructions but presumably also that of the lives of hundreds of people including those of all of the protagonists, which – in a final ironic twist – would have to include the narrator himself.

4. Conclusion

Postmodern irony and overt satire have often been considered harmful rather than helpful in environmental writing. After all, so the argument goes, the problem of ecological exploitation and destruction is far too serious for ridicule. From this point of view, it would be easy to debunk *Grand Canyon, Inc.* as a self-indulgent, postmodern tale that is far too clever to truly care about the environment or invite others to do so. But, as BB Trane insinuates, the story is not as simple as it seems. Although it often challenges and offends ecologically minded readers, the novella ultimately embraces and advances an environmentalist ethics. As Ruffin has pointed out, Everett repeatedly draws parallels "between the individual acts of the eco-entitled Tanner with the American government that mirrors his lack of ecological sensitivity"[52]. It is these parallels, and the resulting understanding that Tanner's environmental narcissism is in fact much more common and widespread than we care to admit – that we in fact are all implicated in it – that mark the political dimension of Everett's satire. As Simpson has observed, "[s]atirical texts are understood as utterances which are inextricably bound up with the context of a situation, with participants in discourse and with frameworks of knowledge"[53]. *Grand Canyon, Inc.* points beyond its own textuality by asking us to gauge the moral and ethical dimensions of our deeply narcissistic attitude that leads us to ignore the needs of sentient others for egoistic reasons and to fail to see our deep implication in ecological processes.

It is one of the greatest, final ironies of the book that at the time of my writing in January 2017 it seems more timely even than in the moment of its original publication. Reading Everett's caustic satire in the first weeks of Donald Trump's presidency is no easy feat. One may be forgiven for detecting similarities between the sociopathic Rhino Tanner and the 45th President of the United States, who has been repeatedly diagnosed with narcissism by the international press and other observers. The Trump administration's muzzling of the Environmental Protection Agency, the National Park Service, and other federal agencies has been accompanied by overt climate change denial and the announcement of plans to open up federal land for oil and gas exploration against the interests of Native American communities, environmentalists, and concerned US citizens. Last but not least, there is an eerie parallel between the present government's hostility toward both science and humanities education and Tanner's insistence that "You don't need college" in response to his son's desire to get an education. "I'm filthy rich", Tanner adds, "You don't need studies. The world doesn't need intellectuals."[54] Donald Trump seems share this assessment and yet he is confronted by a multi-ethnic coalition of American citizens who believe not only in science and education but also in the importance to *resist* injustice, abuse, and exploitation. Niko arrives at the same conclusion and although the prize for his actions is horrendously, indeed absurdly high, his resistance succeeds in ending the exploitation, leaving behind only "the mighty Colorado". This grim ending is bound to make readers uncomfortable, and in doing so it may serve to "expos[e] and possibly correct [...] political follies" – which, according to Butterfield, is satire's "general purpose."[55] In any event, it is a forceful reminder of the considerable dangers implied in unchecked environmental narcissism

Notes

[1] Everett (2001:10).
[2] Bauer (2013:257).
[3] Everett (2001:10).
[4] *Ibid.*, 113.
[5] James (2015:xv).
[6] On the privileging of realism in ecocritical criticism, see Kerridge (2014).
[7] Seymour (2014:62).
[8] Vermeule (2010:xiii).
[9] *Ibid.*, xiii.
[10] Smith, Murray (1999:220).
[11] In the definition of Gérard Genette, focalization refers to the restriction of narrative information in relation to the experience and/or knowledge of the narrator, the characters or other entities in the storyworld (1980:44). If we see the storyworld through the eyes of one of those entities, we are aligned with them and the story is focalized through their consciousness.

[12] For detailed discussions of the role played by mirroring processes in both intersubjective understanding and literary reading, see Iacoboni (2009); and Clay, Zanna and Marco Iacoboni (2014).
[13] Smith (1999:220).
[14] On imaginary resistance, see Flory (2013).
[15] Keen, Suzanne (2010:88).
[16] For a reading of *Native Son* that pays attention to these issues, see Weik von Mossner (2014:chapter 4).
[17] Nabokov's *Lolita* is the story of a literature professor who is obsessed with a twelve-year-old girl and who later becomes sexually involved with her after becoming her stepfather. Nadzam's *Lamb* is a variation of the classical wilderness retreat story that also focuses on a middle-aged man who desires a young girl. In both novels, readers are aligned with morally transgressive protagonists who keep explaining to themselves that there are good reasons for their actions. For a detailed discussion see chapter 1 of Weik von Mossner (2017).
[18] Everett (2001:3-4).
[19] *Ibid.*, 4-5.
[20] *Ibid.*, 18.
[21] *Ibid.*, 11, 12.
[22] *Ibid.*, 11.
[23] *Ibid.*, 90.
[24] *Ibid.*, 15.
[25] *Ibid.*, 22.
[26] *Ibid.*, 22.
[27] *Ibid.* 9.
[28] *Ibid.*, 51.
[29] *Ibid.*, 97.
[30] Everett's novels *Watershed* (1996) and *Glyph* (1999) are typical examples. In *Glyph*, the first-person narrator addresses the reader directly on page 54 with the words "Have you to this point assumed that I am white?" thereby directing their attention to their underlying assumptions (the protagonist is black, but this wasn't specifically mentioned). I have discussed the complexities of the narrative voice of *Watershed* in Weik von Mossner (2017), chapter 3.
[31] Everett (2001:11).
[32] *Ibid.*, 83.
[33] According to the Mayo Clinic website, the Narcissistic Personality Order is marked by the following features: (1) Having an exaggerated sense of self-importance; (2) Expecting to be recognized as superior even without achievements that warrant it; (3) Exaggerating your achievements and talents; (4) Being preoccupied with fantasies about success, power, brilliance, beauty or the perfect mate; (5) Believing that you are superior and can only be understood by or associate with equally special people; (6) Requiring constant admiration; (7)

Having a sense of entitlement; (8) Expecting special favors and unquestioning compliance with your expectations; (9) Taking advantage of others to get what you want; (10) Having an inability or unwillingness to recognize the needs and feelings of others; (11) Being envious of others and believing others envy you; (12) Behaving in an arrogant or haughty manner. See http://www.mayoclinic.org/diseases-conditions/narcissistic-personality-disorder/basics/symptoms/con-20025568.

[34] *Ibid.*, 85.

[35] *Ibid.*, 83.

[36] *Ibid.*, 85-86.

[37] *Ibid.*, 58.

[38] At the time of my writing, the Trump Administration plans to open up federal lands to gas and exploration. For more information, see http://www.climatecentral.org/news/decoding-trumps-white-house-energy-plan-21097?utm_content=buffer7c5b0&utm_medium=social&utm_source=twitter.com&utm_campaign=buffer.

[39] Bauer (2013:258).

[40] *Ibid.,* 73.

[41] Hutcheon, Linda (1994:35)

[42] *Ibid.*, 56. The outdated term pachyderm was commonly used to describe elephants, rhinoceroses, and hippopotamuses.

[43] *Ibid.* 64 and 73.

[44] Ruffin (2010:131).

[45] Butterfield, Stephen (1974:252).

[46] Hoffman (2000:i p. 7).

[47] Everett (2001:107).

[48] *Ibid.*, 124.

[49] *Ibid.*, 125.

[50] *Ibid.* 85-86.

[51] *Ibid.*, 126

[52] Ruffin (2010:131).

[53] Simpson (2003:1).

[54] *Ibid.*, 75.

[55] Butterfield (1974:255).

Works Cited

Bauer, Sylvie (2013). "Percival Everett's *Grand Canyon Inc.*: Self-Reliance Revisited." *Canadian Review of American Studies* 43.2, 257-268.

Butterfield, Stephen (1974). *Black Autobiography in America*. Amherst: University of Massachusetts Press.

Everett, Percival (1999). *Glyph.* Minneapolis: Graywolf Press.

--- (2001). *Grand Canyon, Inc*. San Francisco: Versus Press.

--- (2003). *Watershed.* 1996. Boston: Beacon Press.

Flory, Dan (2013). "Race and Imaginative Resistance in James Cameron's *Avatar.*" *Projections: The Journal for Movies and Mind* 7.2, 41-63.

Gallese, Vittorio (2015). "Finding the Body in the Brain: From Simulation Theory to Embodied Simulation." *Goldman and His Critics*. Ed. Brian McLaughlin, and Hilary K. Kornblith. New York: Wiley-Blackwell, 297-314.

Genette, Gérard (1980). *Narrative Discourse: An Essay in Method. 1972.* Oxford: Blackwell.

Hoffman, Martin (2000). *Empathy and Moral Development: Implications for Caring and Justice.* Cambridge: Cambridge University Press.

Hutcheon, Linda (1994). *Irony's Edge: The Theory and Politics of Irony.* New York: Routledge.

James, Erin (2015). *The Storyworld Accord: Econarratology and Postcolonial Narratives.* Lincoln: University of Nebraska Press.

Keen, Suzanne (2010). "Narrative Empathy." *Toward a Cognitive Theory of Narrative Acts*. Ed. Frederick Louis Aldama. Austin: University of Texas Press, 61-94.

Kerridge, Richard (2014). "Ecocritical Approaches to Literary Form and Genre: Urgency, Depth, Provisionality, Temporality." *Oxford Handbook of Ecocriticism.* Ed. Greg Garrard. Oxford: Oxford University Press, 361–375.

Nabokov, Vladimir (1955). *Lolita.* Paris: Olympia Press.

Nadzam, Bonnie (2011). *Lamb.* New York: Other Press.

Ruffin, Kimberly N. (2010). *Black on Earth: African American Ecoliterary Traditions*. Athens: University of Georgia Press.

Seymour, Nicole (2014). "Irony and Contemporary Ecocinema: Theorizing a New Affective Paradigm." *Moving Environments: Affect, Emotion, Ecology, and Film.* Ed. Alexa Weik von Mossner. Waterloo, ON: Wilfrid Laurier University Press, 61–78.

Simpson, Paul (2003). *On the Discourse of Satire: Towards a Stylistic Model of Satirical Humor.* Amsterdam: John Benjamins Publishing Company.

Smith, Murray (1999). "Gangsters, Cannibals, Aesthetes, or Apparently Perverse Allegiances." *Passionate Views: Film, Cognition, and Emotion*. Eds. Carl Plantinga, and Greg M. Smith. Baltimore: Johns Hopkins University Press, 217–237.

Vermeule, Blakey (2010). *Why Do We Care about Literary Characters?* Baltimore: Johns Hopkins University Press.

Weik von Mossner, Alexa (2014). *Cosmopolitan Minds: Literature, Emotion, and the Transnational Imagination*. Austin: University of Texas Press.

--- (2017). *Affective Ecologies: Empathy, Emotion, and Environmental Narrative*. Columbus: Ohio State University Press.

Wright, Richard (1940). *Native Son*. New York: Scribner.

Contributors' Addresses

Dr. Roman Bartosch, Universität zu Köln, Philosophische Fakultät, Englisches Seminar II, Gronewaldstr. 2, 50931 Köln, Germany.

Prof. Dr. Rainer Emig, Johannes Gutenberg Universität Mainz, Department of English and Linguistics, English Literature and Culture, Jakob Welder Weg 18, 55128 Mainz, Germany.

Dr. Sonja Frenzel, Heinrich-Heine-Universität Düsseldorf, Institut für Anglistik und Amerikanistik V, Anglophone Literatures / Literary Translation, Universitätsstr. 1, 40225 Düsseldorf, Germany.

Dr. Timo Müller, Universität Regensburg, Lehrstuhl für Amerikanistik, 93040 Regensburg, Germany.

Prof. Dr. Birgit Neumann, Heinrich-Heine-Universität Düsseldorf, Institut für Anglistik und Amerikanistik V, Anglophone Literatures / Literary Translation, Universitätsstr. 1, 40225 Düsseldorf, Germany.

Dr. Jan Rupp, Goethe Universität Frankfurt am Main, Institut für England- & Amerikastudien, Abteilung Neue Englischsprachige Literaturen und Kulturen, Norbert-Wollheim-Platz 1, 60629 Frankfurt am Main, Germany.

Dr. Jonathan Skinner, English and Comparative Literaray Studies, Millburn House, Millburn Hill Road, University of Warwick, Coventry CV4 7HS, United Kingdom.

Prof. Dr. John Thieme, University of East Anglia, School of Literature, Drama and Creative Writing, Faculty of Arts and Humanities, Norwich Research Park, Norwich, NR4 7TJ, United Kingdom.

Ioannis Tsitsovits, Katholieke Universiteit Leuven, English Literaturen, Blijde-Inkomstraat 21 – box 3311, 3000 Leuven, Belgium.

Prof. Dr. Pieter Vermeulen, Katholieke Universiteit Leuven, Literaray Studies Research Unit, Blijde-Inkomstraat 21 – box 3311, 3000 Leuven, Belgium.

Assoc. Prof. Dr. Alexa Weik von Mossner, Alpen-Adria Universität Klagenfurt, Institut für Anglistik und Amerikanistik, Universitätsstr. 65-67, 9020 Klagenfurt am Wörthersee, Austria.

Prof. Dr. Wendy Wheeler, London Metropolitan University, 166-220 Holloway Road, London, N7 8DB, United Kingdom.

Druck:
Canon Deutschland Business Services GmbH
im Auftrag der KNV-Gruppe
Ferdinand-Jühlke-Str. 7
99095 Erfurt